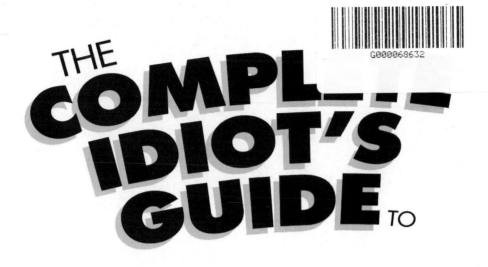

THE COMPLETE IDIOT'S GUIDE TO

Troubleshooting
Your PC

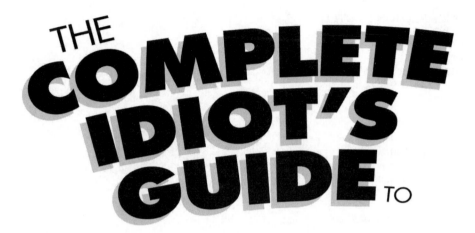

THE COMPLETE IDIOT'S GUIDE TO

Troubleshooting Your PC

by Chris Ward-Johnson

Prentice Hall

An imprint of Pearson Education

London • Boston • Indianapolis • New York • Mexico City • Toronto • Sydney • Tokyo •
Singapore • Hong Kong • Cape Town • Madrid • Paris • Amsterdam • Munich • Milan

PEARSON EDUCATION LIMITED

Head Office:
Edinburgh Gate
Harlow CM20 2JE
Tel: +44 (0)1279 623623
Fax: +44 (0)1279 431059

London Office:
128 Long Acre
London WC2E 9AN
Tel: +44 (0)20 7447 2000
Fax: +44 (0)20 7447 2170
Website: www.it-minds.com/

First published in Great Britain in 2003

ISBN 0 130 45632 2

British Library Cataloguing in Publication Data
A CIP catalogue record for this book can be obtained from the British Library.

10 9 8 7 6 5 4 3 2 1

Typeset by Land & Unwin (Data Sciences) Ltd
Printed and bound in Great Britain by Biddles Ltd of Guildford and King's Lynn.

The Publisher's policy is to use paper manufactured from sustainable forests.

Contents At A Glance

Contents

Introduction

It's taken me over six and a half years to write this book. Since I started the Dr Keyboard column in November 1995 I've answered something like 5,000 questions from real people with real problems, which has given me a unique insight into what really goes wrong with computers – an experience I've distilled down into the few hundred pages of this book.

What really goes wrong with computers? Sometimes it's the hardware, sometimes the software, often the wetware (that's you, the human prodding at it) or, almost invariably, it's a combination of all three. The problem is, when something goes wrong, whose fault is it? Hardware and software manufacturers are all very happy to point the finger of blame at each other so how do you, the poor piggy-in-the-middle computer user, pin them down and make them give you an answer?

Unfortunately for you, their answer is very often to reinstall everything – Windows, your applications, everything. This is akin to taking your car to bits and then reassembling it because it won't start, rather than checking to see if it's just a loose wire. And again, unfortunately, reinstalling everything will almost certainly cure your problem and there are times when it's the only option. But it should be a last resort, not a first answer from a bored and stupid technical support line person.

Where To Start

So how do you find out what to ask? One of the commonest questions I'm sent is, 'Why does my keyboard sometimes stop responding?'. The most likely answer is that there's a problem elsewhere on your PC and the non-responsive keyboard is just a symptom, not the problem, but how could you know that without already knowing the answer? The answer, as Douglas Adams famously pointed out, is easy – it's 42. The problem is knowing what question it's the answer to.

So, I've written this book for two groups of people: it's for those who know that there's something wrong with their computer but don't know what, exactly; and it's also for those who didn't know anything was the matter at all but who are in for a big surprise real soon now. If you're not in the first group you're almost certainly in the second one.

I cover all versions of Microsoft Windows from 95 to XP and all aspects of computing from dealing with a completely dead machine to fine-tuning your internet connection. There are also several chapters on how to help yourself avoid problems in the first place – simple, sensible things you can do to manage your computer, keep it up to date, keep it safe from harm and make sure that, if it does all go wrong, you don't lose anything important.

The book includes many real questions sent to me over the years, along with the answers to them. The experience of answering these questions has taught me that questioners are almost never alone in asking a question – many others will suffer the same problems as you at one time or another, and reading about the solution to their problems can very often help you.

I also point you to the places where, when you're still stuck, you can come for more help. I run a number of websites devoted to helping people find answers to their problems – www.drkeyboard.com contains all the questions I've been asked and the answers I've given since 1995. If you can't find an answer there, I run a message board at www.drkeyboard.net where subscribers can ask as many questions as they like about computers. For you, the readers of this book, I've set up a special message board forum which you can reach via www.drkeyboard.net/trouble where you can ask any questions you like about anything you don't understand in this book.

How To Use This Book

Although you can dive right in and read this book from cover to cover, you can also use it to help you diagnose just what's wrong with your machine and follow through logically to sort it out. Chapter 1, 'What's Gone Wrong?', covers the first steps to take when you think something is wrong, from checking it's plugged in to decoding those mysterious error messages computer programmers love so much. It's full of pointers to other chapters in the book where you can find more help on specific topics.

Chapter 2, 'Identifying The Source Of The Problem', helps you work out what it might be that's causing your problem, explaining how apparently unrelated actions can have an effect on each other – like why upgrading one piece of software will stop another working. This chapter also includes a number of the questions I've answered over the years helping others diagnose their problems.

Chapters 3 and 4 cover setting up a new computer and what's inside the average PC, then chapters 5 to 14 cover different aspects of your computer and the problems you may have with it, from setting it up in the first place to finding out what's inside it, working out what's wrong with the image on your screen, connecting to the internet, printing and more. Each chapter starts with a simple description of the subject, then discusses some of the sorts of things that can go wrong and what you should think about doing to avoid them. At the end of each chapter are relevant questions and the answers I've given to them over the years.

Chapters 15 to 18 are full of hints and tips on how to secure your PC, how to speed it up and how to make sure that, when it all goes wrong, you at least don't lose anything important and can get up and running with the minimum of fuss and delay. If you follow the advice in these chapters then you'll go a long way towards avoiding the sorts of problems you'll find discussed in the previous ones.

At the end of each chapter you'll find a selection of questions I've answered over the years, illustrating typical problems faced by computer users and instructions for solving those problems. Sometimes you may find that you have exactly the same problem and can follow those instructions. Often, your problem may be slightly different – but, hopefully, reading the solution to other people's questions will point you in the right direction to finding the answer to your particular difficulty. Where appropriate, the questions are divided into sections depending on their degree of difficulty and complicatedness. Sometimes, easy-sounding questions can provoke complicated answers – and complicated questions have very simple answers. If you come across any concept you don't understand, use the indexes to look for more information about it – so, if the answer is 'Download and install new drivers', you'll find details on how to do just that in Chapter 12, 'Now You're Online'.

At the end of the book are three appendices. Appendix 1 contains a complete listing of all the questions solved in the main body of the book, both the direct questions I've answered in those chapters and pointers to the other information contained in each chapter. Appendix 2 is a Resource Guide with pointers to websites you might find useful in your quest to beat your PC into a lump of something more useful than just a paperweight. Appendix 3 contains definitions of the terms and abbreviations used throughout the book. If there's a technical term you don't understand, look in Appendix 3 for an explanation.

Finally, there's such a huge range of software and hardware available – with more coming on the market every day – that it's impossible to cover every possible combination and eventuality, so remember that your particular combination may not be in this book, comprehensive though it is. What is in here will, hopefully, set you on the right track to finding the answer to your question and also give you some good habits which may help you to avoid problems in the first place.

You will encounter this special icon and boxed text in the book:

Warning!

Sometimes the troubleshooting solutions I propose are a little bit risky. For example, I might suggest that you open up your computer to make changes to your hardware and if you decide to follow my advice you will need to take care to avoid damaging components or electrocuting yourself! Some of my suggested solutions can have adverse consequences in particular situations, so you will need to weigh up the possible cost of following the solution before proceeding. All of the solutions are designed to help you resolve problems, but please proceed with caution when you see this warning sign.

Good luck solving your computer problem – and remember, if you're still stuck after reading through this book you can get more help on my website at www.drkeyboard.net/trouble.

Acknowledgements

We are grateful to the following for permission to reproduce copyright material:

Figures 5.1, 5.2, 5.3, 5.4, 5.6, 10.1, 10.2 10.3, 10.4, 11.1, 11.2, 11.3, 12.5, 12.6, 12.7, 12.8, 14.4, 16.1, 16.2, 16.3, screenshots reprinted by permission from Microsoft Corporation; Figures 12.1, 12.2, 12.3, 12.4 reproduced by permission of Creative Labs (UK) Ltd; Figure 18.1 © Zone Labs, Inc., 1060 Howard Street, San Francisco, CA 94103 USA. All rights reserved. Used with permission.

Finally, my heartiest thanks to Phil, Jon, Merc, Dave and Michael for all their technical help, advice and counsels. And my very special thanks to my wife, Wendy, for her support and tolerance. May your PCs never crash.

Chris Ward-Johnson
Languedoc, France, July 2002.

Part 1
The Basics – Working out what on earth the problem is

Your computer was working just fine but now, somehow, it Just Doesn't Work. You've turned it on, it's come up with a bizarre message about how you're performing illegal operations and now you're expecting the cops to break the door down and cart you off to a Windows-less prison. Which might be a relief in some ways but isn't much help if you really, really want and need to make the thing work again. The first chapter, 'What's Gone Wrong?' will help you work out just what some of those cryptic messages mean and point you to other chapters in the book where you can delve deeper into the problem.

Chapter 2, 'Identifying The Source Of The Problem', will do just that – help you work out what it is that's started this whole mess off in the first place. Often something unrelated will be causing your problem, and this section of the book will help you with the most difficult part of troubleshooting your PC – not the answering of the question but finding out just what question it is you should be asking in the first place. The answer, as Douglas Adams wrote, is easy – it's 42. Quite what the question is, well that's a little harder.

Chapter 1

What's Gone Wrong?

In This Chapter

➤ How to check the simple things first and make sure you don't make things worse in the process

➤ Dr Keyboard's list of the really obvious things to check when something goes wrong

➤ How to be confident you won't push the wrong button – and how to stop things going wrong in the first place

How To Check The Simple Things First And Make Sure You Don't Make Things Worse In The Process

Something is wrong with your computer. Last time you used it, it all worked splendidly and just how you liked it to. Today, it won't do what you want it to do and keeps giving you bizarre error messages about performing illegal acts. Illegal? Don't worry – you're not breaking the law, just a victim of the way computer programmers mangle the English language to say things no one else would.

The very first thing you should do when 'something' – anything – goes wrong is to think back very, very carefully to the last time you used both your computer and that specific program or piece of hardware. Are you sure you didn't change anything then?

Are you sure that you haven't installed a new piece of software or updated an old one in the meantime? Have you plugged in – or unplugged – anything? Are all the appropriate leads plugged in securely at both ends? Has there been a power cut? It may sound like a stupid question to ask, but there's plenty of evidence that people miss the really, really obvious things while concentrating on the obscure and irrelevant. So, the next section looks at these things.

Dr Keyboard's List Of The Really Obvious Things To Check When Something Goes Wrong

First Things To Check

If you push the 'Start' button on your computer and nothing happens:

1   Check that it's plugged into the mains electricity supply.

2   Physically pull out and replace both ends of the power cord and check that the wall socket is working by plugging in something else.

3   If you have a UPS (an Uninterruptible Power Supply, a large battery which keeps your PC running in the event of a power cut) make sure it's turned on.

4   Look at the front of your computer and see if any lights come on at all.

5   Look at your keyboard – it often has small lights indicating that it's receiving power and that the Caps Lock or Num(ber) Lock keys are depressed.

6   Listen carefully to your computer. Can you hear any noises at all from inside? Modern PCs have several fans to cool them down – can you hear them? Check at the rear of the computer where the power cord is plugged in – there's normally a fan outlet there. Is the fan turning? Can you feel air coming out?

Before opening the computer case take suitable precautions against static electric discharges. See Chapter 4, page 45–6, for details.

7   Is there power to the motherboard (there may be a tell-tale light for this or you may see the fan on the CPU turning if you open the case)? The power switch itself may be faulty or disconnected (see Chapter 4).

If It's Not A Power Failure

If there is power but your PC doesn't start up:

1   When you turn the computer on can you hear any sort of beep? Most computers go through the POST (Power-On Self-Test) when they count their components and beep if they're satisfied that all are present and correct.

2   Normally the 'Everything's OK' signal is a single beep. Anything more than this means that something is amiss and you should consult your machine's documentation to see what the particular pattern of long and short beeps it's emitting means. It could be that the video/graphics card is broken or badly seated, the RAM (Random Access Memory) is failing or that one or more disk drives hasn't been detected.

3   If the beep pattern suggests, or you suspect, that something inside the case isn't functioning correctly either open it up yourself or take it to someone (e.g. a repair shop) who can do it for you. See Appendix 2, page 286.

Before opening the computer case take suitable precautions against static electric discharges. See Chapter 4, page 45–6, for details.

When you've opened up the case:

1   Check that all cards (e.g. sound, video, network) are properly seated and that their top lips are secured with a suitable screw to the case. Just resting them against the case may not make enough contact for them to work electrically. It can help to remove and reseat them sometimes. Do the same with the RAM modules.

2   Check that fans and other components are free from dust – use a vacuum cleaner with a plastic-tipped hose or a specialist canned-air cleaner.

3   Check that leads from the power supply unit are plugged into all disk drives and the motherboard.

On the outside of the case, check that all cables are plugged in for your monitor, power, keyboard, mouse and any other devices. These come in a variety of shapes and sizes:

1   Most modern devices are USB devices, which plug into small rectangular sockets on the back, side or front of your PC. These can be plugged and unplugged at any time.

2   Before this came PS/2 mice and keyboards with small, round, seven-pin connectors.

You should turn off your PC before plugging or unplugging these devices as they're not 'electrically protected' and you could fry a vital chip if not careful, maybe even necessitating a complete motherboard replacement.

3 Before PS/2 came AT keyboards and serial and 'bus' (round plugs with their own slot-in card) mice. AT connectors are large, round, five-pin plugs and serial mice have trapezoid nine-pin plugs, usually female, which fit into COM or RS232 sockets on your computer.

Again, turn off the computer before plugging or unplugging AT or serial devices.

Power and keyboard cables are the most important – nothing works without power and most PCs will stop during their boot-up (start-up) routine if they don't detect a keyboard.

Monitor cables – the signal cable plugged into your PC and its power cable – are also important since, even if your PC *is* starting up you won't know this if you can't see anything on the screen.

If you've assembled the PC yourself or have had the case open, check that the 'panel' leads (technically known as 'headers') from the motherboard to the various LEDs, speaker and so on are all in place.

If the computer passes its POST and gets part way into the boot (start-up) process, do you see any error messages? You can usually pause the screens of information which scroll past on start-up by pressing the **Pause** key on your keyboard. If you get a blue STOP screen with lots of technical jargon, you have a BSOD, or Blue Screen of Death. Read what it says on the screen and follow any advice it gives. Note the reference numbers it gives and look them up, e.g. on the Microsoft KnowledgeBase website (see Appendix B).

If It Starts Up, What Do Those Error Messages Mean?

Do you see the Windows start-up splash screen (telling you which version of Windows you're using)? If you get this far but no further, some hardware or software device or program is interfering with the start-up process (see Chapter 2).

You can investigate this further by restarting the PC in 'Safe Mode' – as soon as you see the 'Starting Windows....' message (immediately after the BIOS start-up information screens about the amount of memory and types of disks installed) hit the F8 function key at the top of your keyboard. Choose the 'Safe Mode' option on the menu – move up and down using the arrow keys on your keyboard and press **Enter** when Safe Mode is highlighted. If you find it impossible to press F8 at the right moment, put a blank floppy disk into your floppy disk drive and restart your computer. Now you'll see an error message about how the computer can't start up from that floppy disk. Eject it and then press F8 twice in succession. The first press responds to the error message's 'Press any key to restart' message and the second opens the menu from which you can choose Safe Mode. This starts Windows with a basic set of drivers and functionality – so your screen will probably look different to the normal one, with larger icons, less 'space' and fewer colours – and will allow you to look in **Device Manager** (under **System** or **Hardware** in **Control Panel**) to see if there are any 'conflicts' – two or more devices inside your computer which can't agree how to work together. Look for yellow circles with black exclamation marks or red symbols on the left-hand side of the listing column. Windows usually automatically 'expands' items with problems or you can click the small + (cross) next to them yourself to see what's going on. Double left-click any problem items (or right-click them and then left-click **Properties**) and you should see details of the problem and be offered the chance to start a 'troubleshooter' which will walk you through solving the problem. You may also find in **Device Manager** extra instances of devices or even devices which you removed some time ago. Remove all of these and Windows will redetect any hardware as necessary the next time you start up your PC.

If you get as far as your regular Windows desktop but then receive error messages about various problems with software, read the messages carefully to see if they give any real clues about what's going on. Unfortunately, programmers haven't always felt it necessary to write these error messages in a language regular mortals can understand – although Microsoft boss Bill Gates has now decreed that future error messages in Windows must be (a) in English (or whatever your local language is) and (b) comprehensible. Quite often there will be some sort of code number associated with the error message and, if the manufacturer is worth its salt, this number will be found in the support section of its website. If you're really lucky, there may even be a solution (but don't forget the old computer programmer's proverb, 'Make it possible to program in plain English, and you will find that programmers cannot write plain English'. (See Chapter 8.)

If the problem is with a particular program or piece of hardware which has suddenly stopped working think very, very carefully about whether you've installed any new programs or hardware since the last time you used the PC. Windows versions before Windows 2000 and XP suffered from what's become known as 'DLL Hell'. This is where installing one program overwrites part of another, preventing the latter from working. The simplest solution is to just reinstall the first, now non-working program. (See Chapter 3.)

Swapping Out Components

If the problem is hardware-based – a sound card doesn't produce any noise, your keyboard doesn't work as you'd hoped – the first step is to swap it with a known good component.

Keyboards and mice are cheap and it doesn't cost a fortune to keep a spare one in the house – but always remember to turn your PC off before swapping out the PS/2 (small round seven-pin plug) variety and, of course, before swapping out any internal hardware too. However, before assuming the problem is with your keyboard, make sure you're not just experiencing system 'crashes', with the keyboard refusing inputs just being a symptom, not the problem itself.

Be thorough when you turn your computer off – some modern computers actually go into a 'sleep' or 'hibernate' state when you push the power button on the front, so read your documentation very carefully and make sure you're doing what you think you're doing.

Swap monitors and cards (such as video cards and sound cards) with a friend if you can. If theirs works on your system but not vice versa, you've isolated the problem.

Checking The Software

If the physical hardware checks out OK, the problem may lie at the interface between hardware and software in what are called the *drivers*. These are small software programs which tell Windows how to work with the particular hardware device – what your sound card can do, how to make the video card show a pretty picture, what commands to send to the printer. (See Chapter 2.)

Many, many hardware problems can be solved by downloading and installing updated drivers from the manufacturer's website. The drivers which come in the box with most hardware are not, despite what the instructions say, going to be the latest, greatest ones available. Indeed, they may be unfinished 'beta' – test – drivers, and the manufacturer's website should be your first port of call if you suspect that this may be the problem. See Chapter 10 for details on downloading and installing new drivers.

When you download and install new drivers be very careful to ensure that you have the appropriate ones *for your version of Windows*. Drivers written for Windows 95 almost certainly won't work if you have Windows XP, and vice versa. Windows Me in particular is *very* fussy about its drivers – accept no substitutes.

When all else fails, RTFM – Read The (Fine) Manual. A *huge* percentage of the questions I receive every day can easily be answered by reading an instruction manual or clicking on Help, either inside Windows or in an individual program. (See Chapter 2 and Appendix 2.)

And if RTFMing doesn't work, come and visit the Dr Keyboard website – you may be surprised to find how common your problem is!

How To Be Confident You Won't Push The Wrong Button – And How To Stop Things Going Wrong In The First Place

The older you get, the more likely you are to worry that, somehow, you'll 'press the wrong button' and delete your files/delete something else important/blow up your computer. Children are much better about this sort of thing than adults – kids know that if it does all go bang then mum and dad will mend it or buy them a new one. So they have no fear and they try pushing every key, clicking every button and testing every link.

Of course, it's different when you're (a) grown up and (b) the person who has to pay to replace whatever goes bang, so here's Dr Keyboard's List of How To Make Sure It Doesn't Go Bang (or, if it does go bang, how to make it all better again).

Don't Be Afraid

You'll have to work quite hard at being pretty stupid to actually make your computer go bang – pouring a cup of coffee into the back of your monitor may produce a minor explosion, for example, but why would you do that? OK, don't answer that one.

RTFM Read The (Fine) Manual. Really

Computers may be supposed to be so simple that an eight-year-old can use them, but you're probably not an eight-year-old so, unless you have access to one who can teach you how to use your PC, read any bits of paper and on-screen instructions which came with it.

In Windows itself you'll find a reasonable Help system with sections called things like 'Getting started online book' and 'Tips for new users'. Windows XP has several useful and interesting video presentations in its help files on what it can do and how to do basic things. (See Chapter 2 and Appendix 2.)

Plan For Things Going Wrong Right From The Start

If you use your computer for e-mailing a few friends and a little light web surfing, you may not have anything you consider valuable on it. But if you rely in any way at all on the information stored inside it – contacts (e.g. your e-mail address book), business information, even your collection of recipes – you should consider how long it would take to put it right if it was all suddenly taken away from you, for any reason whatsoever.

What you need is a *backup strategy*. This means thinking about what would happen if the building where your PC lives were burned down or burgled – backups are no good if they're destroyed or stolen along with the machine they're backing up, so think about what's called 'off-site storage' by the professionals (see Chapter 17).

This could be as simple as swapping CD-Rs or CD-RWs of your backup data with a friend at regular intervals. Your household or business insurance will probably cover you for replacing the hardware, but what do you think your insurer would say if you tried to claim three years' worth of typing to re-input your accounts?

You'll find a full list of items to back up in Chapter 17 – it includes your ISP (Internet Service Provider) details such as your logon username and password and the dial-up telephone number; your contacts book/e-mail address book; any files you create yourself such as letters, invoices, your diary, pictures, archives of digital pictures and scans; copies of both received and sent e-mails, especially if you use them for business; accounts; personalised dictionaries and settings, for example in Microsoft Office; your 'Favorites' or 'Bookmarks' list from your web browser. It means, basically, everything that you can't reinstall from the original CDs and disks which came with your machine and/or you've installed later on. (See Chapter 17.)

Floppy disks used to be the cheapest and most obvious medium of choice for backups but they're actually a very, very poor medium for any sort of long-term storage. Their design means that the disk inside is open to all sorts of dust and other pollution and they *will* fail – guaranteed. If they're your only option, keep two or more copies of every floppy disk, and never, ever, *ever* keep your only copy of any information on a single floppy disk. You *will* lose it sooner or later.

Nowadays, writable or rewritable CDs or even DVDs are an easy and cheap backup medium. Most new computers come fitted with a CD writer and you can add one for less than a hundred pounds. Blank CD-Rs cost less than 50p and will store more information than over 400 floppy disks. DVDs can store the same information as half a dozen or more CDs.

Other options include tape drives, removable hard disks and even online storage where your files are backed up to a computer on the internet.

Have A File And Document Storage Strategy

By default, most Windows programs like Microsoft Word store information in a folder called **My Documents**, which you usually find either on or linked from your standard Desktop. This is a good starting point, but once you've created more than a few documents you'll soon find it hard to track down a particular letter, invoice or diary entry unless you're systematic about your filing. Just as you'll find it hard to put your hand on a bank statement from 1998 if you pile every bit of paper that comes through your letterbox into a giant cardboard box, you'll never find the letter you sent to your accountant about your tax return if there are 50 documents with slight variations on the name 'letter to accountant'.

So, under **My Documents** create folders and sub-folders in a system you find easy to use and remember. For example, have one for invoices and then sub-folders under that for 2001, 2002, 2003 and so on. Or, if you prefer, call them 'Letters about company', 'Letters about pension' and so on – whatever you find easiest to work with, but do establish some sort of system (see Chapter 16).

As well as the files you create on your computer, give files you send sensible names too. This means sending e-mails with subject lines like, 'About the flat' or 'Selling the car' not just 'Hello'. And when you get into correspondence with someone, don't just click **Reply** and accept their subject line – if you're changing the subject, change the subject line. This may sound daft now but you'll thank me for this when you're looking for an e-mail six months from now and discover that you've sent several hundred with the subject line 'Hi!' (see Chapter 11).

As well as filing your documents, file your files. This means that if you download an update to a program or a device driver for some of your hardware, keep the file you download somewhere you can find it again. Have a folder called **Downloads** and then sub-folders called, for example, **Matrox** and below that **G550** if that's the make and model of your graphics card. This way, when you need to reinstall that widget you won't be wondering whether it's the file called 'w2k_533.exe' or the one called 'Q301625_W2K_SP3_x86_en.EXE' that you need.

If you have the chance when buying a new computer, specify one with two hard disks instead of one. In general, two 40-gigabyte (GB) hard disks – or even a 40 GB and a 20 GB – are better than one 80 GB hard disk. It may cost you a few pounds more, but the advantages far outweigh the cost. Having two hard disks allows you to keep your personal data on one and programs and Windows on the other. This means that, when you need to start all over again and reinstall Windows, you don't have to worry about losing all your data – it's safe on the second disk (see Chapter 4).

Keeping Track Of What You Have Done

It may sound obvious and make complete sense that you'd remember what hardware and software you've installed on your computer, but in practice most people can't remember what they've done and when they did it. More importantly, a program you install today may not have any immediate untoward effects until some time later when you run another, unrelated program, which promptly falls over for no apparent reason at all – see the discussion of 'DLL Hell' above and Chapter 2.

It's well worth the effort to note down somewhere the details of what you install and when – a notebook in a drawer beside your PC is fine. A file stored on your PC itself isn't so worthwhile – it's only any good as long as your machine is working, and if you need to read the note about what it was that you installed that made it fall over in the first place, you're going to be out of luck.

Windows Me and XP now include a 'Roll back' function which allows you to set 'System Restore' points. This means that you can undo any changes made to the computer system without affecting the data you've created (e-mails, spreadsheets, letters and so on) – but there's still no substitute for keeping a note yourself of what you've done.

A 'daybook' or journal of some kind – even just a stack of notes on the backs of used sheets of paper can hold everything you do – just remember to date them at the top and add some sort of heading to help when looking through them.

Work Out Exactly What's In Your Computer

When you buy a new computer, keep a copy of the order form, delivery note and any other information which came with it. This will be useful when people like me ask questions like 'How big is the hard disk?' or 'What kind of CPU does it have?'

If you upgrade your computer at all, keep a similar note about what you do or have done to it.

You can get a 'quick and dirty' view of your PC's specification by opening the **System** section of **Control Panel** by double left-clicking on it and looking on the **General** tab. This will tell you what version of Windows you're running and any service packs which have been installed (for Windows NT, 2000 and XP), to whom it's registered, what type of processor (CPU) it has and how much RAM (Random Access Memory) is fitted.

Inside the **System** section of **Control Panel** is also **Device Manager** (under the **Hardware** tab in Windows 2000 and XP), which will give you a full run-down on all the installed hardware. It will also tell you about any immediate problems with the various components.

You'll find a list of installed software under **Add/Remove Programs** in **Control Panel**. NB: Older (16-bit for the technical) programs may not be listed here or even on the **Start > Programs** menu – you'll have to trawl through the hard disk itself (open **My Computer** and double-click the C: drive in most instances) to find them.

Questions and Answers

 While browsing the internet with Internet Explorer I regularly get the message that 'This program has performed an illegal operation and will be shut down'. What am I doing that's illegal? What laws have I broken?

The law that says programmers require you to be as knowledgeable about what they're saying as they are. The only 'illegal' thing you've done is run a program which has fallen over – and by 'illegal' programmers mean 'You shouldn't have done that'. It just means that the program has tried to do something that it's not allowed to do by the operating system (Microsoft Windows, in this case). As for a solution, you'll be pleased to know that you're not alone with this problem but most people I know have managed to solve it by visiting <u>windowsupdate.microsoft.com</u>, clicking on **Product updates** and allowing Microsoft to determine how best to fix what they've done wrong in the first place.

Chapter 2

Identifying The Source Of The Problem

In This Chapter

➤ Digging deep to find the causes of a problem

➤ What have you done to it?

➤ How to check the symptoms

➤ Narrowing down the potential causes

➤ Fixing the problem

➤ Readers Q&A, including solutions to many common error messages

Digging Deep to Find The Causes Of A Problem

Sometimes, it's obvious what's causing the problem – the screen doesn't light up and the power light on the front doesn't come on. At other times the problem is beyond mysterious – a program suddenly refuses to start up, even though it worked just fine yesterday. The obvious is obvious, but how do you narrow down the possibilities when nothing is obvious?

1   What have you done to it recently?

2   Take a very close look at the symptoms and read any error (or other) messages very, very carefully indeed.

3   Narrow down the potential causes.

4   Fix the problem.

What Have You Done To It?

There's no shame or embarrassment in this one, but you'd think that it's akin to eating the last chocolate biscuit to admit having 'done something' to one's PC. Time after time people deny even having touched their computers, let alone having turned them on and installed some new hardware or software. The problem, apparently, occurred all on its own without any human intervention. There is no shame in admitting that you've 'done something' to your computer. There is nothing wrong in trying a new program or device or trying new settings in a program. And if someone's asking what you've done to your computer, be as willing to tell them about it as you would be to tell a doctor what it was you've eaten that's made you poorly. Because if you don't, their job is suddenly a hundred times harder – indeed, they may be unable to solve the problem at all.

Keep, if you can, a note of the software and hardware you add to your computer and any changes you make to program settings. And before you add anything to your PC, do check that it's suitable for your existing hardware and version of Windows. In particular, when adding (or, preferably, when you're thinking of adding) new hardware to your PC check that drivers are available for your particular version of Windows. If you have a Windows 95 machine you may now find that, officially, many manufacturers have stopped writing new drivers for this version of Windows. This is because Microsoft itself has officially stopped supporting Windows 95 – Microsoft promises to support the current version of its operating system and the two previous ones which, now, means it officially supports Windows XP Home, Windows Me and Windows 98 for home users and Windows XP Professional, Windows 2000 and Windows NT 4.0 for business users.

In practice this doesn't mean that your Windows 95 computer will suddenly stop working – but it does mean that you may not be able to obtain telephone or other support for Windows 95 and Microsoft no longer issues security updates and other patches for this operating system. And you may well find that if you buy a particularly popular piece of hardware or software, it will have been made usable on Windows 95. As a last resort you can try using Windows 98 drivers on Windows 95 but there's no guarantee that they will work.

Of course, it's entirely possible that the converse of this is also true – if you *haven't* installed anything new or changed any settings in any program at all, then the cause of the problem may well not be you.

How To Check The Symptoms

If you have an actual error message, take a note of it if possible. With some error messages you can left-click-and-drag across the words to select them, then right-click them, left-click **Copy** and then paste them into a document – open Notepad and right-click inside the blank document then left-click **Paste**. If you can't do this, hold down the left **Alt** key on your keyboard (to the left of the spacebar) and press the **Print Screen** button (sometimes **PrtScn** or a similar abbreviation), usually on the top row of keys above the directional arrow and Home/End block of keys. Now, open a painting or drawing program – Paint in Windows is fine, it's under **Accessories** – and click **Edit > Paste** and a copy of the error message dialog box should be pasted into the program. Now click **File > Save** and put the picture somewhere safe where you can find it again. Not all error messages can be copied in this way – in particular, it won't work on the Blue Screen of Death – and you may have to resort to pen and paper. You're looking for numbers something like 10060 or 0x800CC0D, which are error message numbers. The huge long screens of information at the end of most Windows error messages are useful only to those who wrote the program in the first place and don't mean much to anyone else. These details may then be useful on the support site of the program's manufacturer – for example, the Microsoft support site at support.microsoft.com.

Pay attention to exactly what happens when the 'problem' occurs, for example, if you start up the program and it immediately closes down again without any apparent error messages. Microsoft Word suffered a problem like this which was fixed with a free update from Microsoft, and the symptoms were detailed on the company's website.

Narrowing Down The Potential Causes

Note what other software is running at the same time. Try turning off other programs one by one and see if this removes the problem – then you know that there's a conflict between the two programs which may be caused not by the problem with the obvious symptoms but by something else. And then again, check whether this is a known problem on the relevant websites.

Does the problem only occur if, for example, you turn your printer on before or after starting your computer? Does it only happen after you've connected to the internet and opened your e-mail program?

Open **Control Panel**, double-click on **System** and open **Device Manager** (on the **Hardware** tab in Windows 2000 and XP). Are any problems flagged there (by black exclamation marks in yellow circles, red crosses or red circles with white crosses)? This shows that you have a hardware-related problem, either in the hardware itself or, more likely, in the drivers which allow Windows to control it. See Chapter 10 for details on downloading and installing new and updated hardware drivers, and Chapter 15.

Fixing The Problem

The first rule is not to over-react (i.e. don't just reinstall all your software every time you have a problem). Reformatting your hard disk and reinstalling all your software may solve the problem – but then again it may not, since you may simply be installing the same problem combination all over again.

Sometimes, reinstalling the program which is having problems will solve matters because of what's known as 'DLL Hell'. A DLL is a Dynamic Link Library, a piece of program code which can be used by more than one piece of software. In principle this allows programmers to concentrate on the functionality of their software without having to think about how, for example, to put the toolbar at the top of the screen – they just call upon the relevant DLL and it appears. However, there's usually more than one version of a DLL in existence and this is where the problems start. When you install Program A it installs version four (v.4) of the DLL called toolbar.dll. Then you install Program B, which also wants to use toolbar.dll – but it installs version three (v.3), overwriting v.4 of toolbar.dll. You start up Program B after installing it and it works fine so you assume everything is OK and carry on. Two days later you need to use Program A and start it up – at which point it comes up with a mysterious error about kernel32-this or gdi-that and lots of long, horrible numbers. Which is very strange because it worked just fine two days ago. What you don't realise is that Program B's overwriting of v.4 of toolbar.dll with the earlier v.3 of the same name has 'broken' Program A. Of course, it may not be obvious to you that the problem is actually with toolbar.dll at all, since it's not mentioned in any of the error messages and you're stuck wondering what on earth the problem is. If you're lucky you may find that simply reinstalling Program A will solve the problem – it will overwrite v.3 of toolbar.dll with v.4 which Program B can also use, and this is often the solution to this particular problem. But, occasionally, you'll find that the two programs just can't work together and you have to abandon one of them, or seek out newer versions which are compatible. If you're lucky enough to be using Windows 2000 or Windows XP you'll be happy to learn that Microsoft has taken steps towards preventing this sort of thing happening at all. 'Protected' system DLLs cannot be overwritten – if a program tries to do so, its changes will either be stopped before they can cause any harm and you'll receive a message to the effect that its changes are being undone, or the 'damaged' DLLs will be replaced the next time you start your computer. Much of this problem in the past has been caused by programmers installing component parts of their software into the common **Windows****system** folder – in future, programs will have to keep to their own folders to receive the 'Windows Compatible' certification from Microsoft. Unfortunately there will be times when, no matter how carefully and assiduously you search, you won't find the source of the problem. You can try posting a question on www.drkeyboard.net – you'll be surprised how common most problems are – but, if you're an inveterate 'tinkerer' who likes nothing more than installing shareware applications and trial versions of programs you've downloaded from the internet, the odds are that one day you're going to fall foul of that teetering pile of half-uninstalled, badly-written software and have to scrape your PC back down to bare metal, as the saying goes, and start all over again.

Questions And Answers

Easy Questions And Answers

Q *In the Nero Mix program, when trying to copy a CD I get the error message 'calibration area full'.*

A This is an RTFM question – you'll find the answer on the Nero support site at www.ahead.de/en/helptool/469.htm. This is a good example of how company support sites can help you when you have problems – note the error exactly then check the support section of their website to see if it's a known problem with an easy fix.

Q *I wanted to delete some software that I had installed in my PC, but instead of using the 'undelete' feature, I manually attempted to delete the files from its directory. I now find an error message appearing each time I start my computer, which is intensely frustrating. Can you suggest any solution to this problem?*

A Just reinstall the program and then use either its own 'undelete' facility (check the options available on the **Start > Programs** menu for that particular program) or, if there's none available, use the **Add/Remove Programs** utility in **Control Panel**.

Q *I have a laptop which on start-up displays the message, 'Non system disk or disk error. Replace disk or strike any key' but there's no disk in the floppy drive.*

A You have a problem with your hard disk – it's faulty, unformatted or corrupt. Try booting with a boot floppy disk.

Q *My computer hung when an e-mail download was very slow. I reset and ran ScanDisk and got the error message 'File structure problem found in c:\dir00001/77777777.777'. On clicking 'fixit' ScanDisk started to run and then almost immediately stopped and put up the same error message. There is an empty folder dir00001 in Windows Explorer but as soon as I access it the machine hangs. If I tell ScanDisk not to fix it then it will restart Windows after asking the question twice. How can I stop this happening? Am I doing any damage?*

The error message is caused by Norton Anti-Virus and one of its program updates. Visit their support website via www.symantec.com and you'll find a solution to your problem. If you get an error message like this and don't know what software is causing it, try searching for it (cut and paste the message to get it correct) on Google, www.google.com.

*I keep getting the error message that 'ScanDisk is unable to complete scan due to program writing to hard disk'. My hard disk defragmenter fails to go beyond 3 per cent complete, while my ScanDisk tells me there is a program writing to the hard disk. I have followed your previous advice to close Find Fast and I have followed the Windows 98 CD instructions to install **defrag.inf** prior to restart, as well as closing any program on the icon bar near the clock, but I am still unable to defragment. Any other suggestions would hopefully save me any further tearing out of my hair!*

Try running ScanDisk in Safe Mode – hit the F8 key on starting your computer when you see the 'Starting Windows' message. Your problem is happening because ScanDisk is detecting that the contents of your hard disk have been changed by some other program which is running, and then it has to start all over again – it's like interrupting someone counting out a large number of whatevers who then has to start over. You can also try running it after closing down every other program running on your machine. First, close all programs in the normal way. Next, check in the System Tray – the area next to the time display – and close everything there. Most items here respond either to a right-click or a double left-click. Then hold down **Ctrl** and **Alt** and tap the **Del**(ete) key. Choose to close everything that's running there *except* for Explorer and Systray. Now run ScanDisk and/or Disk Defragmenter.

*Every now and then when booting up my PC gives the message, 'Stuck key. Press ESC to continue'. This is annoying. It happens every now and again when I boot but after pressing **Esc** it is OK again. What causes it?*

This is what's technically known as 'a key that gets stuck on your keyboard'. Strange to say, it's one of those rare error messages which means exactly what it says, and it's caused by a dirty, gunged-up keyboard. The easiest thing to do is just chuck it away and buy a new one – they start at under a tenner. If you're in love with it, wash it with washing up liquid, put it through the dishwasher or take it into the bath with you, then dry it out for at least 24 hours before plugging it back in again (and only unplug and re-plug it while your computer's turned off).

You carry out this procedure at your own risk. There is a danger that you could destroy your keyboard, in particular if it isn't allowed to dry thoroughly and completely before using it again. If you're using a wireless keyboard, make sure you remove the batteries from it before washing it.

I have downloaded Adobe Acrobat 2.1 and Adobe Acrobat 4.0. Whenever I try to open a downloaded PDF document I get an error message.

Quite a lot of software doesn't like to coexist with earlier versions of itself. Indeed, some refuse point blank to do so. Try uninstalling both and then reinstall just Acrobat 4.0 – it can do everything 2.1 can do and more.

I keep getting the error message 'This site contains frames and your browser doesn't support them'. How do I turn frames on?

Frames should just work. Either there's a problem with the website or your browser is broken (or is such an old one that it doesn't support frames). In any case, try installing Internet Explorer 5 or later and, if you already have it, reinstall it and visit <u>windowsupdate.microsoft.com</u> to see if there are any service packs available.

My husband came in one morning last week and his computer was making a lot of noise and the only thing it would give is the 'missing operating system' message. We had some lightning the afternoon before when we left. We called an extended family member who is in the computer business trying to give him some business. He installed another hard drive and we are still getting the same message. He proceeded to talk about replacing the motherboard, CPU, etc. We have not done anything yet because my husband does not think it wise to basically totally rebuild a computer rather than purchase another one. What do you think is the problem, solution and probable cause?

If a new hard disk was installed you'd also need to install an operating system – e.g. Windows 98 – on it before you'll get rid of the error message. However, that's not the only possibility – a lightning strike could, for example, have fried a number of chips on the motherboard like the ones which control the hard disk. So first, try starting up your computer with a boot-up floppy disk – if you have Windows 98, for example, you'll have one. Or perhaps your computer friend may be able to make one. If your computer is of fairly recent vintage it may be able to boot up from the CD drive – try restarting it with the Windows CD in it. If it does start like this, try re-running the Windows installation program. If this proves impossible it may be necessary to change the motherboard and/or the CPU, but I'd advise swapping them out one at a time to isolate the fault. In the meantime you should purchase some sort of surge protection device. I use and heartily recommend those made by APC, <u>www.apcc.com</u>. This should prevent any future similar mishaps, or at least reduce the possibility.

I always get a 'Driver memory error' on start up, what does this mean?

That you have a virus, the KAK worm. See Chapter 18.

I'm trying to install Windows Media Player. I get the error message saying, 'Extracting File Problem. It is most likely caused by low memory or corrupted cabinet file.' I don't believe the problem is due to low memory because if I reboot and do this immediately I get the same message. So what do I do about the corrupt cabinet file? I presume these are the .cab files – there are loads. I did wonder if I could just copy all of the ones on the installation disk.

Well, it could be a corrupt **.cab** file I suppose. You don't say where it's from, but if you've downloaded it then this could be the problem – download it again. If you're installing it from a disk, try copying the files to your hard disk first and install them from there. And if your hard disk doesn't have enough spare space to decompress the files, this could also be the cause of the problem. You can download the latest version of the Windows Media Player program from the Microsoft website. See Chapter 10 for more information on doing this sort of thing.

When my computer turns on it does nothing (it doesn't boot, nothing shows up on the monitor, the monitor acts as if the computer is not on). I have checked several times to make sure everything is plugged in on the inside and it still does not boot regularly, but I don't think it will work, I need some extra tips. Once in a while it does boot and I get the error message, 'Keyboard error or no keyboard present'. I tried plugging the keyboard into the mouse port, but that wire on the inside seems to be disconnected. I don't know where to plug it in. What can I do to fix this? Any pictures will be helpful.

Check the fuses in the plug on the electrical socket, the cable itself, and the plug wiring. Try using someone else's cable to see if that isolates the problem. If that isn't it (and your cable works on someone else's machine) and there's no sign of life at all from the computer (and all the power switches are on – as well as the one on the front, most computers now have a physical on/off switch at the back near where the power cable goes in) you may have a dead power supply. This is the box which takes the power from your regular house circuit and transforms it into the various voltages required by the different bits of your computer. It will have a fan at the back near where it plugs in, and if that's not turning it could be dead. Replacements are cheap and relatively easy to plug in, but you may feel more comfortable getting a computer repair shop to do this for you. The fact that your machine boots occasionally suggests a loose connection somewhere, although that's kind of hard for me to diagnose without sitting in front of it – you'll have to keep checking yourself. However, if it won't recognise a keyboard at all (and again try the trick of replacing it with a borrowed one and try yours on someone else's machine) then there could be some damage to the keyboard socket on the motherboard itself, with more damage elsewhere on the board. This can happen through age with soldered joints working loose with repeated heating/cooling cycles, or because of electrical supply surges frying components. It can also happen if you've plugged or unplugged the keyboard while the computer is turned on.

Harder Questions And Answers

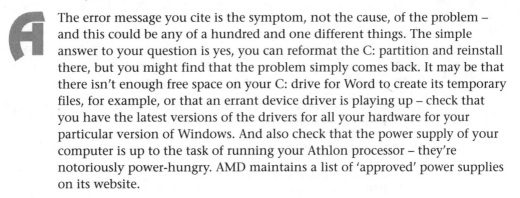

I am running Windows 2000 and have several glitches in programs. I have been advised to reformat my drive and reinstall the software. I have partitioned my hard drive with Partition Magic 6.0, with a C: drive for the OS and programs etc., and another two partitions for 'My Data' [G:] and 'Backups' [H:]. Can I reformat just C: and reinstall Windows 2000 etc. on this drive, without losing the data in the other partitions? An example of the glitches is when I close a document in Word, the program crashes and the error message reads: 'run time error WINWORD.exe has detected an abnormal program termination. You must restart . . .' etc. This error occurs on about 50 per cent of document closures. I have an AMD Athlon with 256 MB of RAM and a 30 GB hard disk.

The error message you cite is the symptom, not the cause, of the problem – and this could be any of a hundred and one different things. The simple answer to your question is yes, you can reformat the C: partition and reinstall there, but you might find that the problem simply comes back. It may be that there isn't enough free space on your C: drive for Word to create its temporary files, for example, or that an errant device driver is playing up – check that you have the latest versions of the drivers for all your hardware for your particular version of Windows. And also check that the power supply of your computer is up to the task of running your Athlon processor – they're notoriously power-hungry. AMD maintains a list of 'approved' power supplies on its website.

I can play music and other information CDs without any problem, but I have a CD-R with wedding anniversary photos on it and every time I try to view the photos from the CD-R on my computer, I get the error message, 'device is not ready'. There's nothing wrong as far as I know with the CD-R as I have had prints taken from it. Is the problem with the CD-R or my computer?

At a guess I'd say that the CD-R disk isn't compatible with your CD drive. These things are very finicky and it can be problematical getting various combinations of CD writer, blank disk and CD readers to work together. Music CDs I copy on my computer, for example, won't play in the CD player in my car unless I use Samsung blanks. Upgrading your CD drive to a newer model – or a DVD-ROM drive which will also read CDs – might be the answer, but unfortunately until you've actually tried it there's no guarantee that it will work. It could also be a CD-R with an 'unclosed session', one still open for writing new information to, in which case probably only the original drive which created it will be able to read it. Or it could be a multi-session CD-R which gives the problems I describe.

*Since installing Netsonic my Internet Explorer 5.5 web browser keeps developing 'internal errors' in **kernel32.dll**. My limited research/knowledge suggests this might be due to Netsonic or some other programme overwriting IE 5.5's **kernel32.dll** with an older version but I have no idea how to rectify this. My diagnosis may also be inaccurate. I use Windows 98.*

You're halfway there – **kernel32.dll** is a Windows file. Try first doing a 'repair' on IE – find it in **Add/Remove Programs** in **Control Panel**. If this doesn't work, try re-running your Windows installation – just put the CD in the drive and do an 'over the top' reinstall, on top of your existing setup.

*My computer keeps going to a blue error screen. It is not when any particular action or program is running. Pressing any key or **Ctrl-Alt-Del** does not do anything, so I have to reboot the machine. I use Windows 98.*

This is one of the commonest problems going, and one of the hardest to solve because there are so many potential causes. It could be faulty software or hardware, and you need to do a number of things to narrow it down.

➤ Delete the temporary files in your **temp** folder and run the Disk cleanup function to free up some hard disk space.

➤ Run ScanDisk and Disk Defragmenter to further clean up your hard disk.

➤ Visit windowsupdate.microsoft.com and click on **Product Updates** to see if there are any updates you need to install.

➤ If the problems continue, you need to look at your hardware. One of the commonest causes of this problem is duff memory chips – if you can, swap out the memory with another stick or two. If you have more than one memory stick, try replacing them one at a time.

➤ While your computer's open, remove and replace all the cards inside to make sure they're securely seated. Check all screws holding them in place.

➤ Check all cables are firmly seated by removing and replacing them. This goes for cables plugged into the outside of your machine too.

➤ If all this fails, try reinstalling Windows 'over the top' by re-running the installer from inside Windows. If that doesn't succeed, you may need to reformat your hard disk and reinstall Windows from scratch.

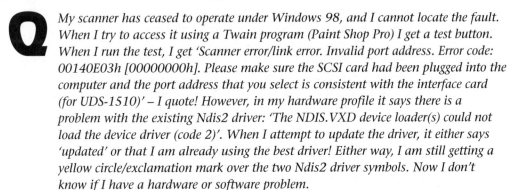

Note that reformatting will delete all information on your hard disk, so you should save it somewhere else first.

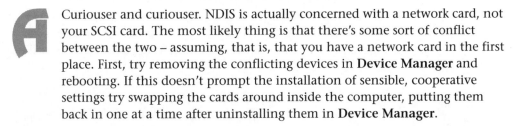

My scanner has ceased to operate under Windows 98, and I cannot locate the fault. When I try to access it using a Twain program (Paint Shop Pro) I get a test button. When I run the test, I get 'Scanner error/link error. Invalid port address. Error code: 00140E03h [00000000h]. Please make sure the SCSI card had been plugged into the computer and the port address that you select is consistent with the interface card (for UDS-1510)' – I quote! However, in my hardware profile it says there is a problem with the existing Ndis2 driver: 'The NDIS.VXD device loader(s) could not load the device driver (code 2)'. When I attempt to update the driver, it either says 'updated' or that I am already using the best driver! Either way, I am still getting a yellow circle/exclamation mark over the two Ndis2 driver symbols. Now I don't know if I have a hardware or software problem.

Curiouser and curiouser. NDIS is actually concerned with a network card, not your SCSI card. The most likely thing is that there's some sort of conflict between the two – assuming, that is, that you have a network card in the first place. First, try removing the conflicting devices in **Device Manager** and rebooting. If this doesn't prompt the installation of sensible, cooperative settings try swapping the cards around inside the computer, putting them back in one at a time after uninstalling them in **Device Manager**.

*I have Windows 95 and at start-up I get all these error prompts. I know I have to fix them in Sysedit, but that's not the problem. The problem is that I want to upgrade to at least Windows 98 or XP, but the computer doesn't recognise my CD drive. When I tried to get the computer to recognise it in Add new hardware, I found I couldn't because there is no 'Add new hardware' in my **Control Panel**. The other problem is I tried to delete everything and start from the beginning by reformatting my C: drive, but in order to recover it I need my CD drive, and also the computer doesn't recognise my boot-up floppy disk. Then the other problem is that when I tried to fix it by typing **msconfig** in the run box, the computer told me it couldn't find it, so you see a lot of files were deleted from my machine, and I don't know how to get it up and* *running properly. I was thinking of rebooting it down in MS mode and typing from the command line, and reformatting it but I don't know how to do that.*

Blimey. I don't want to be rude, but there's an old saying about 'Knowing just enough to get yourself into trouble ...'. I'm not clear where you are right now with all the above, so let's start with some basics. First, if your boot-up floppy disk doesn't work, is this because you've also deleted some files from it? Is it the boot disk which came with your computer? If not, do you still have that? You might also like to check in your BIOS that your computer's looking at the floppy drive before the hard disk – otherwise it'll just carry on booting from the hard disk and never get to the floppy. You get into the BIOS by pressing one or more keys such as **Del**, **Ctrl-F12** or whatever – you may see a message on the screen at start-up telling you which. *Do not*, however, change anything else in your BIOS or you may render your computer even more unusable than it is now. Next, is there any chance you can get hold of a Windows 98SE or Me boot disk from someone else? These include basic drivers which allow you to access the CD drive, and that would sort out your problem completely at the moment. If you can still get into **Device Manager** under **System** in **Control Panel**, see if your CD drive is listed in there and if it has any error messages associated with it. If it's not listed and you're not being prompted to install it on start-up, something more serious has gone wrong and you're looking at a full reinstall of Windows from your original Windows media. To do this you may need to create a boot disk which also contains the DOS-mode drivers for your CD-ROM – these would have been shipped with it when you bought it. (Or, if you or a friend has Windows 98 or Me use the boot floppy disk which is supplied with that version of Windows. It includes generic CD drivers which work with most computers.) I suspect from what you say that this is going to be the only realistic way of getting your machine working again.

*The error message 'A fatal exception has occurred at 9F80:00000804. Current application will be terminated. Press any key to terminate current application. Press Ctrl-Alt-Del again to restart computer. You will lose any unsaved information in all applications' appears in white on a blue screen when I move my mouse or tap the spacebar to resume after I have left my computer untouched for a while, when the screen saver has finished and the monitor screen is blank. I admit that I sometimes shake the mouse or tap the spacebar more than once when wishing to resume. This morning the message appeared after the screen had gone blank and I accidentally jolted the keyboard shelf rather hard. Despite what the message tells me, neither pressing any key nor pressing **Ctrl-Alt-Del** clears the screen and I have to switch off the computer and switch on again (thereby activating the ScanDisk process) if I wish to resume work. I would be very grateful for your advice as to how to avoid this situation.*

The problem is occurring not because of the way in which you move your mouse or the force with which you touch your keyboard, but because of problems between Windows 98 and your computer. Try turning Power Management off in both Windows and your BIOS, restarting, and then using just Power Management in Windows. Windows 98 uses an advanced version of the system with which not all computer BIOSes are compliant.

I have a 486 laptop that I would like to get running again. When I booted up to install an OS, it loads DOS but doesn't read the A: drive – it just says 'I/O Error ... abort, retry, fail' or 'I/O Error invalid drive or sector not found'. I turn it off and now it doesn't load, instead I get 'Keyboard clock inline failure'. I want to give it to my little brother for his birthday. What should I do?

You may have the 'wrong kind' of floppy disk. You're probably using a 1.44 MB floppy and it may only see 720 KB disks. Format a new floppy and check the options to format to this size. Add the system files too – you'll see all these options by right-clicking on a new disk under Windows 9x and choosing the **Format** option. The problem with doing things this way, however, is that you may then have problems if you're installing Windows 3.xx – you don't say which OS you want – because this will format the disk with a later version of DOS. If this is the case and you have your Windows 3.xx/DOS disks, use those instead. However, if your laptop has at least 16 MB of RAM (Random Access Memory) you'll be able to run Windows 95, albeit fairly slowly, and should be able to get up and surfing, e-mailing and so on. The 'keyboard clock' error may indicate that the backup battery has failed, which could also account for the errors. In some machines these are user-replaceable but, in a machine of this vintage, you may be out of luck.

The error message 'Bad or missing Keyboard Definition File' appears when I start up my computer. Things seem to run OK, but how do I go about dealing with the apparent error, please?

Click **Start > Run** and in the box which pops up type **sysedit**. This will bring up a set of configuration files for your PC including one called **autoexec.bat** and another called **config.sys**. The former is a 'batch' file, a file containing a sequence of events, which AUTOmatically EXECutes when you start up your computer, and the second is a SYStem file referring to your machine's CONFIGuration which also runs on start-up – hence their names. Look in them for lines referring to a keyboard definition file along the lines of 'keybuk' or similar. If you find such a reference, type **REM** at the beginning of that line. This is to REMark out that line so it won't run next time you start up your computer – if you have any problems, just remove the REM to go back to the previous position. You're having this problem almost certainly because your computer is trying to load a localised keyboard definition file in

27

DOS (Disk Operating System; the 'real' operating system which underlies Windows 9x) which you don't actually need. The 'localisation' settings under **Control Panel** (**Keyboard and Regional Options**) will take care of this, unless you're going to be running any DOS-mode programs which need to be told about your keyboard.

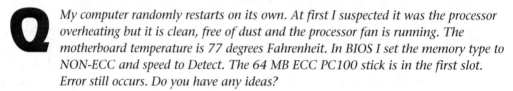

My computer randomly restarts on its own. At first I suspected it was the processor overheating but it is clean, free of dust and the processor fan is running. The motherboard temperature is 77 degrees Fahrenheit. In BIOS I set the memory type to NON-ECC and speed to Detect. The 64 MB ECC PC100 stick is in the first slot. Error still occurs. Do you have any ideas?

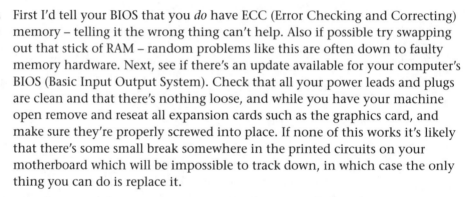

First I'd tell your BIOS that you *do* have ECC (Error Checking and Correcting) memory – telling it the wrong thing can't help. Also if possible try swapping out that stick of RAM – random problems like this are often down to faulty memory hardware. Next, see if there's an update available for your computer's BIOS (Basic Input Output System). Check that all your power leads and plugs are clean and that there's nothing loose, and while you have your machine open remove and reseat all expansion cards such as the graphics card, and make sure they're properly screwed into place. If none of this works it's likely that there's some small break somewhere in the printed circuits on your motherboard which will be impossible to track down, in which case the only thing you can do is replace it.

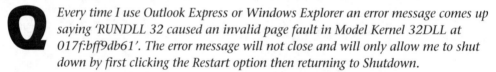

Every time I use Outlook Express or Windows Explorer an error message comes up saying 'RUNDLL 32 caused an invalid page fault in Model Kernel 32DLL at 017f:bff9db61'. The error message will not close and will only allow me to shut down by first clicking the Restart option then returning to Shutdown.

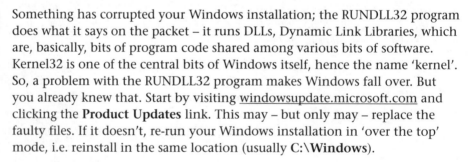

Something has corrupted your Windows installation; the RUNDLL32 program does what it says on the packet – it runs DLLs, Dynamic Link Libraries, which are, basically, bits of program code shared among various bits of software. Kernel32 is one of the central bits of Windows itself, hence the name 'kernel'. So, a problem with the RUNDLL32 program makes Windows fall over. But you already knew that. Start by visiting windowsupdate.microsoft.com and clicking the **Product Updates** link. This may – but only may – replace the faulty files. If it doesn't, re-run your Windows installation in 'over the top' mode, i.e. reinstall in the same location (usually **C:\Windows**).

Setup And Start-up

First Things To Check With A New Computer

Luckily for most buyers of new computers nowadays, they come with middling to good instruction booklets, directions, pamphlets and posters telling you what plugs into what and where all the bits go. Most components, plugs and sockets are colour-coded these days, too, making it fairly obvious what goes where.

If you're lucky, Windows and possibly any other software you ordered will have been installed and, when you've followed the instructions and plugged everything in as appropriate and pushed the On switch, it will turn on and welcome you to the wonderful world of personal computing.

Then again, you may push the button and discover that you've bought the most expensive paperweight you've ever owned.

Obviously, the very first thing to do is panic and blame yourself. And then to sit down and work through carefully what you've done.

1 Check that everything you ordered has been delivered.

2 Have you installed *everything* you're supposed to according to the instructions? Don't be tempted to miss something out because it doesn't look important.

3 Check and then check again that all plugs and cables are where they're supposed to be.

4 Are you pushing the correct button in the correct way on the front of your PC? Some have more than one, others require that you hold them in for a set time before they'll operate.

5 If there are lights appearing on the main system box but there's nothing on the screen, have you actually turned the screen on? Most monitors have a separate power button.

What Goes Where

There are a number of components common to most PCs. Some are essential to the running of your PC, others less so. The important ones:

1 Main system box. Most other parts of your PC will plug into this.

2 Monitor. The display screen.

3 Keyboard. The letter, number and other keys you use to control your PC and to enter information into it.

4 Mouse. Horizontal movements on your desk with your mouse are translated into vertical and side-to-side movements on your screen.

The less important ones:

1 Printer. Used for producing printed output from your computer.

2 Scanner. Looks like a photocopier. It takes a picture of anything put on it by 'scanning' across it, storing an image of what it sees.

3 Digital camera. Takes pictures which are stored electronically and which can then be transferred direct to your computer.

Next Steps

If your computer won't work after working through the obvious points, you'll find more checks to perform in Chapter 1. Other potential problems include:

1 Faulty hardware. If everything is plugged in, it's possible that one or more of the components in your new PC is broken or incorrectly installed. Tracking down such a problem may involve opening the main system box. Doing this, however, may invalidate your warranty and, especially in the case of a brand-new machine,

you should contact the vendor and make them replace or correct the faulty equipment.

2 Missing components.

Installing Windows

If your new computer doesn't come with Windows preinstalled (and now your choice will probably be Windows XP Home or Professional) it will either come with a Windows CD or you'll buy one separately. The simplest method to install it is to check the PC's documentation to set it to boot up from the CD-ROM or DVD drive, insert the disc and turn the machine on, then follow the installation wizard through.

What To Do First When It's All Set Up

The temptation will be to dive right in and start playing. Well, it is for me, anyway, but then my motto is 'When all else fails, read the instructions'. If you have a new computer with Windows XP installed the first thing you'll see when it starts up are a number of screens offering 'guided tours' to familiarise you with what's available. Take the tours – even if you're familiar with earlier versions of Windows you'll be surprised at the useful new stuff that's included. If you've never used a computer before, the tours are invaluable in showing you a few of the basics like using a mouse and keyboard, opening programs and so on.

Once you've done all that you may be tempted to get online and start surfing that there internet about which you've heard so much. And so you should – but first take a few simple precautions.

1 Install your anti-virus software. If none came with your computer, you can download the free AVG from Grisoft, www.grisoft.com. See Chapter 18 for more details on AVG and Chapter 10 for details on how to download and install software.

2 Install a personal firewall. If none came with your computer, see Chapter 18 for recommendations and Chapter 10 for details on how to download and install software.

3 If you have installed Windows NT, 2000 or XP do not install Internet Information Server (IIS) until after you've visited the Windows Update site, windowsupdate. microsoft.com. There's a worm called CodeRed which can infect unpatched (unmodified and older) versions of IIS when you simply connect to the internet. With Windows 2000 and XP, IIS is an 'optional' extra which you normally install after the main Windows installation. If you have Internet Services Manager installed in the **Administrative Tools** section of **Control Panel**, then IIS is installed – turn it off before connecting to the internet for the first time.

4   After updating your anti-virus and firewall software, make the Windows Update site, <u>windowsupdate.microsoft.com</u>, the first place you visit to install 'crucial updates' – security patches and additions – before you go any further. It may seem boring to go through all this the first time you venture out onto the internet but it will stand you in good stead in the future.

5   Read Chapters 10 and 18 before going online. You're at your most vulnerable when you don't know what to expect. If you were visiting an apparently friendly page and a message popped up saying, 'Warning! Your computer is not fully protected against viruses – click here to update!' would you think twice before following the instructions? If you wouldn't think twice, read those chapters carefully as such messages are almost certainly hoaxes designed to get you to infect your own computer.

Questions And Answers

Easy Questions And Answers

I tried to follow your advice about using Backup but it's not installed on my computer – where is it?

Start > Settings > Control Panel > Add/Remove Programs > Windows Setup > Disk (or **System**)**Tools**, tick **Backup** and **OK** twice. Have a look through the other options here – you'll find a number of programs that come with Windows aren't installed by default.

How can I get into the BIOS of my computer, and what is it anyway?

When you turn on the power to your PC the BIOS chip detects this and takes control of the start-up process, working out what types of devices like hard disks and memory are contained within your system. You can change settings in the BIOS by pressing a combination of keys when your machine starts up, e.g. **Ctrl-F12** or **Shift-F1** – check your documentation for the correct combination or watch for a message on-screen when your machine starts up. Unfortunately, there are any number of different combinations for different computers so it's not possible to give full details here.

I want to use the Direct Cable Connection facility between my laptop and desktop computers, but the Windows 98 desktop doesn't appear to have the software. Can I download it from somewhere?

You'll find it on your original Windows CD. Open **Control Panel** and then **Add/Remove Programs**, click the **Windows Setup** tab and left-click once on the **Communications** item to select it and then once more on the **Details** button. Check the **Direct Cable Connection** box, OK your way out and follow the instructions on-screen for installation and rebooting.

 I heard that Windows XP won't support the twin screens I use currently with Windows 98. Is this correct?

 No, it's not. Originally Microsoft had planned that only the Professional version of XP would support dual monitors/graphics cards, but they changed their minds and both the Pro and Home versions support your setup.

 From time to time I accidentally hit Caps Lock with my little finger. How can one link a beep to this action and therefore avoid typing a few lines in upper case, which are rather tedious to remove?

 This is part of the **Accessibility Options**, which may not have been installed on your computer by default. If they're not listed in your **Control Panel**, open the **Add/Remove Programs** applet, click on **Windows Setup** and check the **Accessibility Options** box. Click **Apply** and follow the instructions on-screen – you'll need your original Windows setup disc.

 When I switch on my PC the graphics card details are shown on the screen followed by a large logo of the PC manufacturer. This logo is displayed over the top of the POST and BIOS details, which I would like to see. The manufacturer has now ceased trading and I want to permanently remove this logo. I have looked in the BIOS setup for any details but cannot find anything of help.

 If there's no option in the BIOS to turn off this display then there's probably nothing you can do about it, I'm afraid.

 My computer tries to boot from its CD drive whenever I turn it on with a bootable CD in it. How can I stop this?

 This will be an option in your BIOS – when your machine starts up you should see a message saying you can enter setup or similar by pressing a combination of keys. Do this and you'll find you can change the boot order from there – C: is the best option, then CD and floppy drives.

33

*I've been told recently that I couldn't create more room on my C: drive by moving files to my Desktop, since that itself is part of the C: drive. However, I've now checked and this appears to be wrong – if you open **My Computer** and click to go 'upwards' through the drives, I can see that My Computer and the drives on it – like my C: drive and my D: drive (which is my CD, I've identified) – are below that. So clearly my Desktop is 'above' my C: drive. The question is, moving files from my C: drive to my Desktop doesn't seem to create any extra spare space on my C: drive itself – so I assume that somehow I'm copying, not moving, the files. What am I doing wrong?*

The **Desktop** is a folder on your C: drive. If you look inside the **Windows** folder on your C: drive you'll see a folder there called **Desktop**. Open that and you'll note that most of what's on your desktop will be there, with the exception of 'system' folders like **My Computer** and **Network Neighborhood**. (There is a possibility that you won't find **Desktop** here if you're on a network, for example, or if you have Windows NT, 2000 or XP, when it will be stashed elsewhere in the hierarchy according to whatever system you have – just do a search (**Start > Find**) for **Desktop**). Moving files from, say, **C:\My Documents** to your **Desktop** actually moves them to **C:\Windows\Desktop** (or wherever). There are basically two kinds of storage on your computer, the RAM memory (of which you'll have something like 64 MB), which is used for temporary storage of files and programs you're using at the moment, and your hard disk, which will have something like 10 GB of space on which to permanently store your programs and files. RAM only works when your computer is turned on and has electricity flowing through it, whereas your hard disk keeps things stored when your machine is turned off. From what you say you only have one hard disk on your computer, your C: drive, so I'd ask you to spend a moment thinking about where your files might be going if they're no longer on your C: drive? Your **Desktop** isn't an entity apart from your hard disk – it isn't a magical extra storage space.

Harder Questions And Answers

*Having just built a new computer, when turning it on, it starts to load and then stalls just before the final Windows screen (when your password box is shown). During certain programs the computer freezes again. The computer stops then reloads itself after running ScanDisk. All this is usually cleared by pressing **Ctrl-Alt-Del** or Reset if that doesn't work. It's running Windows 95 with a Windows 98 upgrade on an Abit KT7 motherboard with a 1 GHz Athlon, a 550 watt power supply and four fans.*

First, AMD processors are very fussy about their power supplies – I note you have a 550 watt model, but it's worth double-checking with AMD via their website at www.amd.com that it isn't an approved model. Then you can try a clean installation of Windows 98. You don't need to install Windows 95 first – just run the 98 upgrade disc and, at some point in the installation, you'll just need to insert the Windows 95 CD to 'prove' you're entitled to the upgrade. Do this either on a newly-formatted hard disk or, if that's not possible, into a new folder other than your current Windows one – choose the **Custom** install option to do this. Next, check, check and then check again all the bits you've built yourself. Try using just one stick of memory at a time to see if you can isolate the problem. Remove any non-essential cards like sound and modem cards to see if that's the problem. Remove all the cards and reseat them again, double-checking that all screws are in tightly. Check that all your fans are working properly.

 How can I reinstall Windows 95 from the original CD onto a 'blank' computer? When I put the CD into my computer to which I've had to fit a new hard disk (the old one went south very rapidly) nothing happens, and I can't make it see the D: drive where the CD sits.

 The advent of Windows 98 with installation floppy disks that included 'generic' CD-ROM drivers so you could get to the CD containing the installation has helped a lot, as has the advent of bootable CDs and the hardware to take advantage of them.

But if you have an older machine and need to do a reinstall of Windows 95 while wiping away all of the previous installation, you're in a real bind if you don't have the DOS drivers for your CD-ROM and/or the knowledge on how to use them.

The problem is that Windows 95's boot disk is actually a version of DOS (7.0 to be precise), the operating system on which Windows 9x is based, and to get from the floppy-based boot-up disk to the CD drive you need the DOS drivers for that CD drive. Now, you may have these on another disk which came with the computer, but you may not. Even if you do, getting it all to work is a non-trivial task.

So, instead, do this. Put your Windows 95 CD into the drive of the machine you wish to reinstall Windows on. Cancel anything which pops up and tries to run. Open **My Computer** and then the Windows 95 CD. Open a second instance of **My Computer** and arrange your screen so you can see both windows. On the second, double-click your C: drive to open it, then click **File > New** and make a new folder called **cabs**. Now, right-click and drag the **win95** folder from your Windows 95 CD onto this new folder and left-click **Copy here** on the pop-up menu. Let the files copy – it'll take a minute or two. Copy the file called **setup.exe** into the **cabs** folder too.

Now, in the **C:** drive of **My Computer** delete everything except for your **cabs** folder that Windows will let you delete – it won't let you delete the **Windows** folder, for example, but you'll get rid of a lot, hopefully everything apart from the **Windows** folder itself. If anything else is left, make a note of its *exact* name, including spaces.

Now put your Windows 95 boot disk into your floppy drive and restart the computer. You should arrive at a prompt which says just **A:** or similar. Type the following: **deltree c:\windows** and hit the **Enter** key. Confirm you really, really want to do this. Repeat the process for any other folders left on your hard disk *except* for the **cabs** folder you created yourself.

Then delete all the stray files in the 'root' of your C:\ drive by typing **del c:*.*** and hitting **Enter**. Confirm.

NB: you may not be able to do this from the **A:** drive prompt. If you get a problem, type: **C:** and hit **Enter**, then do the above.

If you do have any folder names or file names with spaces in them, they may not be deleted and/or you may only see them listed in a truncated form. If the former is the case, to delete them you need to enclose their names in double quotes so the delete command for a folder called **My files** would be **deltree "c:\My files"**.

If the file names are truncated you'll see a name like **c:\filena~1** which you should type instead of the full name you see in Windows to delete it, i.e. **del c:\filena~1** rather than **del "c:\filenamedsue"**.

When this is over check there's nothing left on your **C:** drive apart from the **cabs** folder by typing **dir c:** and hitting **Enter**. If anything is left, delete it as above.

What you should have now is a hard drive bare of everything apart from the Windows 95 setup files, so type **cd c:\cabs** and hit **Enter**.

You should now be at a prompt saying **c:\cabs**. Type **setup** and hit **Enter**. This should launch the Windows 95 setup program – follow the prompts through and you should get a new install of Windows 95. This method isn't as thorough as reformatting the hard disk since, theoretically, it's possible for a determined person to recover your data from the hard disk. It also won't delete system and hidden files (with the attributes S and H in their properties). However, unless you suspect your daughter of working for the KGB and/or you store secrets of national import on your computer, the effort is non-trivial enough to make it not worthwhile.

 When I switch my PC on at the initial boot-up (i.e. at the memory check and primary master etc. page) once it has detected master and slave etc. it says at the bottom 'floppy(s) failed(40) press F1 to continue'.

Check the configuration of your floppy drive in your BIOS (the 'Setup' or similar section you should see mentioned during boot-up – you usually access it by pressing a key or combination of keys such as **Del**, **Shift-F1** or similar). Make sure it isn't set to be a 1.2 MB/5.25 inch drive. Next, check the cable into the drive itself, and that the power lead is firmly attached. If none of this cures it, it could just be a duff drive – you can replace them for under £10 nowadays.

My computer is protected from unauthorised use by a password on boot-up. I know my password and have tried to boot up the system several times, but it tells me that I have entered the wrong password. I have removed the battery from the motherboard and left it out overnight then replaced the battery and tried to boot up again. Each time I enter the password it comes up incorrect. Is there a way that I can resolve this and boot up my system to enter setup and delete the password? It's a Packard Bell, 64 MB RAM, 400 MHz processor, 7.5 GB HD, Windows 98.

There may be a 'jumper' connecting two contacts on your motherboard which will clear the CMOS memory and remove the password – check the documentation which came with the machine or the Packard Bell website, www.packardbell.com. I assume you're not referring to the Windows 98 start-up password – you can avoid this by simply clicking **Cancel** or pressing the **Esc** key.

Do you have any advice on the best practices when transferring a PC? I am giving my old one to my daughter and want to remove all my personal records, Favorites and programs, and let her start afresh free from all my clutter, past mistakes and built in faults; including those of which I am ignorant.

The simplest thing to do would be to reformat the hard disk and reinstall Windows 95 from scratch using the original disks which came with the computer. You use the boot disk which came with it to format the hard disk and install Windows, although you may have a problem if the Windows disk doesn't include drivers for your CD-ROM drive, which you will need to access to install Windows itself from the CD – these drivers may have come on a separate floppy disk with the computer/drive itself. The procedure would be to format the hard disk using the **format c:/s** option to make the hard disk bootable, then install the CD drivers from their floppy disk, then install Windows 95 from the CD. A slightly easier option is to copy the Windows **.cab** files from the CD to a directory of their own on your hard disk along with the **setup.exe** file and then boot from a floppy disk and use the **deltree** command to delete all the directories/folders apart from the one containing the **.cab** files, then run **setup.exe** and install Windows. Personally I usually make a small partition on all hard disks where I keep these CAB files to make reinstallation a lot easier – then I can reformat the main C: partition and reinstall from the D: (or whatever) partition where I keep the **.cab** files. If you're not clear on the procedure, do come on over to <u>www.drkeyboard.net</u> for some guidance.

 Having now purchased Windows 98, I seem to be having many little aggravating problems and it was suggested that I should have upgraded to Windows 2000. Should the home user work with Windows 2000 or is that program more suited to business?

 It depends, is the only sensible answer. Probably the best option for a home user is Microsoft Windows XP Home Edition. It's built on the same Windows NT base as Windows 2000 but includes drivers for much more hardware than Windows 2000. Also, more software is compatible with it than with Windows 2000 – probably even more than works with Windows 98, in fact, if you include old DOS programs. Windows XP is much better suited to games in particular. Check to see if your hardware is capable of running it before upgrading, though, since the requirements are for faster processors and more RAM than for Windows 98 – start at <u>www.microsoft.com/windowsxp</u> for more information. If you do decide on Windows 2000 the same caveat applies – have a look at the hardware and software compatibility list on the Microsoft website at <u>www.microsoft.com/windows2000/professional/howtobuy/ upgrading/default.asp</u>.

Part 2
Peripheral Problems

Roll up your sleeves, tell the kids to stand well back and get a good grip on your screwdriver as you prepare to do battle with your PC. Once you've worked out what it may be that's causing your problem in the first place, these chapters will walk you through fixing those problems that are caused by hardware faults. Chapter 4, 'Inside Your PC', will help you become familiar with what all those cards and boxes inside your computer do. Each chapter from 5 to 7 discusses a different aspect of your PC's hardware – that's the bits you can actually touch – tells you how it can go wrong and, when it does, how you can put it right. At the end of each chapter there's a selection of questions I've received and answered over the past seven years which should help you deal with your own problem – and hopefully, show you that you may not be on your own with your particular difficulty.

Chapter 4

Inside Your PC

In This Chapter

➤ Description of the inside of a typical PC

➤ Essential precautions to take if you want to open your PC case

Description Of The Inside Of A Typical PC

If you're lucky you may never see the inside of your PC or, if you do, it may be an excursion limited to watching someone add some more RAM or a new hard disk. But it can still help to know what's inside the magic box and, hopefully, have some of the mysteries revealed as to how and why things work the way they do.

PCs nowadays are based on a design produced by IBM more than 20 years ago to get into the then nascent personal computer market. Early PCs had been self-assembly boxes that required a knowledge of electronics and soldering, but 'ready to use' machines soon arrived which could do something interesting without requiring that the owners had a decent tool kit and an understanding of electrical engineering.

Although the specifics have changed, the interior of a 21st century PC doesn't look that dissimilar to one built in the early 1980s, and many of the components are very similar indeed.

You can see the inside of a typical PC in Figure 4.1. In this case it's a 'tower' system, one which stands vertically – usually underneath your desk. In this picture the front of

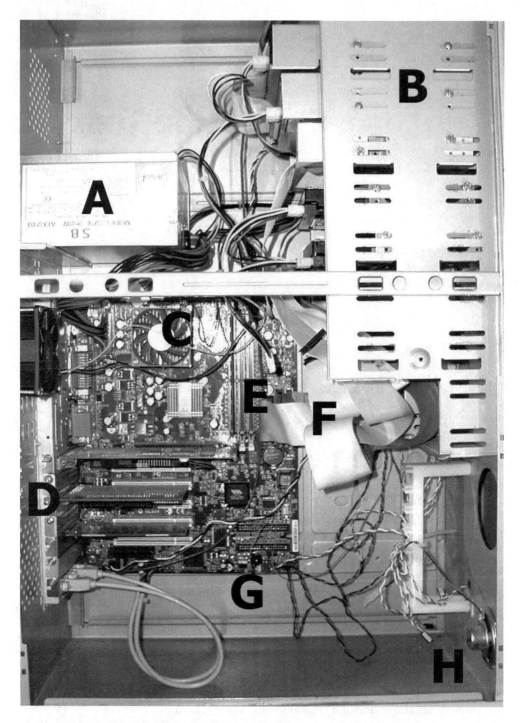

Figure 4.1 The inside of a typical PC

the PC is to the right, the rear to the left. This particular PC case is larger than normal, being designed to be used as a 'server' computer with room for lots of extra hard disks and other components, although it's actually being used as a regular PC at the moment.

The Power Supply Unit

One of the largest components inside the case which holds all the bits is the power supply unit (PSU) (A). This takes in alternating current from the mains at 240 volts or so and turns it into the various voltages required by different components inside your computer – some need 5 volts, others 12, others 3.3 and so on. Power supply units are generally pretty reliable and rarely need replacing, but they're not expensive to replace if they do go wrong. They may wear out after overheating if the air vents underneath and to the sides are blocked or if the fan to the outside at the rear of the computer is blocked in any way. If you're specifying your own components for a new PC, check that the power supply unit is compatible with the CPU you plan to use – this is particularly important with AMD processors – and buy one with a capacity of at least 350 watts if you have a choice (not all system builders allow you to specify anything other than their 'standard' power supply).

Disk Drives

To the right of the power supply in Figure 4.1 at B are the DVD (top) and CD writer drives, with the hard disks in the cage below them. There are two types of cables attaching these. The cables with the white plugs nearest the camera attach them to the power supply; the flat, 'ribbon' cables at point F to the motherboard.

Normally you're limited to a maximum of four drives – either hard disks and/or CD or DVD drives – in a computer using standard IDE connections. However, there is also a SCSI card (Small Computer System Interface, an alternative, add-on method of connecting devices such as these disks to a computer) inside the computer (at D) to which both the DVD and CD drives attach. There is also a standard 3.5" floppy disk drive below these drives. Drives like CDs and hard disks are referred to as being of the 3.5" or 5.25" form factor. This refers to the width of the drive's casing: 5.25" drives are 'full-width' drives and take up the full width of the PC case, as they do here. Hard and floppy disk drives are more usually of the 3.5" form factor. Tower cases are almost without exception 5.25" wide – any 3.5" drives in them come with 'spacers' to allow them to fit into 5.25" drive bays, or are fitted in a small 'cage' of their own inside the PC. Drive bays are divided into those which are accessible from the outside and those which are enclosed – CD, DVD and floppy drives need to be accessible from the outside; hard disks don't normally need this facility. Hard disks are normally described in terms of their capacity for storing data, e.g. 60 GB.

The Motherboard

The motherboard is the large printed circuit board to which everything else is attached. Normally they're green, although for those of you reading in black and white this particular motherboard is red.

The Processor

The fan you see at C is sitting on top of the CPU, in this case an AMD Duron 850 MHz processor. Cooling fans are extremely important, particularly with AMD processors – if the fans fail and the chips overheat they can be destroyed and may even catch fire. CPUs in new computers now all come with hundreds of 'pins' to attach them to special sockets in the motherboard. There was a brief fashion in the mid-1990s for slot-mounted processors such as the Pentium II, but now all CPUs use these multi-pin sockets. AMD and Intel are the commonest makes of CPU but motherboards designed for one type of processor won't work with a CPU from the other manufacturer. CPU speeds are measured in megahertz (MHz), and now there are a number of processors available at speeds in excess of two gigahertz (2,000 MHz) – that's 2,000,000,000 Hertz (cycles per second). CPU speeds used to be a useful way of quickly comparing the performance of two PCs but now many other things also affect the performance of a PC such as the amount of RAM, the speed of the hard disk and the performance of the graphics card. Even two PCs with the same model CPU can perform very differently because they're set up differently, have different architectures and so on. Think of CPU speed as being a little like the capacity of a car engine – two cars each with two-litre engines can perform very differently to each other.

CPUs, as well as having different sockets from manufacturer to manufacturer, also need different 'chipsets'. These are the chips you can see on the motherboard, e.g. below points C and E in Figure 4.1, which control various components such as the BIOS and the expansion cards.

Expansion Cards And Memory

Below the CPU and attached to the rear of the PC case are the (horizontal) expansion cards at D. In this PC the cards you can see are, top to bottom, an AGP video card, an Adaptec SCSI card and an Intel network card. The two cables below these cards connect the external USB ports to the motherboard. The white 'slots' these lower cards fit into are called PCI (Peripherals Connection Interface) slots. There's another, older standard on some PCs called ISA – these are about twice as long and are normally coloured brown. The AGP (Advanced Graphics Processor) slot which the video card in this PC (the uppermost one at point D) fits into is the shortest of all the slots on this PC. The card, a Matrox G400 DualHead card, can connect to two monitors at once, giving a double-sized 'desktop' with different programs on each monitor – handy if you're writing a book chapter in which you need to constantly refer to a photograph, for example, since you can have Microsoft Word on one screen and the image on the second screen. Versions of Windows from Windows 98 on can also work with two video cards to give the same effect. Nowadays most video cards are sold on their 3D capabilities – that is, their ability to show on a two-dimensional screen a realistic representation of a three-dimensional landscape. This is mostly useful – at the moment, anyway – for playing games, although there are hints that Microsoft may make use of the 3D capability of modern PCs in a future version of Windows. If you're not interested in playing games, though, you don't need a very expensive 3D graphics card, which can cost several hundred pounds.

Windows 9x can become 'confused' about the expansion cards installed inside your computer, since there are a limited number of internal 'addresses' they can use. Sometimes the only answer is to remove the cards and change their locations, putting them back one by one into different slots inside the case – but first see below on precautions to take before opening up your PC.

The RAM memory slots are at E – one of the three, the leftmost, is filled here with a single 256 MB 'stick' of PC2100 DDR RAM.

Below the memory at G, at the edge of the motherboard, a number of thin wires are attached – these connect to the power switch, the PC speaker (at H), the reset button and various LED lights on the case to indicate, for example, that the hard disk is being accessed.

This PC has an additional black case fan above D designed to improve cooling by drawing cool air into the case. In general if you're adding extra fans to a PC they should be taking warm air out of the top of the case. You may also find that adding a fan drawing in cool air at the bottom of the front panel helps cooling.

Sound

There is no additional sound card on this computer since the chips doing this job are actually included on the motherboard, immediately above the AGP graphics card at point D. The built-in sound on new computers is generally 'good enough' for the sounds produced by most programs and for the playback of MP3 music files and CDs, although if you want anything more complicated you should look at Chapter 6.

Essential Precautions To Take If You Want To Open Your PC Case

If you plan on opening your own PC case for any reason you need to take precautions against static discharges – those little electrical shocks you sometimes feel, e.g. after scuffing your feet across a nylon carpet. They may feel small to you but these shocks can do real damage to the delicate components inside your PC. The conventional way to protect yourself is to buy a strap which goes around one wrist and then connects to a suitable earth, e.g. a bare bit of metal on a central heating radiator. A better idea is to just leave your PC plugged into the mains electricity but to turn it off. Read the documentation with your computer very carefully about where to find the 'real' on/off switch on your computer, since the power button on the front of many these days does NOT cut power completely to the machine. Some need to be held for a certain number of seconds and/or pressed a number of times. Some computers have a separate, 'hard' power switch at the rear near the point where the electrical supply cable is plugged into the power supply.

If you are in any doubt at all about this, *do not* open your computer case yourself – take it to a professional repairer and get them to do the work. If you do decide to open the case yourself, to eliminate the possibility of electrical shock (which is what the PC manufacturer is worried about when they advise you to always disconnect the electrical plugs), plug your PC into a power strip or surge protector with an on/off switch and turn that off. This should leave the supply 'grounded' and allow you to work without worries about static but check the documentation on your surge protector before relying on this method.

Questions And Answers

Easy Questions And Answers

My computer worked fine at home in New York but now I've moved to France it won't start up. What's up?

This is a virtually impossible problem to diagnose at a distance, but there are a few things to check. If this is a desktop computer, check that all cables are in properly and that nothing has become loose inside the main system box during your move. Whether it's a desktop or laptop, check that you have the correct voltage adapter/power supply – most desktop power supplies are switchable between the USA's weedy 110 volts and Europe's mighty 240, so make sure you've switched that over. Check the power 'brick' on your laptop to verify that it auto-detects the European voltage. If you plug a 110 volt supply into the 240 volt mains you may fry the power supply/adapter if you're lucky, or the entire PC if you're unlucky.

My keyboard plug has a broken prong caught inside the socket on the computer that I can't get out. Is there another way to plug in the keyboard so I can use it?

If you have a USB keyboard and your computer and operating system support USB (Windows 95b/OSR2 or later, not including NT4) you can plug it into your computer's USB socket – you could also buy a new USB keyboard if your setup is compatible. Otherwise, unless you can get the damaged prong out you may be stuck.

I currently have a UMAX SCSI scanner which appears to have given up the ghost. Since most scanners now seem to be USB, I would like to replace the SCSI scanner with a USB one. Is this possible on a Pentium 200 simply by fitting a USB PCI card or are there other hardware issues?

Assuming that there's nothing wrong with your SCSI card, you'd probably be better off going for another SCSI scanner. If you're determined, though, I can't think of any reason why fitting a PCI USB card wouldn't work, assuming you have a version of Windows which supports USB. Note, UMAX in the USA started trying to charge for updated drivers in May 2002, although if you follow the links through from their website at www.umax.com to Europe and then the UK you may still be able to download them for free. They may change their minds but, on balance, I'd suggest looking at a different manufacturer such as Epson or Canon.

A few days ago I was unfortunate enough to sustain a lightning strike close to my TV aerial. Happily, no damage occurred to my house, but the voltage pulse destroyed my satellite DigiBox and thence the video and television via their respective SCART leads and my computer's modem card via the internal telephone wiring, not to mention the phone handsets themselves. I consider it fortunate that the damage to my PC stopped at the modem and that the whole machine was not a write-off too. Is there anything that can be done to protect against such circumstances, other than the crude but effective 'unplug everything' when you leave home?

Yes, you can – and should – buy surge protectors which should protect against electrical failures like this. They usually look like the trailing socket devices you can buy to plug several items into one socket, but have protection circuitry built in to protect against such things as lightning strikes. I use and recommend APC, www.apcc.com. They have models which also filter out spikes on telephone lines and TV aerial cables, which you should also buy.

My PC resets itself for no reason. I know that if my GeForce2 MX 400 card overheats it'll reset the PC, but I solved that problem by putting a table fan blowing right at the opened CPU casing. My GeForce card has its own fan too but the PC still resets itself. I also heard that improper mounting of the hard disk will cause the PC to reset but mine is mounted as well as any hard disk can be screwed in and my PC still resets. My processor's temperature is 42–50°C so it can't be the CPU overheating.

There are a number of reasons why your PC could reset itself, but leaving the case open with a desktop fan pointing at it is unlikely to cure any of them – as you've found. In fact, there's a good chance that the various components in your machine will receive *less* cooling with this system than if you simply closed it up. Cases are usually designed to draw in cool air over warm components and then exhaust that warmed air to the outside, and interrupting that by leaving the case open can cause more problems. There are other things you can check. Are all the fans working correctly for a start? Are they dusty? If so, clean them out gently with some canned air every six months to one year. Are the fans working in the correct direction? Apart from the power supply fan, which will need to work as designed, other fans at the top of the case should be drawing warm air out of the case, not bringing air in, and fans at the bottom of the case should be drawing in cool air so check they're facing the right way. If none of this solves the problem, your RAM could be at fault. If you have more than one strip of memory, try using them one at a time to see if that isolates the problem. It could also be a faulty PSU, a crack in the motherboard itself which, when it heats up, breaks an electrical connection, or a poorly seated component such as a modem or video card.

I already have two hard disks in my computer. Can I add a third?

If your computer has two IDE channels you can add a third HD on the second channel, or you could opt for SCSI, but this would require an additional card and is also a more expensive option. This presumes you don't have more than one CD or DVD device – the normal limit is a total of four devices (hard disks, CDs, DVDs, CD writers), two on each of the two IDE channels.

Harder Questions And Answers

*My computer won't boot up consistently. When I turn it on, it sounds like it is not accessing the hard drive. I also get nothing on my screen. This happens a lot. At this point, it shuts down automatically. Occasionally though, the system does boot up (I get the 'Compaq' screen) and gives me a message regarding my display settings being wrong. I just close this window or hit **OK** to get to Windows. Is this a power supply problem? It seems as if it's not passing all the tests(?) needed to boot up properly, so it just shuts down. It's a Pentium II 450 with 128 MB of RAM running Windows 98.*

It could be your power supply failing, it could be the hard disk failing, it could be a loose power lead, it could be a virus, it could be … well, the list goes on. The error message you mention about screen resolution suggests that you don't have the correct drivers for your video/graphics card installed – visit the manufacturer's website and download the latest drivers available for your particular version of Windows. There are also a number of troubleshooters for Windows 98 start-up problems available from Microsoft. Check in your help files first and then look at support.microsoft.com/default.aspx. Also check that all the computer's cables are secure and, if you're up to it, that all the cables and cards inside the box are seated firmly – it doesn't harm to take them all out and reseat them. If none of this makes any difference, it could be either a failing power supply or hard disk, in which case they'll need replacing as a matter of urgency – the specification of your computer suggests that it's several years old so this is a distinct possibility, and you should make sure that all your data is safely backed up somewhere other than your hard disk.

Q *I have a 200 W ATX power supply unit (PSU) to power an Intel SE440BX-2 motherboard. After powering up, the PSU fan starts then cuts out after a second. The PSU was working fine and powering the board, but Windows 98 reported a problem with the mouse driver on boot-up and it shut the PC down. I've been unable to power up since.*

A Well, it could be the power supply going bang – it sounds to be of a fairly ancient vintage. New ones are pretty cheap and they're easy enough to replace, so that may be the way to go. Before you splash out, just double-check all the connections first and also try powering up just the PSU. Also vacuum out all the dust inside the fans.

Q *My computer locks up after the splash screen. I have replaced all major items but still the computer hangs. It has a GB motherboard and Maxtor hard disk. If left on at start-up, i.e. in the BIOS setup program, for approximately 5 minutes the computer will then boot OK. I'm running Windows 98SE on an Athlon XP 1700+ with 512 MB of RAM.*

A If you've replaced all the 'major' items it implies that one of the 'minor' components is causing your problem. Have you carried some RAM over from an older machine? Or the power supply? AMD processors are very picky about what power supplies they'll work with, and there's a list of 'approved' ones on the company's website at www.amd.com. Leaving the machine on for a while and it then starting up implies that a connection is loose somewhere and heating it up makes a previously broken connection – this is typical of a hairline crack on a circuit board, e.g. on a motherboard or video card. Try removing all components apart from the CPU and video card and seeing if you can get the machine past the POST (Power-On Self-Test). Add the RAM one stick at a time to see if that's the problem. Also, check with the Gigabyte website to see if you have the correct type of RAM and whether or not there's an update for the BIOS. And if your Maxtor hard disk is getting on a little it could be just wearing out/seizing up and needs to be warmed a little before it starts up. If this is the case you should make sure you have all your data properly backed up (see Chapter 17).

 I have fitted a second-hand Cirrus graphics card to my system. How do I disable or remove the onboard graphics card to stop the system recognising it at boot-up and use only the Cirrus?

 You usually do this via the BIOS, the small program which tells your computer what to do with itself between you powering it up and it finding the operating system (like Windows 98). You get into it by pressing a key or combination of keys such as **Del**, **F1**, **F10** – there's usually a message on-screen telling you what key to press immediately after turning your PC on. There are hundreds, even thousands of BIOSes out there and it's impossible to predict exactly what you'll have to do. Check your system documentation for further details.

 I am building a computer using some parts from one that was put together for me. The previous system seemed to have problems recognising hardware that was installed at times, but yet it worked using them. Anyway, to make a long story short, I purchased a new motherboard (with onboard sound), an AMD Athlon TB 850 processor, 256 MB of PC133 SDRAM, and a 300 watt ATX tower case. My video card is a several months old ATI Rage whose drivers did not appear to load properly in the old system. I installed the following components: motherboard with processor, RAM, hard drives, 24x CD-ROM, 1.44 MB 3.5 " floppy, and video card. I powered up and I got a long continuous beep, no display, and approximately 30–45 seconds later the system just shut down. I disconnected the CD-ROM and the second hard drive and I get the same result. What do I try next?

 The beeps you hear on start-up are different depending on what BIOS your computer uses. Check your documentation – it should have come with the motherboard – as to what this might mean. At a guess, I'd say it means that something's not seated properly in the board. Try removing everything and then add bits one at a time – memory, video card and so on. If you still get a beep with nothing installed, it could be a problem with the power supply – I assume you checked the AMD website to make sure yours is rated as capable of supplying the rather high power levels their processors need? If this is the case, as it were, you should take it back and get a replacement.

 I have a P120 IBM Aptiva. Can I upgrade the RAM and what type should I use? Two of the current 16 MB are taken for the on-board graphics. Secondly, can I disable the on-board graphics to install a graphics card? And can I install an extra hard drive bigger than 2 GB, and if so how do I go about it?

Perhaps, depends, possibly, maybe and … well, you get the idea. The problem with proprietary computers like your IBM Aptiva is that manufacturers often used proprietary components – memory, hard disks, motherboards, the lot. Sometimes they didn't and you can upgrade them, but there's no way to tell without opening the box, consulting the documentation and poring over the company's website. Luckily, IBM are quite good in this respect. Go to their Upgrades and Services website at www.pc.ibm.com/us/upgradecenter.html where you can type in your machine's reference number and it'll tell you about it. Also, have a look at the Crucial memory website for RAM – there's a direct link from my message board at www.drkeyboard.net (which earns me a small commission if you buy via the link). They may be able to tell you if you can add more memory. Having said all this, your machine is pretty ancient by modern standards, so look carefully at what you're going to spend upgrading it and compare this with what you'd get by putting the same amount towards a new machine – personally, I've given up trying to upgrade computers by doing anything other than adding more RAM and, possibly, a new hard disk. Note, when you do fit RAM into computers it usually only fits into the appropriate slots one way round, and sometimes needs a harder 'push' to seat it than you think might be necessary. Also, modern computers have little clips at each end of the 'stick' of memory – these need to be fully closed.

 I have a home-built PC which has worked fine for a year. I use a Creative GeForce DDR graphics card. A few months ago I got a snazzy new case and transferred everything over from my old case. This included the actual PSU as I knew that the GeForce and Athlon had issues with insufficient power and I didn't want to take any chances on the new PSU. Ever since then I've experienced lockups that can only be resolved by hitting the reset switch. Any sound playing at the time gets stuck into a loop so it sounds like the new Chemical Brothers single (i.e. 'It came from Afrika-ka-ka-ka-ka-ka-ka-ka-ka-ka-ka'. You get the point). Sometimes it can be on all day before it happens, but normally it locks anywhere between 5 minutes to an hour and a half after being switched on. It also happens regardless of what I am doing, including just being turned on and left without me touching anything. Thinking I may have to do a complete reinstall, I installed Windows 98SE on to a freshly formatted 1 GB hard disk and booted that instead of my main system. I only installed Detonator Graphics drivers and then left the machine running. When I returned hours later it had locked up, leading me to believe that it's a hardware issue instead of a problem with Windows.

 If the only thing that's changed is your case then it is unlikely to be the cause of the problem, unless it's changed the airflow so drastically through the case that something is overheating – if this could be the problem (check the direction of airflow in the old and new cases), fit one or more extra case fans – they're not expensive. More likely is either that you've disturbed a bit of hardware during the transplant or that some other bit of software you've installed is causing the problem. Could it be some duff/badly-seated memory? A crack in the motherboard (this one's almost impossible to detect, unfortunately)? A problem with a cable either being not quite inserted properly or having been damaged in the move? Could it be a thermal problem? Are all the fans on your CPU, PSU and expansion cards working properly? Did you take the opportunity when you moved to vacuum out all the dust? Finally, have you tried putting everything back in the old case to see if that cures the problem? Sorry to ask so many questions, but this is a classic case of the 'can't diagnose it at a distance' problem. Come on over to the Message Board at www.drkeyboard.net and we can work through the options.

Chapter 5

Monitors And Displays

In This Chapter

➤ Some definitions

➤ Picture quality

➤ Step-by-step guide to optimising your display settings

➤ How to work out what kind of video card is inside your computer

➤ Adjusting your display

➤ Types of screens

➤ Other screen adjustments and screen problems

Some Definitions

It's very easy to run your computer screen at less than optimal settings. In fact, the odds are that if your computer came with Windows preinstalled then it won't have the optimum settings.

The commonest problems with the picture you see on your monitor screen concern its size, resolution and a couple of other settings. To understand why these are important, there are a few things you should know first about computer screens.

Size

The *size* of your screen is its most obvious feature – 15 inches, 17 inches or whatever. These, like television screens, are measured across the diagonal and usually refer to the size of the whole tube, not the visible area. Changes in legislation in the past few years now mean that manufacturers also have to quote the actual visible size of the screen, hence a 17-inch monitor may be cited as having a visible screen size of, say, 15 inches. Laptop and 'flat panel' TFT (Thin Film Transistor) LCD (Liquid Crystal Display) screens are generally the size they're quoted as being – and this may mean that, for example, a 15-inch laptop screen actually has the same visible screen area as a 17-inch CRT (Cathode Ray Tube – a conventional computer monitor) screen.

Resolution

The *resolution* of computer screens is measured in *pixels* (short for picture elements), or the dots which actually make up the picture. If you take a magnifying glass you'll see that the picture on your computer screen is made up from millions of tiny dots which, when viewed from a distance, make up the whole picture. A typical 14-inch screen will have a resolution of 640×480, that is 640 pixels across the horizontal and 480 pixels down the vertical axes. A 15-inch screen typically has a resolution of 800×600 pixels and a 17-inch screen 1024×768. There are many variations on these figures, and a 14-inch screen may be perfectly able to display a resolution of 800×600 or even 1024×768 pixels. Laptop and flat-panel TFT screens have fixed resolutions and you'll find that they will only work properly at, say, 800×600 or 1024×768 pixels.

Colour Depth

Next comes *colour depth*, the number of different colours your monitor can show at once. After the original monochrome (black and white or, sometimes, dark-green and light-green) screens came the first colour models which could show 16 different colours at once. This original specification – 16 colours at a resolution of 640×480 pixels – was called VGA (Video Graphics Array) and is still the standard resolution most, if not all, combinations of video card and monitor can show, a sort of 'lowest common denominator' resolution. Then came monitors and video cards capable of showing 256 colours at 800×600 pixels and, for a time, this became the standard computer screen resolution. Now we have screens which will support millions of colours at gigantic resolutions.

Refresh Rate

Your screen's *refresh rate* is the final thing to consider, and the magic number is 72 Hz (Hertz). The picture on your computer screen is made up of hundreds of thousands of tiny red, green and blue dots drawn in lines across the screen. The electron beam which draws the image sweeps across the entire screen (usually left to right and top to bottom, one row at a time) and then starts all over again with the first dot, refreshing the picture it's just drawn. The number of times it does this per second is called the refresh rate, and to avoid the image appearing to flicker it has to do this quickly enough to fool the human eye into believing that the image is not actually being constantly redrawn – similar to the way that movies are actually composed of many thousands of individual frames projected very quickly one after the other, fooling the human eye into believing that the image is moving smoothly. A refresh rate of 60 Hz means that the whole picture is redrawn 60 times per second, and while this sounds like a lot, most people will notice any refresh rate lower than this. In fact, many people notice some sort of flickering up to 72 Hz. Above this rate very few notice any difference, particularly once the rate goes above 80 Hz – monitors now being sold with refresh rates of 100 Hz or more may well be overkill and you shouldn't consider this a 'must-have' feature. Note also that using fluorescent lights, which themselves flicker many times a second, can cause interference with what you see on the screen. In the UK fluorescent tubes flicker at 50 Hz, whereas in the US, Canada and Japan it's 60 Hz. This may cause additional problems if you're using your PC in one of these countries.

Interlacing

Modern computer monitor screens now have what's called non-interlaced displays and you're very unlikely to come across interlaced screens unless you have a computer that's more than five years old. If you do, consider upgrading it for a new model – the display quality is very inferior. An interlaced display means that as the electron beam sweeps over the inside of the monitor, instead of drawing each line in turn it actually only draws every other line. On the next pass down the screen it draws the lines in between those it drew on the previous pass. Although this can give higher apparent refresh rates, you actually get a much worse picture which may flicker noticeably.

Picture Quality

The commonest definitions of the quality of picture you see on your monitor are:

➤ **MDA:** Monochrome Display Adapter, text-only monochrome screens showing 80 characters on 25 rows at once, each character 9 pixels wide by 14 high at 50 Hz.

➤ **Hercules graphics:** a proprietary graphics card from the Hercules company, which was the first to support monochrome graphics in charts, for example in spreadsheets like Lotus 1-2-3 on MDA displays.

➤ **CGA:** Colour Graphics Array from IBM, which actually produced worse quality pictures and graphics than Hercules cards. It supported 80×25 characters in 16 colours, but each character was formed from an 8×8 instead of a 9×14 grid. The graphics mode supported a 640×200 monochrome or $320 \times 200 \times$ four-colour screen at 60 Hz.

➤ **EGA:** Enhanced Graphics Array from IBM supported 16 colours from a palette of 64 at 640×350 pixel resolutions at 60 Hz. This was the minimum requirement for Windows 3.x and some older computers may still run at EGA resolutions.

➤ **VGA:** Video Graphics Adapter was the last widely accepted standard produced by IBM and is still a standard lowest-common-denominator resolution for all screens and video cards. It supports 640×480 pixel screens in 16 colours or 320×200 in 256 colours chosen from a palette of 262,144 colours.

➤ **8514/A:** a less common standard than VGA introduced at the same time, supporting 1024×768 displays in 256 colours but only at 43.5 Hz (interlaced) or 640×480 at 60 Hz (non-interlaced).

➤ **XGA:** eXtended Graphics Array, introduced by IBM on their late-model PS/2 (Personal System Two) model computers. Using either 512 KB or 1 MB of VRAM (Video Random Access Memory), XGA displays up to 1024×768 pixels in 256 colours or 640×480 pixels in 'high colour' (16 bits per pixel). There was also an XGA-2 standard supporting 1024×768 displays in high colour at higher refresh rates.

➤ **SVGA:** Super VGA (sometimes called UVGA, Ultra VGA). There are many definitions of SVGA, from $800 \times 600 \times 256$ colours on up, but with the decline of IBM's dominance in the computer market there's no official body defining such standards any more.

Nowadays the VESA (Video Electronics Standards Association) sets standards for computer displays, and more and more manufacturers are following their guidelines. The VESA BIOS Extension or VBE can be implemented in a number of different ways, either in software or hardware. Their website at www.vesa.org/standards.htm has much more information on this sort of thing than you're ever likely to want.

Before you start, check very carefully the maximum refresh rate your monitor is capable of displaying. *Do not* try to set it to a higher refresh rate as this can, in theory, cause permanent damage. In practice, Windows usually checks the settings you input and the worst that happens is that the display goes bonkers for a few seconds, then reverts to the original settings but there is *no guarantee* that this is what will actually happen. If you're in any doubt at all, err on the side of caution, check your documentation and the manufacturer's website and *do not* set higher refresh rates than your monitor can cope with. Also, many video card setup routines know about the most common brand-name monitors and can automatically adjust to show the best picture in any case.

In a nutshell, almost any new monitor you buy these days will far surpass the capabilities of the human eye to detect any flickering or lack of depth of colour. That doesn't mean you can get away with buying a cheap one, since other concerns such as focus of the picture come into consideration, and, as with televisions, in general the more you pay the better the overall quality of picture you can expect.

What you can do, whatever brand of monitor and card you buy, is make sure that you set up your display to show the best picture it can, and this means adjusting the screen size, colour depth and refresh rate to their optimum settings.

Step-by-step Guide to Optimising Your Display Settings

If, when you turn on your computer, the icons on your desktop (**Recycle Bin**, **My Computer** and so on) look large and colourless, right-click on a blank section of the **Desktop** and click **Properties** on the pop-up menu, then click the **Settings** tab. If you see something like Figure 5.1, it's pretty certain that your display could look a lot better than it does.

Figure 5.1 Display Properties dialog box

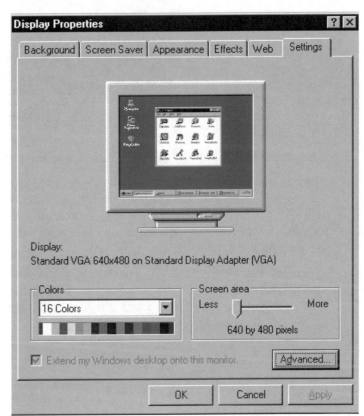

*Figure 5.2 Standard
Display Adapter
Properties dialog box:
Adapter settings*

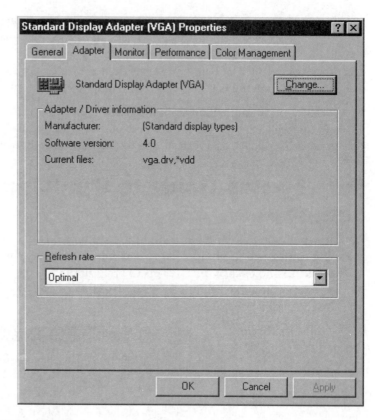

Left-click the **Advanced** button and then the **Adapter** tab at the top, and you should
see a dialog box like Figure 5.2.

Click the **Monitor** tab and you should see something like Figure 5.3.

These screens show that Windows has not detected either the kind of video card
(sometimes called graphics card) or the kind of monitor you have installed. Instead, it
has installed drivers for the lowest-common-denominator hardware it knows about –
drivers which every video card will work with and show some sort of picture on your
screen, but which isn't very pretty to look at or easy on the eye.

If you're lucky, clicking the **Change** buttons (top-right in the Figure 5.2 and Figure 5.3
dialog boxes) will start up the **New hardware** wizard and Windows will, this time,
recognise your hardware with a dialog box something like Figure 5.4.

If you're unlucky it won't, and it will invite you to try to install the card and/or
monitor manually.

*Figure 5.3 Standard
Display Adapter
Properties dialog box:
Monitor settings*

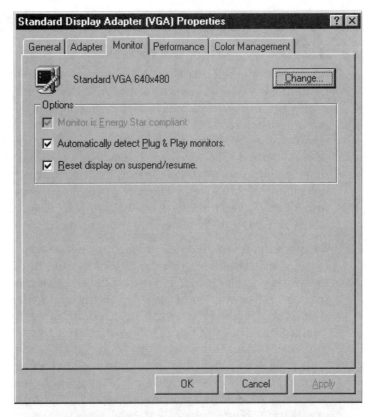

*Figure 5.4 Update Device
Driver Wizard*

How To Work Out What Kind Of Video Card Is Inside Your Computer

Now, generally speaking it's more important to know what kind of graphics card you have than the type of monitor, although knowing both will both help to fine-tune the quality of the picture you see and offer more options. If you don't know what sort of monitor or card you have, first check any documentation you have very carefully. In the case of monitors, you'll usually find some sort of identification either on the front or on a sticker or plate on the rear detailing things like the voltage it uses, serial number and so on. With video cards, if it's not recognised automatically and you have no documentation to tell you, you may need to open up your computer box and look for some sort of identification on the card itself. Figure 5.5 shows a typical, older card which you may find Windows not recognising.

There are thousands of different video cards available, all looking different, so it's hard to generalise about what you should look for. In this case, the clue to the card's identity is given by the large, square chip in the centre with 'Trident' on it. Why not the 'Quadtel' or another of the chips on the board? Here, the PCB (Printed Circuit Board, the green board everything is fixed to) itself has 'Trident Microsystems' stamped on it, but this sort of information isn't always available and it can be a process of trial and error to narrow things down. Typing the number immediately underneath the Trident logo, plus the word 'driver', into Google points to a number of websites, including the very likely looking www.video-drivers.com, specifically the page at www.video-drivers.com/companies/1072.htm which, about halfway down, has information about a driver for the above card. In this case, it points to both Trident's own site at www.tridentmicro.com and another very useful site, www.driverguide.com.

The driverguide.com website can even sometimes provide drivers for products whose manufacturers have disappeared completely, so bookmark it now.

Figure 5.5 An older type video card

If you have a PC with the video card chips included on the motherboard (often called 'on-board video'), you may need to check with the original manufacturer of the PC and/or the motherboard itself for drivers which will work with your computer. Check any documentation which came with your machine very carefully for clues as to exactly what's included.

Once you've downloaded or otherwise found the correct driver for your specific video card *and* for your version of Windows, install it as directed by the manufacturer or, if there's no specific instructions, see Chapter 12.

Adjusting Your Display

Once you've installed the new drivers, you can start adjusting your display – you'll know you've been successful if the **Display Properties** box shows the name of your video card and/or monitor and also allows you to set a screen area greater than 640 × 480 pixels and the **Colors** drop-down box allows a selection of something other than just 16 colours, as in Figure 5.6.

The usual preference is to set the **Colors** setting as high as possible – to 16 bit at least –

Figure 5.6 Display Properties dialog box

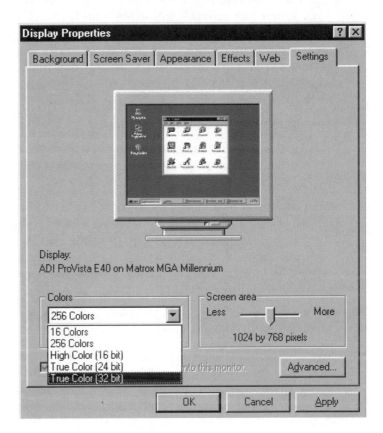

and then adjust the **Screen area** slider to something that looks comfortable. As you move this slider and change the number of colours, you may find that the other option changes automatically. If Windows wants to restart each time you change something, click the **Advanced** button and on the **General** tab, under the **Compatibility** section, you'll see you can change the 'After I change color settings:' option to 'Apply the new color settings without restarting' (This will read 'display' rather than 'color' in Windows 2000/XP). Check this and click **OK**, but do note the warning that some programs may 'operate improperly if you do not restart your computer after you change display settings'. This varies from program to program and between versions of Windows. Generally, the later the version – especially if you're using Windows 2000 or XP – the less rebooting you have to do.

Once this is adjusted, the next thing to check is the monitor's refresh rate. Click the **Advanced** button and on the **Adapter** or **Monitor** tab you'll see a section allowing you to set the 'refresh frequency' or 'refresh rate' or similar. This may be set to 'Optimal', although it often isn't. Remember that 72 Hz is the 'magic number', so try setting the refresh rate to something above this – again, remember that monitors can, in theory at least, be damaged by setting them to a higher refresh rate than they can cope with, so do check your documentation before trying this. That said, most modern monitors can cope with refresh rates of at least 85 Hz, some up to 100 Hz or more, and Windows is quite clever at just turning your screen fuzzy for a few seconds if the options you've chosen don't work. Also note that the combination of number of colours, screen area and refresh rate are interdependent. So, a card and monitor may cope with $1024 \times 768 \times$ 32-bit colour at 75 Hz, but only $800 \times 600 \times$ 16-bit colour at 85 Hz, and you may need to experiment to find the best settings for you.

If you get stuck, set things this way round:

1 The screen area – choose whether you want 800×600 or 1024×768 or whatever first, and check that screen icons and text in the main programs you use are comfortable at normal viewing distances.

2 The number of colours – try to go for at least 16-bit colour (which, confusingly, may be called something else – it's usually the first option higher than 256 colours and could be called 'High color'). If you're working with photographs you should try to use 32-bit colour if at all possible – if you use anything less you may suffer from on-screen 'banding' where changes between two different colours don't occur smoothly. This will have some relationship to the next thing to set.

3 Refresh rate. As long as you can run your setup at 75 Hz or higher, you probably won't notice any difference, so trade down on this one to get better colours and/or more screen area.

Getting all this right may sound complicated, and indeed some of it is – particularly if you're having problems identifying your video card so you can install drivers for it. However, a properly-sized, decently-coloured and non-flickering display on your computer monitor is something that's well worth striving for, since the alternatives – wrongly-sized, poorly coloured and madly flickering – can do actual harm to your eyes.

Types Of Screens

Until fairly recently, most standard PCs came with a CRT (Cathode Ray Tube, like a television screen) monitor sized between 14 and 21 inches. There are smaller ones available, larger ones too, but this covers more than 99 per cent of the possibilities.

Now, LCD (Liquid Crystal Display) monitors are starting to creep into some higher-end packages as the price of the screens themselves plummets. Laptops have always come with such screens, of course.

Don't confuse LCD screens with so-called 'flat screens'. The latter are just CRT tubes with, as the name implies, a flat (or nearly flat – the monitor market is prone to exaggeration) front to the tube. This can give less reflections on the glass screen, making it easier to read, but there are inherently more problems and difficulties in making a tube front flat (the electron beam creating the picture has to travel further to reach the corners of such a screen than it does the centre of it, unlike in a curved screen where the distances are the same). This can give a worse, more poorly-focused picture or cost more to get right. Or be both worse and more expensive.

Similarly, LCD screens are very trendy at the moment but unless you really, really need the extra space they liberate (conventional CRTs can take up a huge amount of room in larger sizes) look at what you'd get for the same money with a conventional monitor first, too.

With all monitor purchases it's well worth making the effort to see one before you buy. Magazine reviews are all very well, and it's tempting to just accept whatever manufacturers bundle with their machines, but you're going to be spending an awful lot of time looking at your new monitor over the next few years and it can, potentially, do a lot of harm to your eyes. Also, a good monitor will last many more years than most PCs – I have one 14-inch screen which came with a computer that I bought in the early 1990s and it's still going strong.

Other Screen Adjustments And Screen Problems

You make many adjustments to your screen and the picture it shows using the **Display** utility in Windows' **Control Panel**. However, most monitors – certainly just about all new ones – have varying On Screen Display (OSD) functions which allow you to adjust many aspects of the screen's functions. These concentrate on things like the shape and size of the picture on the screen, its focus both overall and in specific areas (e.g. the corners, the centre) and correction of various types of distortion to the picture. The way these adjustments are made varies very widely from monitor to monitor, but is usually via a series of menus controlled by buttons on the lower front edge of the monitor surround.

Cleaning The Screen

Before you do anything, check the manuals and manufacturer's instructions – many monitors have various anti-glare and other coatings on them, and anything other than approved cleaners can destroy this coating and ruin your screen. If your monitor has a conventional glass-fronted screen, you may be able to use a conventional glass cleaner as you would with a normal TV set, but check the manual first. Laptop screens are particularly susceptible to damage; *do not* use anything other than the manufacturer's approved cleaning methods on them.

Questions And Answers

Easy Questions And Answers

 *Every time I switch my computer on the desktop resolution is set at 640 × 480. I prefer it to be 800 × 600 so I have to manually set it by going to **Display** in the **Control Panel**. How can I permanently set the resolution to 800 × 600 without having to manually set it back every time I switch my computer on?*

 It sounds as though you don't have the correct drivers installed for your video card – the card inside your computer which sends the picture out for your monitor to display. Click **Start > Settings > Control Panel**, double-click **Display**, then click the **Settings** tab at the top. Click the **Advanced** button and the system should tell you what sort of card you have installed. If it doesn't sound correct, **Cancel** your way out, and back in **Control Panel** double-click **Add/Remove Hardware** and let the wizard find your graphics card. If it doesn't have the correct drivers already installed it will ask for your installation CDs, which should have come with your machine. You should also be able to download new drivers from the video card manufacturer's website. See Chapter 12 for more details on doing this.

 Unsurprisingly, my somewhat aged computer is creaking at the seams. The latest problem is with the screen display (the monitor is an ADI Microscan 4V), which seems to be getting progressively darker and with an intermittent but very annoying flicker. I do not know whether this is a sign that the monitor is about to pack up or whether there is another cause. If this is relevant, the graphics card is a Diamond Stealth 64 Video 2001 and the drivers are up to date. I would be very grateful for your advice.

It seems likely, as I think you suspect, that your monitor is simply suffering from old age. You could try attaching it to a friend's computer, or attaching theirs to your PC, but the odds are that it's had it and you should think about replacing it before you're left with no way to look at the data on your machine. You'll find some sensible recommendations at www.hardwareguys. com/picks/video.html or you could ask in the hardware section of my message board at www.drkeyboard.net.

I have installed a game called Who Wants to be a Millionaire? *on my PC. However when I try to play the game the sound is choppy and distorted and the graphics are not as they should be. It's a bit like a video tape appears to play when it is slipping. I have tried the CD in a friend's PC and it works perfectly. Is there a problem with my sound card? Or is it that my PC is not configured correctly?*

It's impossible to diagnose this at a distance. Check you have the latest version of Microsoft's DirectX (check their website starting at www.microsoft.com/windows/directx/) and that you have the latest versions of the drivers for your sound card and video card for your version of Windows via the relevant manufacturers' websites. Also, check the minimum hardware requirements for the game – they'll be printed on the box – and make sure your machine matches up. You could also try turning off all other programs when running the game.

My machine only has a basic 4 MB graphics card, and I would like to upgrade. Could you please advise a suitable card? Although I am not an experienced gamer I would like the card to be capable of handling fairly sophisticated games.

The hottest gaming card of the moment changes from week to week – day to day sometimes – and can cost in excess of £400. It also probably won't work in a PC more than a year or so old, but luckily there are a few places on the web where you can at least try to keep up: www.overclockers.com is a good starting point. Other sites which may clue you in to the latest possibilities include www.hardocp.com, www.aceshardware.com, www.viahardware.com; a personal favourite of mine is Tom's Hardware at www.tomshardware.com, and www.nvnews.net, as its name may suggest, specialises in information about Nvidia graphics cards.

The screen of my Cyrix M 300 computer with 32 MB of RAM, a 3.2 GB hard disk and Windows 98 has started to go purple intermittently. This is almost impossible to read. Sometimes it stays like this for ages, sometimes it goes back to white again after a few minutes. This problem doesn't seem to be associated with any particular program or key. I have jiggled all the connections at the back and this doesn't make any difference. Can you help? Or can you tell me whether the problem is most likely to be the monitor or the computer?

It could be your monitor on the way out, the graphics card in the computer, the computer's own motherboard, the cable between them all or any combination of the above, unfortunately, and it's the sort of thing that's impossible to diagnose at a distance. Try removing all the connections between the computer and monitor, along with the power leads, and replacing them. If you're up to it, also try taking out the graphics card and gently cleaning the connector along the bottom edge and then replacing it. Also, if you have access to someone else's computer try swapping your monitor and/or graphics card to see if you can isolate the problem. A worn cable is most likely, then the monitor then the graphics card, so eliminate them in that order.

*Whenever I try to minimise a window the graphics from the previous opened window remain on the screen. Ten minutes later when the previous problem has occurred the computer will freeze on me. I've tried everything. I bought Norton SystemWorks 2001 and did a full diagnostic and virus check and everything came back normal. Thinking it might be the Windows program I wiped out the hard drive and reinstalled Windows Me. Again, nothing works. Also whenever my computer freezes the mouse still operates. I have to press **Ctrl-Alt-Del** three times in order to reboot. When it does reboot and starts, my computer no longer detects my modem. In order to fix this problem I have to restart the computer by shutting it down and waiting ten minutes to restart it. I'm pulling my hair out just trying to figure it out. Is it something to do with my video card or my modem? I've also gone under my startup option and closed out all the programs in the background.*

The problem is almost certainly, as you suspect, your video card. Windows Me is notorious for needing different drivers to every other version of Windows, and those which came in the box with it (or with your computer) are probably for an earlier version. Visit the card manufacturer's website and download and install the latest version they have available for Windows Me.

*While surfing the net my screen freezes, often after a short time, for example 10 or 15 minutes, resulting in my having to use reset to restart the computer with screens still up. Obviously this is not doing the hard disk any favours, so what can I do to fix this? I have tried **Ctrl-Alt-Del** to no avail.*

The single biggest cause of this problem is graphics card drivers. Visit the manufacturer's website and download and install the latest available for your specific version of Windows – don't rely on those which came with the card being the best ones you can get.

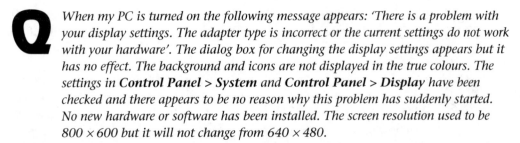

*When my PC is turned on the following message appears: 'There is a problem with your display settings. The adapter type is incorrect or the current settings do not work with your hardware'. The dialog box for changing the display settings appears but it has no effect. The background and icons are not displayed in the true colours. The settings in **Control Panel > System** and **Control Panel > Display** have been checked and there appears to be no reason why this problem has suddenly started. No new hardware or software has been installed. The screen resolution used to be 800 × 600 but it will not change from 640 × 480.*

The problem is with your graphics card drivers. For some reason, Windows has reverted to the 'standard' VGA drivers which give you the basic 640 × 480 × 16-colour display and you need to change it back to the appropriate drivers for your card. Check with the manufacturer's website to see if there are new versions available for your version of Windows and install them.

My PC has been switching off when I use 256-colour settings and I suspected a driver problem, so I completely reinstalled Windows 98 from my CD – for me that was simpler than downloading drivers from the Microsoft website. That sadly hasn't sorted out the problem. It has been suggested that my graphics card has packed up. What do you think? And if so, is installing a new card something I can do myself?

You should check the graphic card manufacturer's website to see if there are any new drivers for the card itself. Reinstalling Windows 98 will simply reinstall the old, defective drivers and won't do anything to help the problem at all – and it's the card manufacturer's website you need, not Microsoft.

I've just installed Windows Me on my computer and there is a very poor colour analysis. It's as if my screen is too small for what I'm seeing.

I'm not sure what you mean by 'colour analysis' but it sounds as though you're running at a resolution of 640 × 480 pixels with just 16 colours – the basic lowest-common-denominator resolution used by Windows when it can't work out what kind of graphics card you have. The mention of Windows Me makes me suspicious that you don't have the correct drivers for the card – drivers are small programs that interface between the hardware itself and Windows, telling them how to cooperate. You should visit the card manufacturer's website and download and install the latest drivers available for your specific card for Windows Me – not for any other version.

I recently bought a new Dell Dimension XPS800. When I came to transfer my scanner SCSI card from my older Dell Dimension PC and my Video Capture Card I find that physically they are too big to fit in the slots. Could you tell me what the old cards were called and what the new cards are called so I can go about ordering the correct thing.

It sounds as though your old cards may have been of the ISA variety, and that your new machine has only PCI slots. You'll need PCI versions of the cards.

I have a GeForce 256, 32-bit video card in my computer. It seems that every time I play a video game on there it looks really dark. I go through the settings on the game and turn the brightness up all the way but still it doesn't seem to go that bright. I even used the monitor buttons to turn it up from there but it still didn't seem to help. Can you help me figure out the problem?

I've heard of others suffering from this problem – it happens with the early versions of the drivers. You need to install the latest drivers for your version of Windows, available from the manufacturer's website.

How can I have two computer monitors in Windows, both running from the same computer? I don't want to have to have a second machine in addition to my current laptop.

Many laptops can run a monitor showing the same image as on their built-in screen – look for a Video or VGA socket around the side or rear. You almost certainly won't be able to display different images on the two screens, though, unless you have one of the latest laptops which specifically offers this function and you have a version of Windows which supports this, too. Check the specification of potential purchases if this is important to you.

I've been notified that the drivers for my video card are obsolete and I should update them, yet they seem to be working fine on my Windows 95 computer. Do I have to do anything?

No, probably not. You don't say so, but I'm assuming that perhaps the card manufacturer has sent this message out as part of its regular mailings to owners. What it probably means is that if you want to use Windows XP, for example, you'll need new drivers to make it work. Alternatively, the message could simply relate to the manufacturer's support of Windows 95 – now that Microsoft has officially ended support for it, the card manufacturer may be doing the same, too. However, it may be worth checking with the company's website, just in case there are new drivers which offer some additional functionality you might find useful. If this isn't the case and the card and drivers do all you currently need them to do, you needn't upgrade anything.

There's one, two or more horizontal lines across my screen – what's that about?

Essentially these are thin wires which support a 'mask' inside the front glass of your screen. The mask is pierced with holes or slits through which the electron beam projects the picture onto the inside of the glass.

When I turn my computer on there's a loud 'Twang' from my screen. How can I stop this?

I suspect that this is a normal part of your monitor's start-up routine called 'degaussing', designed to remove the magnetic fields around it which can distort the image. It's nothing to be concerned about.

Harder Questions And Answers

I remember you saying a year or two ago in your column that the best way to view movies is not on a computer screen but a television, because of the different physical characteristics of the two types of screen. Is this still true? I ask because I'm keen to buy a DVD (Digital Versatile Disc) player for use both on my laptop computer and on my family's television.

Computer screens are designed to show images, usually words, which stay on the screen for some time. Television screen images change many times a second. The coating on the inside of the two types of screen is therefore different, in the former case to allow some 'persistence' of the image, in the latter to allow it to change extremely quickly. This means that if you watch a movie on your PC screen you won't be getting the best possible picture, and vice versa for viewing computer images on a TV screen. However, the arrival of DVD and your mention of a laptop (whose screens, incidentally, are by far the worst for watching movies) brings to mind a cunning plan: buy a laptop with a DVD drive and MPEG 2 hardware decoding. This latter point is important – MPEG is the format in which DVDs are encoded and the decoding can be done in software, but a dedicated bit of hardware will do the job much better. Then you can use it as a computer, obviously, but also plug it into your television when you want to watch a movie. Clearly if you can site your home computer within cabling distance of the TV it would perform the same function.

Can you tell me what the specification of a Intel 815E Internal Graphics card is? I suspect that the card does not support a game I want to play and I will need to upgrade, but I don't want to go out and blow the cash on that, just to find out there is another problem.

You'll find details of the integrated Intel Graphics Technology at developer.intel.com/design/chipsets/815e and you can, as it says on the Intel site, add a regular 4× AGP graphics card.

69

Is it now possible to download TV programmes using a TV tuner on PCs and copy them onto CD discs? Can you advise what length of programmes occupy what amount of space on the discs?

It depends on the resolution at which you're recording. For example, if you save the video in 320×240 pixel at full colour resolution at 24 frames per second – an image taking up approximately a quarter of your television screen – you'll get about half an hour of video onto a 1 GB hard disk. This means that if you're trying to store four times more information on a CD holding 650 MB, you'll get about 10 minutes or so of footage onto your disc. Then again, it also depends on how you're encoding the video – MPEG 2 will compress more so you'll get more footage on your CD. Zip it up and you'll get even more. There's a handy beginners' guide to video on the PC at www.matroxusers.com. The idea of using a PC as a video recorder is becoming more and more feasible now, with several video cards offering this sort of facility. Indeed, the Tivo set-top box and others such as the Sky Plus system designed to allow you to 'pause' live TV broadcasts and have your favourite programmes recorded automatically are all, essentially, built from standard PC components with customised operating systems. Also, recordable DVD discs make it easier to store the large amount of information needed to record live video streams. This is a subject worth a book all on its own, but a few starting points include www.digiguide.com (a very good online and PC-based programme guide), www.tivo.com and tivo.samba.org. There's also a lengthy discussion on this topic with many more recommendations and personal experiences on my message board at www.drkeyboard.net.

I've installed the correct software in Windows 98 for my Belinea 10-70-20 monitor but when I try to alter the settings to improve the image (it is giving me 16 colours and 640×480 pixels), it won't alter (i.e. the advanced settings simply doesn't respond; it gives me only a choice between 2 and 16 colours and no choice in pixels). I've tried altering the adapter but it tells me that the one I have is the optimal one. I've tried reinstalling Windows with no success. Can you suggest where I've gone wrong?

Your mistake is in believing Windows, which is lying outright to you about your adapter (i.e. your video card). Undoubtedly, you're actually running the standard, built-in video drivers which come with Windows and are designed to do no more than put up something readable on the screen to allow you to do more. What you need to do is work out what kind of video card you have and install the drivers for that – a disk or two may have come with the card or the computer, but I always recommend checking the manufacturer's website to see if, as is likely, there are more up-to-date ones available for your version of Windows. Download them and follow the manufacturer's instructions to install them and you should get a lovely view through your monitor in future.

My monitor (AOC-5e) does not turn on at boot up. Only after several attempts it turns on. I have this problem only if my computer has been turned off for a long period of time (more than 30 minutes). I use Windows XP Pro, ASUS A7V266, Athlon XP 1600, Radeon 7200 (64 MB), 1 GB of DDR RAM, two Maxtor HDs (40 GB/7200 and 20 GB/5400), SB Live Value, Realtek network card, NEC 7800A CD burner, Afrey 50X CD-ROM, Enermax 360 watt PSU. My computer is only 2 months old and the problem first appeared after 2 weeks of use. I know it would sound silly, but does something in my computer need to warm up before starting to work normally (video or CPU etc)? I tried to use my friend's AOC-5e, but I got the same result.

The fact that a friend's monitor behaved the same way indicates a problem either with your video card or your power supply – are you plugging the monitor into its own power socket? Also, are you plugging the monitor into any sort of power strip surge protector and turning off the strip when closing down your PC? This could cause a slow restart. Check the graphics card to make sure that it's seated properly – take it out and put it back in again and make sure the contacts are clean. Then check the manufacturer's website and download the latest drivers available for your specific version of Windows – anything which came with the card itself won't be up to date, especially for Windows XP.

71

Sounds, CDs And DVDs

What To Check First If Your Computer Won't Produce Any Sounds

Back in the olden days (before 1989) PCs went 'beep' in such a limited fashion that they made mobile telephones sound like symphony orchestras. Then Creative released the SoundBlaster sound card and gave every computer the ability to play and make music. Nowadays every computer comes with some type of sound card, from the simplest variety embedded on the computer's own motherboard (aka 'on-board sound') to devices costing hundreds or even thousands of pounds which could put recording studios of only a few years ago to shame.

It's usually fairly easy to diagnose when the sound on your computer isn't working – you can't hear anything coming out of the speakers. Working out why that might be may be a little trickier but, as always, there are a few simple things to check first.

1   Power. If your speakers need either mains power or batteries, check and then check again that the appropriate leads are plugged in and that the batteries are fresh. Many speakers now have an indicator light on the front to indicate when they're powered up – check this is on.

2   Cables.

a   As well as the power lead there will be a cable from the main computer box to the speakers carrying the sound signal. It will be plugged into a socket possibly on the front of the computer box, but more usually (and awkwardly) on the back. New computers have colour-coded plugs and sockets but on older machines you'll need to check carefully that you're really plugging the speaker lead into the speaker socket. You'll find one, two and possibly more sockets near it, one for a microphone, another for a line-out feed and possibly others. If you accidentally plug the speakers into the microphone socket you'll probably hear nothing, but you may get some sort of sound from the line-out socket, which may account for a lower volume than you expected. There will probably also be a lead between the two speakers (or five speakers if you have a 'surround sound' setup) – make sure this is plugged in correctly, too.

b   If your PC makes 'beep' noises through your speakers (as opposed to beeps coming from the small speaker inside the main system unit) and plays sounds in games but you can't hear music from audio CDs, there may be a cable missing inside your computer connecting the CD-ROM or DVD drive to the sound card. If you installed some or all of these components yourself, check that you installed this cable correctly – it's normally a round wire with small, flat four-socket plugs at each end. Also, modern CD and DVD drives in Windows 2000 or XP can use 'digital transfer'. Open **Control Panel** > **System** > **Hardware** > **Device Manager** and click the + cross symbol next to DVD/CD-ROM drives. Right-click on your drive and left-click **Properties** > **Properties** and check the 'Enable digital CD audio for this device' box. Note the warning in this dialog box that this may not work with all drives – if it doesn't work, repeat the process above and uncheck the box.

3   Volume. First, check any volume control on your speakers. Some sound cards, irritatingly, also have a volume control on the panel next to the sockets described in point 2 above – check that's turned up appropriately, too. Next check the

volume control in Windows. Normally you'll see a small speaker icon in your System Tray next to the time display. Click it once and a simple slider volume control with a single 'Mute' check-box should appear. Make sure the slider's towards the top and that the 'Mute' box is not checked. If this doesn't make any difference, double-click the speaker icon to open the full volume control range. Click **Options** > **Advanced Controls** so that a tick appears next to the words 'Advanced Controls', then click **Options** > **Properties**. Check the **Playback** radio button and then scroll down the list under 'Show the following volume controls' and make sure each box on the left of the list is checked. Click **OK**, and back on the main **Volume Control** panel make sure all the sliders for the various volume controls are towards or at the top of their range and that no **Mute** boxes are checked. If any individual controls have an **Advanced** button click it and check any settings in there which may be preventing you hearing anything. Click the 'X' box top-right to close this control panel.

How To Check Your Sound-playing Software And Drivers

If none of the simple things work, the next thing to look at is the drivers which control your sound card.

1   Open the **System** applet in **Control Panel** and then **Device Manager** (on the **Hardware** tab in Windows 2000 and XP). Look for any yellow circles with black exclamation marks in the middle or red and white marks over the symbol for your sound card. If you see one, double-click the offending item and check what Windows tells you about the problem. It may be that there's a conflict with another device – this means that they're trying to use the same resource inside your computer and Windows needs some help sorting things out. Run through the troubleshooter offered and you should solve your problem. Note that PCs only have a limited number of resources which can be used by add-on devices like sound cards and if your computer has run out of them you may be stuck with the only option to remove something before everything will work properly again. This resource-sharing issue is much worse with Windows 9x than with Windows 2000 and XP and may be a good reason for upgrading.

2   If running the troubleshooter doesn't help, you may need to download and install the latest drivers available for your particular model card and your specific version of Windows. See Chapter 12 for details on how to do this.

If you've checked all the cables and volume controls, troubleshot your resources, installed the latest drivers and *still* can't hear anything then it's most likely some sort of hardware failure, either with your sound card itself or your speakers. Swapping out the latter to try something else is easy – you can even plug headphones into the speaker output socket on your sound card to see if anything's going on. Swapping your sound card may be more problematical, especially if you don't feel comfortable opening the box yourself, so you may need to find a local repair shop or, if your PC is still under warranty, contact the manufacturer.

Improving The Sound Quality From Your PC

If you're any sort of hi-fi buff then you probably won't want to go any further than the basic sound card that your PC comes with. There's just too much interference inside your PC box to get decent quality sound out of it unless you use a completely digital path for your music (see point 3 below), and PC CD-ROM and DVD drives aren't designed with the idea of extracting the best possible quality music out of your CDs either.

That said, if you just want a little music to accompany your web surfing and word processing, there are a few things you can do to improve the quality of what you're listening to, depending on just what it is you want from the sound capabilities of your PC.

1   If you want just the basic beeps and sounds from your PC and perhaps to play the occasional CD or MP3 music file, you'll probably be happy with the sound card that came with your computer. Built-in sound (PCs where the chips from the sound card are built into the motherboard itself instead of being on a separate card) used to be appalling, although these days it is getting better. I use the Via Avance sound chipset on my PC's MSI motherboard to play MP3 music through my hi-fi and it's good enough for my low-resolution ears. However, for under a hundred pounds you can buy a new sound card which will probably improve on whatever came with your machine originally. New sound cards come out all the time so it's difficult to recommend specific models, but Creative, www.creative.com, the inventor of the original SoundBlaster, is always at or near the top of the heap for quality and value for money, along with Turtle Beach, www.tbeach.com. AOpen, www.aopen.com offers good value-for-money sound cards and Yamaha ups the price range a little. Pay a little more and you'll find you can get away from having to grovel around at the back of your PC to plug and unplug cables with sound cards that include a 'break-out box' which sits either on top of or beside your PC, or which may be installed on the front panel to give you the sockets and volume controls you regularly access more easily (with the speakers normally still plugged in at the rear of the computer box).

2   If you don't want to mess with your sound card or are happy with the one you have, you could try adding better speakers to your PC, and there are a couple of ways to do this. First, you could junk the cheap desktop ones which came with your machine and either buy better, powered computer speakers – or even splash out on a set of surround sound speakers complete with a 'sub-woofer' bass speaker if you have a sound card which supports multiple speakers. These speaker systems

76

are usually designed to work with Dolby soundtracks, for example on DVD movies, and the sound from many newer DirectX computer games, but may also improve the regular sounds coming from your PC. Or, if you have a hi-fi in the same room as your computer you can take a lead from the line-out socket (or speaker-out if it doesn't have line-out) to the line-in or aux/auxiliary input socket on your amplifier and play your computer sounds through your hi-fi speakers.

3   Use a completely digital path for your music. Enable digital reads from your CD as in point 2b in the list at the beginning of this chapter (see page 74) and pass that through your sound card to a digital output socket (optical or SPDIF). This can considerably reduce interference.

4   If you are interested in delving deeper into the sound capabilities of your machine – sample editing, using MIDI music files, mixing and so on – you need multi-channel, multi-effect DSP (Digital Sound Processor) capabilities. Look at Steinberg's software, www.steinberg.net, for starters.

5   For playing games and watching DVDs with surround sound, you'll need a sound card with multi-speaker outputs and, for Dolby Digital, a card which can cope with this sort of signal. Optionally for Dolby you can use a separate decoder which will process the signal instead of it being done on the sound card itself.

Recording From External Sources Onto Your PC

It's one thing to be able to pop a CD into the CD-ROM or DVD drive of your PC and have the music play – Windows even includes a basic CD player program to allow you to do this, while Windows XP includes a version of Microsoft's Media Player which does this and shows you pretty pictures at the same time. But what if you'd like to record some of those CDs and play them from your PC without having to put the disc into the CD drive each time? This is where the now-famous acronym MP3 enters your computing life. MP3 actually stands for Moving Picture Experts Group MPEG-1, Layer-3 Audio. MPEG-1 is a format for digital video and Layer-3 is the sound layer for it. Put simply, it's a way of making music files smaller without losing too much of the quality of the sound – although generally the quality direct from a CD will be better than an MP3 file of the same track. If you look at a regular music CD in Windows Explorer, you'll see that the tracks are called something like **Track01.cda** – the 'cda' at the end stands for Compact Disc Audio and is the standard format for music on compact discs. Windows will also show the files as being extremely small, in the order of 50 bytes, when, in fact, they're much, much larger. An MP3 file can be considerably smaller than a music file from a CD, perhaps 10 times smaller, and hence easier to store on a PC depending on the bit rate you use. A typical MP3 file is encoded at 128k on up to near-CD quality at 256k or more. To convert files from CD format to MP3 format and store them on your computer you'll need what's called a 'ripper' program such as

MusicMatch Jukebox, www.musicmatch.com, which works well for me, or AudioCatalyst from Xing, www.xingtech.com, but you'll find a plethora of recommendations at www.mp3.com.

If your existing music collection is on vinyl records instead of CDs you can still transfer them to your PC, although the process may be slightly more involved than just popping the CD into your CD-ROM drive. First, you'll need to establish a link between your record player and your PC's sound card, either direct or via an output on your hi-fi amplifier. Then you'll need some software to record the output from your record player – MusicMatch Jukebox can do this, as can programs like Cool Edit or Cakewalk Express. Also Easy CD Creator (now called Roxio) and the Nero Burning ROM CD-creating software are capable of recording either direct onto CDs or via your PC. At this point you'll have a WAVE format file (ending in **.wav**) which you can then convert and compress into an MP3 format file.

MP3, Audio Copyright And What You Can Do With Your Own Music

The music recording industry is not known for its hatred of lawyers and, indeed, as soon as you scratch the surface of this subject you'll find that there's a veritable legal hornet's nest waiting to engulf you for daring to try to copy a music CD which you own. The law about what you can and can't do varies from country to country, but in general while this may be technically illegal you probably won't get into trouble if you're copying a CD for your own use, for example to listen to music from your PC hard disk via an MP3 file instead of popping the CD into the machine. It's when you start making copies for your friends and uploading copies for the rest of the world to use that you'll get into trouble as you get noticed.

And now you need to be on the lookout for 'copy-protected' CDs which, while ostensibly designed to be impossible to copy, are in fact impossible to play on PCs – indeed, if you try to play them on some Apple Macintosh computers they can mess the Mac up so badly it needs to be returned to the manufacturer for repairs. If you play CDs on your PC you may want to avoid these types of discs completely – I certainly do.

There are, of course, shades of grey, not black and white issues involved here – just type **MP3** into Google and settle down for a good argument.

CD And DVD Drives (Including CD/DVD Writers)

CD and DVD drives (read-only and writers) are collectively known as 'optical' drives; hard disks and floppy disks are known as 'magnetic' drives. The word 'optical' is given because CD and DVD drives work by focusing the light from a laser onto the surface of the disc to read its contents (or write new contents), while hard (and floppy) disks work by recording data magnetically, in the same way as a cassette tape works.

If your CD or DVD drive is working without any noticeable problems then, by and large, you should just leave it alone and not mess with it. This includes not using any proprietary drive cleaner, no matter what promises the manufacturer makes for it. These cleaners usually work by scraping off the dirt the manufacturers claim encrusts these lasers with some sort of liquid, brushes or a combination of the two. In fact, unless your drive is suffering some sort of problem (see below), you don't need to clean it at all and you could easily do more harm than good. CD and DVD drives have fairly delicate mechanisms and the laser assembly in particular isn't intended to ever come into contact with anything, let alone an alcohol-soaked plastic brush whizzing by at several hundred revolutions per minute.

The Main Problems Encountered With CD And DVD Drives

The two main problems you're likely to encounter with an optical drive are:

1   The drive suddenly stops playing music discs and/or ceases to recognise that you've put a data disc (such as an installation disc for a new program) in it.

2   Your PC itself suddenly refuses to acknowledge that the CD or DVD drive exists.

If your PC suddenly refuses to recognise a disc, try the following steps:

1   Eject the disc and inspect the data side (the shiny side opposite the side with the label or writing on). This should normally be shiny side down in the drive with the label uppermost (but check your documentation to verify this).

2   Is the disc clean and scratch-free? Dust and dirt can be removed by gently dusting from the centre hole towards the outside of the disc. *Don't* wipe around it in a circular direction (as if along the grooves of a record). Grease and sticky items can be washed gently using mild soaps and warm water – make sure the disc is thoroughly dried before using it again. Scratches may be polished out using proprietary products, e.g. CD Doctor, www.cddoctor.com/cdindex.htm.

2   Will the drive recognise any other discs? If other discs are read without problem, the original CD may be faulty. If the CD is read in other drives, the original drive may be the problem.

3   Is the kind of disc appropriate for the drive? DVD drives will generally recognise and read CDs but CD drives won't recognise or read DVD discs. Also, many CD drives more than a couple of years old may have problems reading CD-R or CD-RW discs you've created yourself (or which someone else has burned).

If you've established that the drive appears to be faulty, check the following:

1   Is it receiving power? If you push the 'eject' button and the tray opens or, in the case of slot-loading drives, you can hear the mechanism whirring, the drive is powered. Many also have power-on lights on the front.

2   Is the data cable connected? This is trickier to check, since it involves looking inside your computer casing. The CD or DVD drive will be connected to the motherboard by a flat ribbon cable with either 40 or 80 strands. This needs to be inserted the correct way around both at the drive end and at the motherboard end. Many cables now have a 'key' which fits into a corresponding cut-out on the socket into which it fits. The ribbon cables also have one edge coloured red – this goes to Pin 1 on the motherboard and towards the power-in plug on the drive end. If you don't feel comfortable checking this yourself, you may need to take the machine to a repair shop or call the manufacturer for repairs.

If the drive is receiving power and the data cable is fixed, next check in **Device Manager** to see if your PC is recognising it (see Chapter 2 for details on how to do this).

Also check to see whether or not the 'Autorun' facility is enabled on your PC. Double-click your CD or DVD's entry in **Device Manager** and on the **Settings** tab click the 'Auto Insert Notification' check-box to put a tick in it (you can uncheck this box if you don't like the Autoplay facility).

If you can see your CD listed in **My Computer** but nothing happens when you insert a particular disc, it may be that that particular CD doesn't have an Autoplay facility – double-click the disc in **My Computer** to open it and browse the contents.

Types Of Drives Available

The commonest type of CD and DVD discs are of the IDE type. These are cheaper to produce and use than the second commonest type, SCSI drives. SCSI used to be preferred particularly for CD writers and rewriters because much of the processing involved in creating a CD is done by the SCSI card itself. With IDE drives the processing for the burning operation has to be done by your PC's CPU, and this used to mean that if you did anything else while trying to burn a CD the operation would fail as it was interrupted when your CPU thought about something else momentarily. Now, most CD burners are available with some sort of 'Burn Proof' technology which allows the process to be interrupted and then restarted without failing, making the more expensive SCSI drives less popular.

External drives are also available, with USB (1 or 2), parallel (printer) or Firewire port connections. These can be useful for a laptop which has no internal CD drive or CD writer. Parallel (printer) port models are extremely slow, especially for burning discs, and should be avoided wherever possible.

You'll find more information on CD and DVD burners, including details of the various formats available, in Chapter 14.

Questions and Answers

Easy Questions And Answers

I understand that the 'MP3 revolution' is, apparently, about to bring the music industry to its knees. And, indeed, it may well do so – but what is it?

MP3 stands for 'MPEG 1 layer 3' – MPEG is the Moving Picture Experts Group, the bunch of tall-foreheads who work out how to send video pictures and sound over the internet. An MP3 file is a sound-only file which has been 'encoded' by a piece of software to allow it to be compressed and, therefore, downloaded over the internet more quickly than if it were uncompressed. An entire album in MP3 format typically takes up between 50 and 100 MB; a CD of the same album would take up anything up to 650 MB. As an ordinary user, you just need a piece of software to listen to the music and, if you feel so inclined, to convert your existing CDs to the MP3 format. The MusicMatch software (from www.musicmatch.com) will do this very well – put a music CD in your computer and it will look up its name and track details on the internet and convert it to MP3 format for you. To find MP3 tracks to download, start at www.mp3.com – but remember that, although you may be able to download tracks you may not have permission to do so. There are an awful lot of 'pirate' music sites out there; avoid them if you have any respect for other people's property.

My keyboard makes sounds. I've disabled sound but the beeping remains. Please help – I am computer illiterate.

It sounds as though you have the **ToggleKeys** option in the **Accessibility Options** turned on. Click on **Start > Settings > Control Panel > Accessibility Options**, click the **Keyboard** tab and towards the bottom of the dialog box you'll see the **ToggleKeys** section. Uncheck the box, click **OK** and the sounds should stop.

I have been trying to install my Tsunami 4100 PCI Soundcard which my computer cannot detect. I have installed the drivers, tried to install hardware through the Control Panel, removed the network card (that works fine) and tried the slot to make sure the other slots weren't broken, and tried it in both other available slots. Do you have any ideas on how to proceed? It is actually the second soundcard I have tried and the shop gave me this one after I asked them to see if the first one was working.

It's almost certainly a driver problem – visit the manufacturer's website to check if there are any newer ones available for your particular operating system. Which, by the way, may not be Windows if the information in your e-mail is correct – the form you submit also checks the version of the operating system you're using, and it reckons you're using an Apple Macintosh PowerPC, which could be your problem.

I recently listened to my favourite football team via an online web broadcast; it was excellent with good quality and no drop outs. Can you tell me how I can use streaming video and audio on my website? I have DV capability etc. How do I set up the site so that a user clicks on a link and (I presume) it buffers some of the footage etc. and plays while the rest comes in?

Have a look at the Real website, www.real.com for details of their RealAudio client and server software. You'll then need to talk to your ISP about hosting such content – many won't let you do so because of the bandwidth it occupies.

Why do I get minimal CD output unless I turn the volume way up, which distorts the normal Windows sounds?

Double-click the little yellow speaker icon on your taskbar and then on **Options > Properties** and check the box for CD Audio. Now you should be able to turn up the volume.

Nothing comes out of my computer's right-hand speaker, although all the settings are correct. Why?

If you're really, really sure all the settings are correct then it could be a duff speaker. Try someone else's.

Windows Me doesn't support sound in old DOS games. Is there a software sound card emulator that would allow me to get sound in my old games?

I don't know of one but you may be interested to know that Windows XP does offer sound for old DOS-mode games without adding in any extras.

When listening to radio stations on the net the audio breaks up when I am also downloading web pages. Is there anything I can do about this?

This happens because the 'bandwidth' of your connection is suddenly being shared by the radio station and the web page you're downloading, and so the distortion happens. Only a faster internet connection would cure this.

I have a reference CD to which I refer frequently. Is it possible to fit a second CD-ROM drive so I can keep it permanently available?

Yes, you'll have no problems doing this although you may find it cheaper and quicker to simply copy the contents of the CD to your hard disk and run the program from there if your hard disk has sufficient free space. Theoretically you can just create a folder on your hard disk and use Windows Explorer to copy all the files on the CD into that folder, then run the CD's installer program from the folder on your hard disk. However, some manufacturers try to stop you doing this by various means in an effort to prevent software piracy. Other programmers, of course, have found ways to get around this with 'virtual drive' software which makes the program think it's still being run from a CD. There's one called Virtual Drives, details at www.farstone.com. Another from Paragon is called CD Emulator, www.paragon-gmbh.com.

I have about 30 out of date catalogue CD-ROMs that I have no further use for. Can they be recycled?

I have one friend who uses them as coffee mug coasters, another who's turned them into a lamp stand and a third who's planning to turn them into a frock for his partner (although she doesn't sound too keen on the idea). By far the most popular use seems to be as bird scarers – tie a few to bits of string, hang them from a pole in the vegetable patch and the sunlight reflecting off the shiny side keeps the pigeons away, I'm told. The only problem with this, of course, is that you need sunshine too. If you don't have a garden yourself, contact your local allotment society who may be delighted to receive them. You can also recycle old printer ribbons to tie them up with. Other uses include in place of wallpaper to decorate teenagers' bedroom ceilings; slotting them into the pockets in a plastic shower curtain; and as garden sculpture (very good when you need to reproduce the effect of fish scales, apparently). Personally I just chuck them away – they're not much good for anything else, unfortunately. Unlike floppy disks, you can't reuse them.

I have bought a new motherboard which I have installed successfully except when I first booted I got a message 'Load from CD-ROM' then it came up 'failed'. Windows then loaded properly and the CD-ROM worked OK. I have now changed the BIOS so it does not read the CD-ROM when it reboots, but I am not happy with this solution – any ideas? The other problem is that my floppy drive does not work and the drive

light is on all the time. Again I changed the BIOS to check the floppy and now it comes up with the message 'failed (40)'. I swapped the floppy with an old one but it still does not work. I need this drive as I need to clear the hard drive to load Windows 98SE.

 I'm not sure why you're unhappy with the solution to booting from the CD – many BIOSes offer the choice of whether or not to boot from the CD, which is handy when you're installing Windows (although only later versions – Me onwards, I believe – are bootable CDs). Turning the feature off in the BIOS is the best way to stop this happening. You'll probably find that you can set the order in which the PC looks for a bootable disk, e.g. floppy first, then hard disk, then CD (or a variation thereon). As for your floppy problem, it's because the cable is in the wrong way round either in the motherboard or the drive itself, or the cable is faulty.

 Can I add a CD-ROM drive and sound card to my old laptop?

 Yes, look at the 'Backpack Bantam' range of CD-ROM (and other) drives from Micro Solutions which can plug into a PC Card slot or your parallel/printer port, www.micro-solutions.com.

 My computer pusher, sorry retailer, is urging me to install a DVD drive in my computer when he upgrades the memory and hard disk next month. Will I still be able to read my old CD-ROMs and play music CDs?

 Yes, DVD drives are what's called 'backwards-compatible' with CDs.

 Can I read DVD discs in a CD-ROM drive?

 No, you'll need a DVD drive.

 How can I reformat all the CDs I've received on computer magazine covers? It seems a shame to waste them.

 You can't – they're called CD-ROMs because they're Read Only Memory Compact Discs.

Harder Questions And Answers

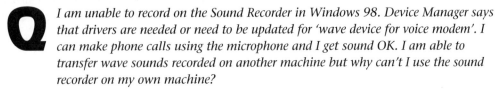

I am unable to record on the Sound Recorder in Windows 98. Device Manager says that drivers are needed or need to be updated for 'wave device for voice modem'. I can make phone calls using the microphone and I get sound OK. I am able to transfer wave sounds recorded on another machine but why can't I use the sound recorder on my own machine?

The device you describe, wave device for voice modem, is usually only intended to allow you to use your modem as a hands-free telephone and/or a telephone answering machine, but you'll need to check its particular specifications to make sure of this. If it can function as a regular sound card, you'll need to check the manufacturer's website for new drivers for your specific version of Windows. If, as I suspect, it can't do the job you want, you'll need to buy and install a separate sound card – come on over to www.drkeyboard.net for help choosing one if you need more information.

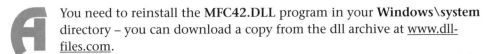

*My Montego sound card was working happily. When I recently installed QuickTime I lost sound on the computer from all sources. I uninstalled QuickTime using the uninstall option without any improvement. I then decided to reinstall the Montego. As it does not come with an uninstall option I used **Add/Remove Programs** to remove Montego AudioStation 2 and the Montego Drivers. Having now reinstalled the Montego, I get the error message 'Error Starting Program: The POPEXAM.DLL file is linked to missing export MFC42.DLL:6467' each time I boot the computer. I still do not have any sound. I would be eternally grateful for some suggestions as to where I should go next.*

You need to reinstall the **MFC42.DLL** program in your **Windows\system** directory – you can download a copy from the dll archive at www.dll-files.com.

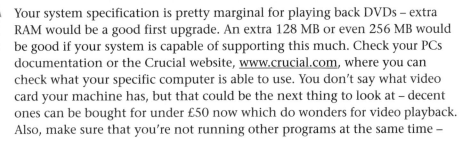

My DVD unit does not play DVD home videos correctly. I only hear the sound but I can't watch the video. Do I need a special video card to play DVD or is this a problem of software? I have a Windows 98 Pentium 500 with 64 MB of RAM.

Your system specification is pretty marginal for playing back DVDs – extra RAM would be a good first upgrade. An extra 128 MB or even 256 MB would be good if your system is capable of supporting this much. Check your PCs documentation or the Crucial website, www.crucial.com, where you can check what your specific computer is able to use. You don't say what video card your machine has, but that could be the next thing to look at – decent ones can be bought for under £50 now which do wonders for video playback. Also, make sure that you're not running other programs at the same time –

85

hold down the **Ctrl** and **Alt** keys and press **Delete** and end all programs apart from Explorer and Systray. You don't say which DVD player you're using but check that you have the latest version available for your version of Windows. And finally, I've found a program called DVD Genie, www.inmatrix.com, useful for 'tweaking' many settings in many DVD player programs.

Q *My Sound Recorder won't work. The reason according to Windows 98 System Information is that two drivers are shown as 'disabled 0' and this is confirmed by Regedit. The drivers are CD Audio Device Media Control **mcicda.drv** and Wav Device **mciwav.drv**. The problem is I haven't a clue why they became disabled a long time ago and I just don't know how to get them active again. I have tried reloading both Windows and the sound card disc without result. The sound card is a Crystal PNP Audio System CS4232/36/37/38 and in all other respects it works perfectly. I would appreciate seeing the little green line wiggle again.*

A It's probably a fault with the drivers themselves which aren't the correct ones for your version of Windows – the ones which came with the card are probably for Windows 95 and only make it partially work. You need to go to the manufacturer's website and see if they have later ones designed to work with Windows 98.

Q *I've uninstalled my CD burning software and now I can't access my CD drive at all. **Device Manager** says it's not working properly because 'Windows cannot load the drivers required for this device (Code 31)'.*

A You may also see Code 19, 32, 39 and 41 errors. The solution to this involves editing your Registry, so first read Chapter 17 for details on how to back it up first. Then look at the Microsoft support site at support.microsoft.com and read article Q314060 which details the steps you need to take to correct the problem.

Q *This is a self-built system and so I only have myself to blame (or warrant). I cannot get the CD-ROM – a Panasonic/Matsushita CR585 – to play audio CDs. I have linked the digital audio output (2-pin) to my SB-Live! soundcard's SPDIF input. I have not linked the analogue output (4-pin) – mainly on account of having misplaced the cable in the 'move' to this system/incarnation – but this surely shouldn't matter(?). Each time I load an audio CD I get a message from the Creative CD player saying that it 'can't play this track/file it may be corrupted or damaged'. This appears for all CDs regardless of quality (both cleanliness and musical). I get cracking sound from games and the Windows Sound System but would like to purchase a DVD/CD-R box and among other things cut some compilation CDs from my existing collection. Am I missing something obvious?*

If it were just that you could play CDs but not hear anything then yes, I would suspect the cable joining the back of your CD-ROM drive to your sound card. However, this only carries the sound once the music CD is actually playing – it doesn't carry any control or error information. It could then be a problem with the IDE cable connecting the drive to the motherboard, a problem with the drive itself or incorrect drivers. Try swapping components wherever possible and check for new drivers for the drive and the sound card on the appropriate websites. You could do a quick check by plugging a pair of headphones or speakers into the phone jack on the front of the CD drive – you should be able to hear music playing through them. You might also try the 'digital transfer' method of listening to music from CDs. See page 74 for details.

 The CD drive on my Windows 98 PC has suddenly stopped reading any discs.

 Is it still listed in My Computer? Check Device Manager in **Control Panel > System** and see if it's still there. Can you open the drive bay by pushing the button on the front? If not, it may not be receiving power. If it is powered, the data cable may be loose at the rear of the drive.

Printers And Printing

How To Choose The Right Kind of Printer For Your Needs

In these days of electronic communications, the internet and e-mail it's all too easy to forget the humble piece of paper. But, when it comes to portability, ease of use and cheapness it's hard to beat a simple sheet of A4. The question is, how do you get your information out of your computer and on to something that's easy to read in bed?

There are, right now, a plethora of inkjet and bubble jet printers available, many of them offering near or actual photographic quality colour. And while many can offer that, you need to look at the total cost of producing such a print, and how useful the same machine might be if what you really want to do is produce several hundred pages of black words printed on ordinary white paper.

As ever, the golden rules of buying computer equipment are:

1   Work out what you want to do,

2   Work out what software/machinery combination best achieves that end.

3   Find a combination that also matches your budget.

If you do want to print lots of boring type with the occasional colour illustration thrown in, think about buying both a laser printer and a colour inkjet. It may sound like an unnecessary extravagance, but in the long term, perhaps even in the medium or short term, you'll save yourself money. Neither type of printer does the other's job very well, and the extra couple of hundred pounds you spend buying two machines will be repaid very soon in the cost of consumables.

Inkjets, in particular, are expensive to run. The ordinary paper they print on is slightly different to the cheap photocopier stuff with which most laser printers are happy – and two or three times more expensive, too. The ink cartridges they use are horrendously expensive and, while you will undoubtedly meet people who refill them with needles and syringes, this is really only for those who are happy with permanently inky fingers and pullovers. If you do buy an inkjet printer at least make sure it has a separate ink cartridge for black ink – some even have different cartridges for the three or more colours they use, which means you don't have to throw away part of your ink supply when just one colour is finished.

You can now also buy 'generic' replacement ink cartridges, which cost much less than those from manufacturers. However, be aware that they may not be manufactured to the same high tolerances as those from the printer manufacturer and that in some cases you will be invalidating your warranty by not using original cartridges. I used to be quite a fan of non-original cartridges until I got four in a row that either didn't work at all or poured ink all over my desk.

Personal laser printers are now available for a couple of hundred pounds and can be well worth the money if you do want to print lots of black type on white paper.

As for qualitative differences, these days anyone will be very hard pushed indeed to tell the difference between a page printed by a laser printer and the same page produced by an inkjet. Indeed, in terms of definition – measured in DPI, dots per inch, literally the number of dots of ink in one inch of printing – many inkjets offer higher resolutions than the average laser printer. The biggest difference between the two types used to be the speed of printing, both in producing the first page and in the number of pages per minute (ppm) they can print. Inkjets used to struggle to produce two or three pages a minute, but now, like the humblest laser, they can usually produce six pages in a minute, and many can print 10 or more, although even expensive inkjets will struggle to match these figures if graphics are involved.

Brands to look for: among inkjets, Canon are first in my book, followed by Epson and

Lexmark. With lasers, look at the same brands plus Kyocera's Ecosys, whose refill system makes them cheaper to run than most, and Samsung, whose ML-6060 comes highly recommended in many comparative tests. I base these recommendations on the number of letters of complaint and praise I receive about problems with printers – HP used to be a firm favourite but their change in attitude recently (especially in taking so long to make their printers work in Windows 2000) has seen them fall from favour. There's no doubt that their laser printers, especially the earlier ones, are extremely reliable – many people who bought HP printers 10 years or more ago are still using them without any problems.

Whichever brand you buy, do check that the manufacturer has decent drivers for your computer – so that it will work with your particular version of Windows or the Macintosh OS.

Why Won't It Print?

Troubleshooting problems with printers means looking at three things:

1   Has it run out of consumables (ink or toner and paper)?

2   Is the hardware (including the cables) broken?

3   Have I installed the latest drivers available for my version of Windows?

Unfortunately, what can happen when you're trying to diagnose a problem with a printer is that you get involved in a major round of the Blame Game. PC manufacturers, printer manufacturers and Microsoft are notorious for blaming each other when a printer just won't print and you end up playing piggy-in-the-middle as they pass your problem around and around each other.

So, here's a simple guide to the things to check when your printer won't print.

1   Check all the cables – very often just removing and re-inserting plugs will correct problems.

    a   If your printer plugs into the parallel port – usually a large 25-pin socket on your computer – check that it's secure at the computer end and at the printer end. Many printers have small wire clips which secure such cables firmly to the socket.

    b   If you have a USB printer, remove and replace the plugs at each end of the cable and see if this kick-starts the process.

    c   Check that the power cable is plugged in at both ends and that the power supply is on and working (e.g. by plugging something else into the socket).

2   Check the ink. How you do this varies from printer to printer – many now have some sort of indicator on the printer or in the Windows software to indicate this.

Check your manual for details. You may find a small program specifically referring to your printer in the Control Panel. If not, open the **Printers** program in **Control Panel** and right-click your printer's name, then left-click **Properties** and see if anything is detailed there. With inkjets you may notice lines or characters missing or only partially printed right towards the end of the ink cartridge's life, and with a laser printer the printed output usually gets uneven and faint as the toner runs out.

3   Clean the printer. As well as checking the printer visually for any evidence of dirt build-up and stuck sheets or small pieces of paper, run any cleaning application routine it has. Check your documentation for details – often you can start it either from the printer's control panel (see point 2 above) or by pressing a combination of buttons on the printer itself.

4   Check the drivers. Assuming you've the basic ingredients for printing – a printer, electricity, cables firmly pushed in and plenty of ink – the single biggest cause of printer failure is incorrect drivers. Drivers are the small programs which interact between Microsoft Windows and your hardware, in this case your printer. The first time you connected your printer and turned your computer on, you may have been prompted to put in a disc or choose your printer from a list. This is when the drivers are installed. However, while it may seem obvious that you should use the disc (usually a CD-ROM these days) to install your printer's drivers, in fact you're virtually guaranteed that these will, at best, be out of date and, at worst, obsolete by the time you pop that disc into your PC. Printer manufacturers will be developing their hardware – the printer itself – right up until the last moment, and the specification may be finalised too late to allow the software developers who write the printer drivers to finish them properly in time to make the CDs to go in the box with the printer. So, those on the CD – while they'll probably work, albeit only after a fashion sometimes – will not be the latest available since the software developers at the printer company will have used the time it takes to manufacture the printer, put it in a box and ship it around the world to you to refine and improve their drivers. Indeed, the writers of the software drivers may not even have had a finished version of the printer to test their software on until after it was shipped out. And, by the time you open the box there will almost certainly be more up-to-date drivers available for your printer on the website of the manufacturer – so check. See Chapter 12 for details of how to find, download and install new driver software for your hardware.

How To Buy A Printer

The basic choice for printers is between fast and cheap-to-use lasers and more flexible, colour-capable, cheap-to-buy but expensive-to-run inkjets.

Inkjet printers seem like an obvious choice for the home user, and indeed they are very versatile. You can print regular text documents, documents with pictures in them, photographs – even very high quality photos with the right kind of paper – in fact, just about anything any computer can print, you can use an inkjet printer to produce it. And, if you're ever planning on printing anything in colour, right now a colour inkjet is the only realistic choice for the home or small business user, with many colour laser printers costing around £1,500 – and then producing colour prints which will probably be inferior to most colour inkjet printers anyway. However, if you print anything more than a few dozen pages of black text on white paper a day you may be spending much, much more money than you need to, so ask yourself the following questions.

1   Realistically, how often do I need to print anything in colour? When you print a page from a website, for example, you may end up printing it in colour simply because it appears in colour on your screen. But if you're only looking to be able to read, say, a news story over your breakfast or a report away from your computer screen, ask yourself if using colour really enhances the information. It may be useful if you're examining a graph but a waste of money for simple text.

2   Do I ever need to print out photographs, either taken with a digital camera or scanned in to my computer? Unless you're in a profession or business which requires large numbers of extremely high quality colour prints, a colour inkjet will satisfy your printing requirements for photographs.

3   How many pages do I print per day, week or month? If you print hundreds of pages of text a month, you should consider buying a laser printer.

4   Examine the 'cost per page' of your printing needs. Add up the price of the printer, the cost of the paper and the ink for your specific needs and work out how much this will cost you over a period of, say, two years. You may be very surprised – that colour inkjet printer you buy now for £75 could end up costing you an absolute *fortune* in ink, especially colour and photographic inks. A typical ink cartridge for an inkjet printer will last a few hundred pages; toner cartridges for laser printers typically last for up to 10,000 pages or more. There are exceptions to both these, of course, notably inkjets which have the facility to use large, external bottles of ink, but these are normally used for specific purposes.

Making The Most Of What You Have

Whatever kinds of printer(s) you buy or own, make the most of what you have.

1   Check your printer's documentation to see if it has an 'economy mode'. Many inkjets and some lasers can print at reduced, 'draft' quality if all you need is a rough print, using a fraction of the ink used in producing full-quality prints.

2   Use print preview in all your programs to check that the document or picture you're about to send to the printer fits on the page(s) as you expect and hope it

will. If you're about to commit an expensive lot of ink to some expensive photographic paper, consider printing a draft, black-and-white version on scrap paper first to make sure it's of the correct dimensions.

3   Reuse paper which has only been printed on one side for 'drafts'. When a 'proper' print job fails for some reason, don't throw the paper away – stack it somewhere handy so you can use it for printing out those non-essential, breakfast-reading print jobs.

4   Do you really need to print it? Ask yourself if there might not be a better way to read and preserve the information you're committing to all those dead trees.

    a   Save web pages on your computer instead of printing them out automatically. See Chapter 12 for details.

    b   Save e-mails on your computer rather than printing them all out. Set up folders in your e-mail program to file messages appropriately rather than printing and storing them on paper. See Chapter 11 for details.

    c   If you really do have to print out e-mails or web pages, aggregate them onto one page rather than printing them all out separately. In the e-mail or web page, hold down the **Ctrl** key on your keyboard and press the letter **A** then **C** to first select all the text and then copy it. Switch to your word processor and hold down **Ctrl** while pressing **V** to paste the text in. You can use the word processor's normal editing facilities to tidy the text up and make it a readable size and shape before repeating the process as necessary.

    d   Look into PDAs, Personal Digital Assistants, like the Palm and PocketPC ranges. These allow you to carry large amounts of text and pictures around with you and can be used to edit many types of documents, including those produced in Microsoft Office. Using programs and websites like Avantgo, www.avantgo.com, you can carry around copies of any website you like, and 'synchronise' the information on your PDA with the online version automatically so that you always have, for example, the most recent edition of the *Guardian* newspaper with you.

5   Look for 'compatible' cartridges:

    a   Printer manufacturers, especially inkjet manufacturers, work on the 'razor blade' principle – i.e. they sell the printers at apparently bargain prices while actually making their profits on the ink cartridges you have to buy. It's been said that Xerox is actually in the business of selling toner cartridges, not printers and photocopiers. When you do have to buy new ink cartridges, as well as looking at 'original' models also check to see if there are any 'compatible' cartridges available. These are made to fit many printers, especially inkjets, and can cost a fraction of the price of the 'proper' cartridges. Do be aware, however, that many manufacturers state that using cartridges other than the ones they make will invalidate any warranty or guarantees on your printer. Then again, they would say that, wouldn't they?

b   Buy online – check the internet for places offering ink cartridges at a good price.

c   Refilling cartridges is possible if you have a steady hand when it comes to using syringes and needles, but this can be tremendously messy. Also, some printers need to have the 'print head', the nozzles through which the ink is squirted, changed every time they're refilled with ink, so this isn't always successful. It can be fun in a mud-pie-making sort of way, though.

6   And I know it's been said a lot in this chapter but *do* check to see if there are any new drivers or widgets for your printer on the manufacturer's website. Often when the drivers for a new version of Windows are released, new facilities are included too – you might be pleasantly surprised at the new lease of life they give an old printer.

What Next If It Won't Print?

If you've checked all the obvious things, open the **Printers** section of **Control Panel**, right-click your printer's name, left-click **Properties** and look for an option to print a test or trial page (the location of this option varies from printer to printer). If nothing appears Windows will prompt you to start the Printing troubleshooter. Work through this and see if any of its suggestions help. If none does, try uninstalling your printer and reinstalling it with the latest drivers you've downloaded from the manufacturer's website. Some printers require that you first remove any existing drivers, so follow instructions to do this. If you can find the actual driver file (it may be called something like **Canon800.drv**) you can try renaming it (don't delete it, just in case) and then reinstall the drivers. Also, if your printer can use both parallel and USB cables try one of each to see if that helps – I've had printers refuse to work with a USB cable and then perform perfectly using a standard parallel cable.

Then check with your printer manufacturer's website to see if your symptoms are a known problem for which there's an existing cure.

And if all that fails, it could just be time to buy a new printer.

Questions And Answers

Easy Questions And Answers

In Windows 98 when I have typed a document in Word and try to save it or print it, the error message 'Insufficient memory' comes up. I hardly use it for typing and saving documents. It is only about two years old. I use it mostly for e-mailing and

the internet. It's a Dell Pentium machine with 64 MB of RAM and a 500 MB hard disk.

If your computer really does only have a 500 MB hard disk, this could well be the source of your problems. The 'insufficient memory' message is referring to space on the disk, not the RAM of which you have an adequate (although not overwhelming) supply. You should clear some of the non-essential files off your computer – see Chapter 15.

I have an HP LaserJet 6L printer, which I find excellent for monochrome printing. I plan to get an inkjet printer soon for colour, using USB, but I would like to keep the LaserJet in service as a good workhorse connected to the parallel port. Does this sound reasonable or would it create problems?

It sounds perfectly reasonable. You'll need, when you install the second printer, to choose one of the two to be the 'default' printer, but apart from that you shouldn't have any problems. I note that you're using Windows Me – do make sure that you have the correct drivers for this version of Windows, which is particularly fussy about this sort of thing.

Quite often I get the error message 'Communication error, printer out of paper' when using my Epson Photo 870 printer. Connections are OK and restarting Windows always cures it.

Check you have, as I so often say, the correct/latest version of the drivers for your printer for your specific version of Windows on the manufacturer's website. Also, try cleaning the relevant bits of the printer – a speck of dust or ink could be causing the problem. Check the handbook for cleaning details.

I have a Hewlett Packard printer which I bought about two months ago. I expected the ink in it to last several months since that's what the salesman told me was normal. However, now it has stopped printing in black. Could it have run out of ink already? Do I have a case against the salesman for telling me it would last for months?

Well, clearly the time the ink in a printer lasts depends entirely on how much printing you do rather than how long you've owned the ink cartridge. Unless, of course, you've owned the cartridge for so long that it's dried up anyway, but that doesn't seem likely in your case. I'm guessing that it's just run out of ink and you'll have to buy a new cartridge. I really don't think you have much of a case against anyone.

My screen seems to have a wobble, but sometimes it is OK. My brother told me that it is because I have my printer and speakers too close to it and they are interfering with each other. He said I could damage all of them. Do you agree?

Yes, the printer and speakers will have magnets in them which will distort your screen and, potentially, cause damage to it in the long term. So move them away.

If I keep a laser printer for regular black and white printing and a colour inkjet for more artistic work, can I have two sets of printer drivers operable at the same time? Presumably I would have to disconnect the printer I'm not using and connect up the chosen channel of the moment. I have an HP LaserJet IIIP and am going for a colour printer as well.

You can do that or buy a switch box.

I know how to display web pages in Internet Explorer 5 without the background visuals and pictures but can I also print pages without these features? Some pages are covered by background visuals, which means it takes ages to print them off – wasting time and printer ink.

Click **Tools** > **Internet Options**, then click the **Advanced** tab. Scroll down the list to the **Printing** section and uncheck the 'Print background colors and images' option.

I've created a letterhead template in Word 97 but it prints the header and footer in the second and subsequent pages. How can I instruct the programme to print these on the first page only?

Click **View** > **Header and Footer** with a blank template page open. On the Header and Footer toolbar click the **Page Setup** button – it looks like an open book – and check the 'Different First Page' option. Now use the **Page Down** button to move through your headers and footers. When you get to the headers/footers on second and subsequent pages, just delete them. Then save your edited page as a template again and the header and footer should only appear on the first page.

I wish to transfer my personal address book in MS Outlook to another PC and/or send my address book to a printer for a hard copy. It seems that MS Outlook allows one to do neither, nor it seems can I 'copy-paste' my address list.

Click the **Contacts** folder to open it. Click any of the contacts' title bars to select it, then hit **Ctrl-A** to select all the contacts. Now click **File** > **Print** and choose the formatting options you'd like. To save the contacts elsewhere, click **File** > **Import and Export** > **Export to a file** > **Next** > **Personal Folder File (.pst)** > **Next**, select the **Contacts** folder (and check the 'Include sub-folders' box if you have sub-folders you'd like to save as well), click **Next**, choose a location and name for the file and click **Finish**.

97

*Help on the **Print screen** key tells us: 1. To copy the window or screen contents ... press alt+print screen. 2. To copy an image of the entire screen press print screen. Now what?*

Paste into another program like Paint, which comes with Windows. Open it and click **Edit** > **Paste** or hit **Ctrl-V** and your image will be pasted into a new picture, and you can now manipulate and save it as you wish.

*I have recently upgraded from Windows 95 to Windows 98. I use MS Office 97 and print to an HP720C printer. Since upgrading I am having difficulty in printing in 'Econofast' mode in greyscale. When requesting to print, the entire PC freezes up. Using **Ctrl-Alt-Del** doesn't work and I have to reboot the system. Things appear to work fine when printing in 'normal' mode. This problem doesn't happen every time and seems to happen only when printing from Word and/or the internet. I have experimented by uninstalling and reinstalling Word and the printer drivers many times but with no success. I have even tried it on a 'bare-bones' machine (just with Windows 98, Office and the printer) and it's just the same.*

The key to your problem, I think, is in the upgrade – the drivers for your printer which worked fine under Windows 95 aren't suitable for Windows 98, as many users have discovered. Check with your printer manufacturer for a version of the drivers which works properly under Windows 98 – you'll almost certainly find them on their website.

*How can I get my web pages printed out without losing parts of what is displayed on the Internet Explorer 5 screen? Frequently when I print web pages the right-hand edges of documents disappear, also whole and part lines are lost between the end of one printed page and the next. The only adjustments that I can find in **File** > **Page Setup** are the margins, which I have set to zero, and the headers and footers, from which I've removed all entries. Reducing the text size of the displayed page will sometimes shrink the document to the point where the whole width gets printed, but not always; and bits will still be chopped out where the printout runs on beyond a single sheet. All this is especially exasperating when an online form is to be printed out.*

Printing web pages is not an exact science even now, unfortunately, although there are a few things you can do to help. With extra-wide pages you could try printing in landscape instead of portrait mode. If this doesn't help, cut and paste the contents of your web page into, say, Microsoft Word which gives you greater printing control. Internet Explorer 5 seems to have cured many problems associated with web page printing – it's certainly much better in my experience – and it allows the option to print only specific 'frames' on web pages made up this way. To use this facility click once on the section of the web page you want to print and then click **File** > **Print**. You could also try clicking the **Edit** button in Internet Explorer 5 which should fire up FrontPage Express, if you have it installed. Again, this gives more control over the printing process. You have to realise, unfortunately for you, that the designers of the pages with which you're having problems have only really thought about how their sites will look on screen – perhaps you should move into the digital age with them.

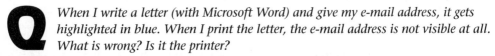

When I write a letter (with Microsoft Word) and give my e-mail address, it gets highlighted in blue. When I print the letter, the e-mail address is not visible at all. What is wrong? Is it the printer?

In Word, click **Tools** > **AutoCorrect** > **AutoFormat As You Type** and uncheck the 'Internet and network paths with hyperlink' box.

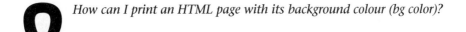

How can I print an HTML page with its background colour (bg color)?

You'll need a colour printer (sorry to state the obvious) and then, assuming you're using Internet Explorer, click **Tools** > **Internet Options** > **Advanced**. Scroll down to the **Printing** section and make sure the 'Print background colors and images' box is checked.

How can I print e-mail messages which have been forwarded to me without the quote characters? I do receive many such messages second hand and wish to copy out part of the message without the print quotes and preferably display it on a full page as in Word.

Stripmail, www.dsoft.com.tr/stripmail, is good for removing all the >>> stuff from e-mails. I've also had Clipmate, www.clipmate.com recommended, which works slightly differently but can be used to the same end.

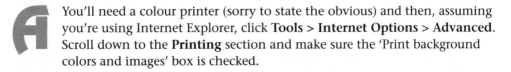

I'm having problems installing both an Epson 680 Stylus Color and an Epson 640 U scanner in Windows Me on a USB port. Incidentally, the printer installs and runs fine off the parallel LPT1 port. Both devices are found as 'unknown USB device' when attached to the USB ports and when I try to update drivers (and I have the latest ones from the Epson website, as well as the original CD) I get a message to say that the .inf files do not contain information about the hardware device. Neither device is listed in the Me list of supported devices, yet I have tried to install the correct drivers as per the Me specific instructions supplied with both the printer and the scanner.

The answer is right there in your question; the drivers you're trying to use don't work with Windows Me, only with earlier versions of Windows like 98 or 95. It is, unfortunately, the case that the drivers for the two types of Windows aren't necessarily compatible. However, you can download new Me-compatible drivers for the printer and scanner at www.epson.co.uk.

I have a car club, and we need to exchange information on members. In Outlook Express, can I print or send an e-mail of names, e-mail addresses and phone numbers?

Yes. To print them out, open the address book (click **Tools > Address Book**), select those you'd like to print (**Ctrl**-left click to select more than one or, if they're contiguous, left-click the first and then **Shift**-left click the last to select all between the two) then click **File > Print**. You'll see you have a choice of methods of printing – Memo, Business Card or Phone List. It's probably the last option that'll suit you best.

*On my old computer I used to be able to print Excel spreadsheets together with the comments in yellow boxes. Now in Excel 2000 under **Print options > Sheet**, the comments option is not available (greyed out). Any clue as to what I can do?*

First you need to have the comments showing on the worksheet – **View > Comments**. Then click **File > Page Setup > Sheet** and then, in the **Print** section of the dialog box you'll see there's a drop-down box next to Comments from which you can choose 'None', 'At End of Sheet' or 'As Displayed on Sheet'.

I have a printer problem. Using an HP8150 I'm having problems when trying to print underlined text. Using some document templates the underline is not actually below the text, but rather strikes through the bottom of the letters, although strangely this problem doesn't occur with all documents. Is this a problem with Microsoft Word? Or with my printer? I'm sure it's very easy to resolve. I've downloaded and installed the latest software drivers to no avail.

Problems with printers are almost always down to either a faulty cable – which doesn't seem to be the problem in your case – or the wrong drivers. You say you've installed the latest ones, but it's worth checking that you really have done so – check on their website that you have the latest ones for your specific version of Windows. I note that you have Windows 2000, and HP have been very tardy releasing Windows 2000 drivers for much of their hardware, so it's worth checking again. The other potential cause of your problem might be that you're using different fonts for things like equations and macro fields in your templates. If this is the case, it will make the underlining go funny as you describe. The only remedy here is either to use a different emphasis – bold, for example – or use the same font for all the underlined text.

Every time I have some type of Windows error (which is sometimes quite frequently), I lose my printer driver connection. I have to reinstall with my installation disks each time I need to use the printer. Any idea why I have to keep reinstalling my printer driver?

I note that you're using Windows 98SE and have rather an old printer. There's a possibility that the drivers you're using from the original disk are specifically for Windows 95 rather than 98, and it could be this which is causing the problem. Have a look at the manufacturer's website and see if there are any new drivers for your model printer and your version of Windows and install them. There's a chance your regular crashes may go away too.

Although it prints OK from Windows, my Canon BJC 1000 will not print from DOS.

Printer drivers (the software which tells your computer how to use your printer) in DOS come with the program which is trying to print, not from Windows or elsewhere. It's unlikely that any DOS application will have drivers for your Canon, but you may find that it can 'emulate' another printer which the software knows about.

How can I get Outlook Express to print in portrait mode?

File > Print > Layout.

How do I obtain a printout of my list of Internet Explorer Favorites?

In IE click **File > Import and Export > Next**, select **Export Favorites** and click **Next**, click the **Favorites** folder (or a sub-folder if you want just one), click **Next**, save it somewhere you can find it, then click **Next > Finish**. Now open the file **bookmark.htm** in IE and print as normal.

If I write a letter and after printing it I cancel it, does some file remain on my hard disk?

If by 'cancel' you mean that you shut down your word processor then no, no permanent file will remain on your hard disk, unless the act of printing creates a 'temporary' file which somehow doesn't get deleted. Check under 'paranoia' in your help files!

101

I have recently upgraded to Internet Explorer 5.5. Now any e-mails I print from Outlook Express have a black border. How do I stop this?

Microsoft says that it knows about this problem. Check windowsupdate.microsoft.com and click on 'Product Updates' or, in IE, click **Tools > Windows Updates** for a fix.

*How do I print long single scrolled web pages? **File > Print** or highlighting the whole text then right-clicking and choosing **Print > Print whole frames** merely gets a single page which is a small part of the total text highlighted.*

When you click **File > Print** click the **Options** tab and then choose 'As laid out on screen' under the **Print frames** section.

My computer doesn't recognise my scanner. I was told it's a SCSI (whatever that is) and the cable it came with fits my printer socket.

Plugging SCSI devices into your printer port can damage both irreparably. You'll need a separate SCSI card for your scanner.

I use cut and paste to move a few lines from an e-mail to print it out. I'd like to save paper and cut and paste from another e-mail and print on same page. Possible?

Yes. Cut and paste the first set of text, leave a line blank, then repeat for the second and subsequent e-mails.

Is it correct that there are different size cartridges for the HP895Cxi inkjet printer?

Yes, it's often sold with the 'economy-sized' 30 ml black cartridge whereas replacements are usually twice this size.

My son's school has been given a Star LC200 dot-matrix. Where can they get a printer driver?

Try Driver Guide, www.driverguide.com or search on Google, www.google.com.

How can I make the 'Printer' icon appear on my taskbar?

It only pops up when you're printing something.

How can I print my own e-mails?

You'll find a copy in the 'Sent' mail folder. Click once on the message you want to print and then click **File** > **Print**.

Harder Questions And Answers

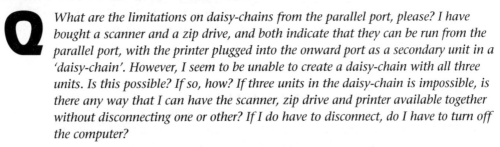

What are the limitations on daisy-chains from the parallel port, please? I have bought a scanner and a zip drive, and both indicate that they can be run from the parallel port, with the printer plugged into the onward port as a secondary unit in a 'daisy-chain'. However, I seem to be unable to create a daisy-chain with all three units. Is this possible? If so, how? If three units in the daisy-chain is impossible, is there any way that I can have the scanner, zip drive and printer available together without disconnecting one or other? If I do have to disconnect, do I have to turn off the computer?

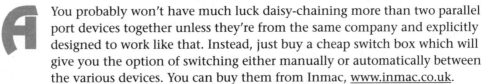

You probably won't have much luck daisy-chaining more than two parallel port devices together unless they're from the same company and explicitly designed to work like that. Instead, just buy a cheap switch box which will give you the option of switching either manually or automatically between the various devices. You can buy them from Inmac, www.inmac.co.uk.

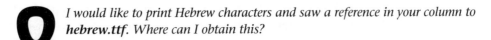

*I would like to print Hebrew characters and saw a reference in your column to **hebrew.ttf**. Where can I obtain this?*

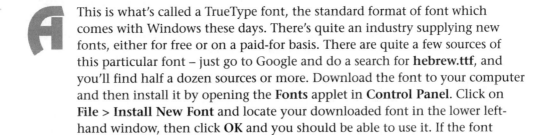

This is what's called a TrueType font, the standard format of font which comes with Windows these days. There's quite an industry supplying new fonts, either for free or on a paid-for basis. There are quite a few sources of this particular font – just go to Google and do a search for **hebrew.ttf**, and you'll find half a dozen sources or more. Download the font to your computer and then install it by opening the **Fonts** applet in **Control Panel**. Click on **File** > **Install New Font** and locate your downloaded font in the lower left-hand window, then click **OK** and you should be able to use it. If the font arrives in a compressed format, e.g. as a zip file, you'll need to decompress it before installing it.

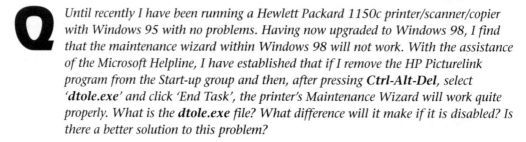

*Until recently I have been running a Hewlett Packard 1150c printer/scanner/copier with Windows 95 with no problems. Having now upgraded to Windows 98, I find that the maintenance wizard within Windows 98 will not work. With the assistance of the Microsoft Helpline, I have established that if I remove the HP Picturelink program from the Start-up group and then, after pressing **Ctrl-Alt-Del**, select **'dtole.exe'** and click 'End Task', the printer's Maintenance Wizard will work quite properly. What is the **dtole.exe** file? What difference will it make if it is disabled? Is there a better solution to this problem?*

Microsoft says that this is all Hewlett Packard's fault – **dtole.exe** is, I presume, a widget installed by the HP installer. The bad news is that HP has been very slow writing new drivers for anything other than Windows 95. However, the good news is that there's a new driver available for your particular machine at <ins>www.hp.com/cposupport/nonjsnav/multi.html</ins>, which HP claims supports Windows 98 in all its glory. This is a good lesson for all of us – it's always a good idea to check the website of the manufacturer of any hardware regularly, and certainly when you first install any new equipment. Don't rely on the drivers which come in the box – they're almost always out of date.

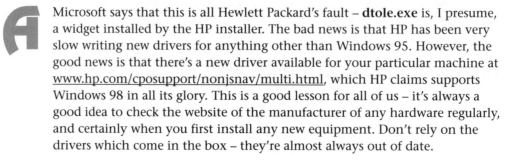

*When I click on the command **Print**, four times out of five I get the message: 'There was an error writing to LPT1. Cannot access that port. Quit other programs and try again.' Quitting all other programs makes no difference. If I keep repeating **Print**, it eventually complies. Can I make it obey first time?*

You don't say what program is causing these problems, but I guess that it's something from the Microsoft Office suite – probably Word. It needs a lot of spare hard disk space – 100 MB at least – to create temporary files when it's printing. Clear some room and run Disk Defragmenter and ScanDisk over your hard disk. Also, check your printer manual and see what type of printer port it requires, then check that you've set your parallel (printer) port to this in your PC's BIOS – you get into this when your machine starts up by pressing a key or keys in combination. There will be a message on your screen telling you that it's **Del** or **F1** or similar. Try ECP, EPP, Bi-directional and Output Only in that order until you find one that works. Also check that both the power cable and the cable between your printer and computer are correctly plugged in at both ends, and that neither is damaged.

I am working with a Family Tree Maker program, to print a family tree. If I save it to disk, I can only save it as a PRN file. I want to email it to my son-in-law, who owns an art gallery, so that he can print it on one large piece of paper instead of me printing it on 30 pages and having to tape it all together. The problem is that he needs it in a TIFF format. Is it possible to cut and paste it into another program, and then save it as a TIFF? Or is there any other way to change it into a TIFF so that he can use it?

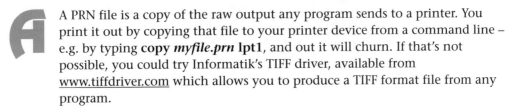

A PRN file is a copy of the raw output any program sends to a printer. You print it out by copying that file to your printer device from a command line – e.g. by typing **copy** *myfile.prn* **lpt1**, and out it will churn. If that's not possible, you could try Informatik's TIFF driver, available from www.tiffdriver.com which allows you to produce a TIFF format file from any program.

I can't print anything from Outlook Express 4. The printer test works, and I've printed a test page to make sure the printer is set up correctly with no problem. I can print from the internet and all other programs but nothing will print from Outlook Express. I have tried updating drivers for both my printer (HP DeskJet 932) and Outlook Express with no luck.

First, try upgrading to Outlook Express 5 or 5.5, which often seems to cure this problem. Also, try opening messages before printing by double-clicking on the message in the upper-right pane in OE. Next, in Internet Explorer click **View > Folder Options > File Types**, scroll down to the entry for TMP files. The Content Type (MIME) should be text/html – if it's not, click **Edit** and from the Content Type (MIME) drop-down box choose text/html. **OK** your way out.

*Word is taking an inordinate time to print to an HP720c with v.10.3 driver which I believe to be the latest. The response between clicking on **Print** in the **File** menu and the commencement of printing – even for such a short amount as an envelope – is over a minute. I have uninstalled Office 2000 Professional then defragmented the drive before reinstalling Office 2000 and still the delay occurs. Can you please help?*

I've been less than impressed recently with HP's devotion to writing new drivers for their older hardware with newer versions of Windows – there's little or no support for their one- or two-year-old printers. Anyway, in your case I'd check that the 'latest' drivers you've installed are in fact for your version of Windows – the 98 drivers are different to the 95 ones and the Me ones, for example. Also, check to see how much free hard disk space you have – if it's almost full Word will be struggling to make the temporary files it needs to print. Remember that colour prints will take much longer to produce than black and white ones, and graphics-intensive pages will also take time to 'render'. Check in your BIOS that your printer (parallel) port is set appropriately for your printer – see what the documentation recommends – and in the **Printer** properties what the Spool settings are. Try 'Raw' to see if this makes a difference.

I use Outlook 97 and will soon be upgrading to Outlook 98 and I wish to print the Contacts (names, phone numbers, e-mail addresses – all fields including dates of birthdays, not shortcuts) onto Filofax-size pages. I do not need the field headings to be printed for all fields, e.g. full name is self-evident. The paper is perforated and tears down to two pages wide, each of 95 mm × 170 mm and will need to print on the front and back of the paper. Can you help? Many thanks if you can help this poor person who cannot afford/does not want to carry an electronic personal organiser around with me.

With the **Contacts** folder selected in Outlook, click on **File > Page Setup > Define Print Styles > Phone Directory Style** (or whatever style you prefer) > **Edit** > **Paper** and then set the paper size to what you need.

My PC has suddenly taken to printing out a single page with ü and é on it after booting up and loading Windows 98. This never used to happen, is very irritating and wastes a page of paper on every restart. I have not, to my knowledge, changed anything, but the strange thing is that my laptop has done this following a hard disk crash and clean system reinstallation. They share a printer. Is it possible that the laptop has somehow 'infected' my PC?

I don't know of a virus with this behaviour, although I suppose it's possible. What seems more likely is that you've got either a duff printer, printer cable or printer driver. When Windows starts up it checks the printer which is installed and yours is misinterpreting this check signal as telling it to print these characters. You can find out which by a process of elimination. Try using your printer on someone else's computer, if possible, or by using their printer on your machine. If the problem continues it could be the printer cable – again, try swapping it for someone else's. Finally, try replacing the printer driver software on your computers – uninstall it completely by deleting it from the **Printers** applet in **Control Panel** or on the **Start > Settings > Printer** menu and then deleting the actual driver file itself, which you'll probably find in your **Windows\system** folder. Its name will vary depending on what printer you have – the Canon BJC800, for example, has a driver called **Canon800.drv**. Re-run the **Add A New Printer** applet and reinstall the printer.

We have two computers on opposite sides of the same room which we wish to connect so that they share folders and a printer. It appears from Windows 95 and 98 Help that it is possible to connect the computers directly by cable, without network cards, through serial ports (both computers have DB9 male connections). I have been unable to find a supplier of a suitable cable (length 6 metres DB9 female both ends). Any ideas? Is there a limit on the length of connection?

There are indeed limits on the length of such cables. Serial cables top out at 50 feet, parallel (printer) cables normally only run to 10 feet and the latter also offer higher connection speeds. Inmac (www.inmac.co.uk), however says it offers a high-quality 10 metre parallel cable, part number DCA4910, although I suspect this may be a misprint. However, you may be better off looking at a 'proper' network – you'll find a 'starter kit' with a cable and two networking cards for under £50 in most computer stores. See Chapter 13 for more details.

 I need to produce reports for many students, all of which use the same basic form. I have scanned the document into my computer and opened it in Word 97. However, I do not want the base document to be printed, just the text I have inserted in text boxes drawn in the spaces I have to fill. Can you please tell me how I can set Word to show the base document but not print it, allowing me to use photocopies of the original in my printer and just printing in the text I have added? Creating a template based on the scanned-in document doesn't seem to work and Word offers little help.

 Just click on **Tools** > **Options** > **Print** and check the 'Print data only for forms' box. You may also like to investigate the wonders of 'mail merge' which can bring together sets of data and standard forms or letters. Have a read through the help files on the subject – you may become enlightened.

 In January 1998 I purchased a PC with an Epson 600 Stylus printer. Recently I was given a Hewlett Packard DeskJet 635 which now occupies the parallel port of the PC instead of the Epson. The HP is great for scanning, faxing and copying but as a normal printer is inferior to the Epson. I would like to be able to switch between the two without having to unplug/plug them. Is it possible to obtain a cable so that I can leave both plugged in and use whichever one is required? Someone suggested installing another parallel port, but the PC's technical support team say this is not possible.

 Actually you could install a second parallel port if your computer has a free expansion slot, but it would be much easier to instead use a simple switch box which will allow you to have both printers connected to the box which in turn is connected to your PC's printer port. You can buy manual ones which work with a simple dial-type switch on the front – you just choose printer A or B as appropriate – or, more expensively, automatic switch boxes which will make this decision for you. Try Inmac at www.inmac.co.uk.

Part 3
Software And Hardware

If Windows won't open and you can't get into Office, this is where you start to look. Windows 95 tried to make everything look simple by hiding all the difficult bits beneath the surface – but the problems have a horrible tendency to come bulging out the sides of your computer and, it seems, no matter how hard you push one in, another will come out of the other side. This section of the book covers the particular problems different programs have working with each other and with Microsoft Windows, and how to get them all to play nicely together and behave.

Operating Systems

What Is An Operating System?

Think of your computer as being like a trifle made up of several layers. At the bottom is the hardware, the physical components that make up your system. Just above that is the BIOS, the Basic Input Output System software which tells your PC's components how to wake up and do basic things like talk to each other. The next layer up is the operating system, the software which interacts between the hardware and BIOS and the really interesting stuff, the application software layer, like your e-mail program and web browser.

Microsoft Windows is by far the most popular operating system around now, with something in the order of 90 per cent of all personal computers running one version or another of it.

If you buy a new computer now, unless you buy an Apple Macintosh it will almost certainly have Windows preinstalled on it. The only competition for it at all at the moment, apart from the Mac OS, is a Linux variant – and the odds are that, if you're reading this book, you really won't want to be messing with Linux (but start at www.linux.org if you do).

New PCs will almost certainly now only be available with Windows XP (the Home or Professional version) and, officially, Microsoft no longer 'supports' Windows 95 – this just means that it won't answer technical support questions via e-mail or telephone, or issue any new 'patches' to correct problems with it; it doesn't mean that Windows 95 will cease to work.

The following subsection gives a short history of the various versions of Windows that you may come across.

A Potted History Of Windows

3.xx

The 'xx' here means that there are a number of versions of Windows beginning with the number 3 – Windows 3.0, 3.1 and 3.11 (and there were other versions before, including Windows 1.0 and Windows 386). Windows 3.0 was the big breakthrough for Microsoft in the battle against competing operating systems and the first version of the OS which gained widespread acceptance; you may still find it on older computers here and there. It sits on top of DOS, the command-line Disk Operating System.

Windows 95

The launch of this version of Windows in 1995 was, at the time, the largest ever such event and tens of millions of copies of Windows 95 have been sold. It promised a new age of '32-bit computing' but actually, like earlier versions of Windows, sat on top of DOS and, as a result, used lots of 16-bit code too (16-bit essentially means it deals with 16 individual bits of data at once, 32-bit that it deals with 32 at a time). This balancing act, sitting some 32-bit code on top of 16-bit code on top of DOS with a pretty user interface sitting over all of it, made Windows 95 pretty vulnerable to crashes and it was unable to cope with large amounts of RAM and big hard disks (over 2 GB). In 1996 came Windows 95 OSR2 which cured some problems (but not all) and introduced support for USB.

Windows 98

Windows 98, launched in 1998, wasn't that different from Windows 95, although a number of bugs were fixed. The 1999 launch of Windows 98 Second Edition (SE) fixed many more problems and introduced Internet Connection Sharing (ICS). Many users chose to stay with Windows 98SE and this is still regarded as the most stable and useful of the Windows 9x line.

Windows Me

Windows Millennium Edition, aka Windows Me, was originally going to be a bringing together of the separate Windows 9x and Windows NT lines of operating systems. Instead, it remained part of the Windows 9x line and Windows 2000 carried the Windows NT torch onwards. Me introduced many features which later actually worked properly in Windows XP, such as System Restore and DLL Protection. The former allowed users to 'roll back' their PCs to an earlier configuration before whatever it was they'd just installed messed things up; DLL Protection made it much harder for programs to overwrite vital system files and stop other programs working. Unfortunately, these and other widgets in Windows Me were very resource hungry and slowed down anything but the most modern of computers.

Windows NT

Windows NT 3.1

Windows NT 3.1 was launched shortly after Windows 3.1 – hence the numbering – and was quickly followed by version 3.5 and then 3.51, but it wasn't until version 4.0, with the Windows 95 interface, was released in 1996 that it gained real popularity as a desktop OS (as opposed to a server operating system). Unlike Windows 95, Windows NT (and subsequent versions) is a fully 32-bit operating system from the bottom up with no 16-bit code inside it. This made it much more stable than Windows 9x. It was designed as both a server operating system and a workstation OS and proved very popular because of its stability, especially when Windows NT 4 was launched with the same user interface as Windows 95.

Windows 2000

Windows 2000 replaced Windows NT 4.0 as both a server and desktop operating system in the year 2000. It added some of the 'fun' functionality previously only available in Windows 9x and, most crucially, brought support for USB to the Windows NT family of operating systems.

Windows XP

Windows XP for desktop computers is available in two versions, Home and Professional. It finally brings together the Windows 9x and NT lines in an operating system that combines the robustness of Windows NT with the multimedia and 'fun' features of Windows 9x. Windows XP Home isn't able to join certain types of business networks and can only support one CPU. Windows XP Professional is a 'superset' of XP Home – it has all the features of Windows XP Home plus further network and multiple CPU support.

Other OSes

Unix

Unix was developed in the late 1960s to work on large 'mainframe' computers as a way for many people to use one computer at the same time. It's now available in many versions.

Linux

While widely regarded as an excellent server operating system, it has yet to make a breakthrough into the desktop arena currently dominated by Microsoft Windows. See www.linux.org for more information.

Macintosh

The Macintosh operating system, currently at version X (10), is only available on proprietary Apple computers. See www.apple.com for more information.

Keeping Windows Up To Date

On the one hand, there's no real reason to upgrade your version of Windows if the one you have already does everything you want it to and the newer version doesn't have any features which tempt you.

On the other hand, it is worth keeping up to date with security patches and fixes for your current operating system until, eventually – as has now happened with Windows 95 – Microsoft stops releasing such patches. At this point you'll probably find that the hardware running the now outdated and unsupported OS is out of date and about to fail anyway and that, in any case, it's not up to running Windows XP – if you have any doubts check the guidelines at www.microsoft.com/windowsxp, where you'll find you need something like 128 MB of RAM and a 300 MHz processor as a minimum specification. The dilemma is that if a new security threat of some kind appears which threatens Windows 95, there will probably be no way to avoid it if you go online at all. Personally, while having to use every single version of Windows that Microsoft releases because I need to answer questions about it, my 'personal workstation' – the computer I use from day to day – tends to lag one release behind the leading edge (or 'bleeding edge', as it's sometimes better known). So, right now, I'm working mostly on a Windows 2000 computer, although the computer which I use second most frequently, my laptop, does run Windows XP.

Only you can decide when the time is right for you to upgrade – for example, you may find that some vital piece of hardware such as a printer or scanner isn't supported by the new OS at first, so always check this before upgrading. On the other hand, you will want to weigh this against new features, improved security and stability and so on. In general, if you're happy with what you have then I usually advise people not to upgrade unless the new version of the OS has something they want particularly badly – for example, if you're running Windows NT 4.0 and want to connect some USB devices to your PC then you should move to Windows 2000 or XP. If you have a laptop which you need to synchronise regularly with a desktop PC or network, the extra features offered for this in Windows 2000 and XP make it a worthwhile move from any earlier version of Windows.

If you're a home user running Windows 95 you should seriously consider moving to a later operating system simply because of the lack of support patches and upgrades for your version of Windows now, although you may also need to upgrade your hardware too (see Chapter 15 for more information on hardware upgrades). If you have Windows 98, visit the Microsoft update site at windowsupdate.microsoft.com where you'll see a link on the left through which you can order an update CD to give you most of the functionality of Windows 98SE (you don't need to order it if you already have this version of Windows), a well worthwhile update.

If you have Windows 98 or Me, have a look at what's offered by Windows XP to see if you can use any of its new features – you'll find comprehensive details at www.microsoft.com/windowsxp. The main new 'feature' is more a lack of something – many, many fewer crashes. Windows 9x is terrible at managing memory and other system resources, problems corrected by Windows XP. While Windows 9x computers need to be rebooted at least once, and probably several times per day, Windows XP will probably run for days and even weeks at a time without needing to be restarted. Windows XP also manages sound and image files much more sensibly, and has a system for burning CDs built into it: you can simply drag-and-drop files onto it as if it were another hard disk.

Types Of Upgrade

'Over The Top' Upgrade

This is the most obvious type of upgrade to perform. You start up your computer as normal, pop in the CD for the new version of Windows and let it do its thing. The advantage of this system is that you don't normally lose any of your data or your program settings. The disadvantage is that you will still have on your hard disk older versions of drivers for your hardware which may cause conflicts and problems with their replacements. It's worth trying this type of upgrade as a first step, just in case it works – but be prepared for a 'blank sheet' upgrade.

'Blank Sheet' Upgrade

This involves completely erasing everything on your computer before you start to install the newer version of Windows. Note, this doesn't mean that you have to buy the 'full', more expensive version of the new operating system. If you own an earlier version all you need is its original CD – when you install the new version of Windows at some point it will ask you to 'prove' you're eligible for the upgrade by just popping the old CD into your PC. The advantage of this is that you only have the newer version of Windows on your computer without any old baggage to mess up the new one. The disadvantage is that you lose all the data and settings on the hard disk where you install the new version of Windows – but see Chapter 17 for steps you can take to preserve all this information and make reinstalling your data and program settings as easy as possible. You may have a problem if your computer manufacturer shipped only a 'recovery disc' instead of a proper Windows CD – such CDs may well not qualify you for upgrades to later versions of Windows. Check with the computer vendor for details.

'Side By Side' Installation

This is a compromise between the 'over the top' and 'blank sheet' upgrades which leaves you with two versions of Windows installed on your computer. There are a number of caveats to doing this. First, you *must* install each version of Windows with a different drive letter. Windows 9x has to be installed on the C: drive, Windows NT, 2000 and XP can go on any drive. Note, you don't have to have two physical hard disks: you can 'partition' a single disk to give it two or more different drive letters, e.g. C: and D:. Also, you can only have one instance of any version of Windows 9x installed at a time (unless you use a third-party 'boot manager'), although you can have multiple versions (and copies) of Windows NT 4, 2000 and XP. After this you will see a menu on starting your computer asking you to choose which operating system you want to use. Finally, if you're mixing Windows 9x with Windows NT 4, 2000 or XP you *must* use the FAT32 file system format (FAT16 in the case of Windows 95). While Windows NT4, 2000 and XP can read all file systems, Windows 9x cannot read Windows NT's native NTFS file system. You'll need to install programs you want to use in each version of Windows from that version itself, although they can be installed to the same location. So Microsoft Office, for example, could be installed in Windows 98 and Windows XP and in both cases be on the C: partition, meaning that it's only installed in one location on your computer and doesn't take up two lots of disk space. The advantage of a 'side by side' installation is that you can have the best of both operating systems and gradually get used to the new one. You can also continue using hardware and software which isn't compatible with the newer version of Windows (and vice versa). The disadvantage is that you use more hard disk space and may find the whole process confusing.

Questions And Answers

Easy Questions And Answers

Q *I am an English teacher in Japan and intend purchasing a laptop in the near future. I am in two minds whether to buy one at home (i.e. Ireland or the UK) and have it shipped over or whether to buy one here in Japan. I was wondering, if I buy one in Japan is it possible to have it converted to an English language operating system? After ringing up the manufacturer's customer support in Japan they told me that they didn't do it, but not that it was impossible. Does this mean that my warranty will be invalid if it is possible and I do?*

A You'll almost certainly be able to simply reformat your machine's hard disk and install an English-language version of Windows (I'd recommend 2000 or XP) simply by popping in the CD-ROM and running the setup program. However, you will have to cope with, possibly, a Japanese-language keyboard which will be 'mapped' with English letters – i.e. the letters on the keyboard won't match those Windows thinks you're pressing. You may be able to get round this by buying a laptop with English keys on it, though – I'm not hugely familiar with the Japanese marketplace. You should also be aware that you may be liable for various taxes and import duties on arrival in the EU, too, so look into that first. Also, note that some manufacturers will wash their hands of you if you've change the OS on your PC and then have a problem – even if it's a hardware problem. You should check carefully with both the Japanese and UK offices of the manufacturers first.

Q *I've just bought a Macintosh iBook and can't find what version of Windows it uses – can you tell me where to look, please?*

A Apple Macintosh computers don't run Windows – they run the Macintosh operating system. iBooks are currently up to version 10 – called OS X by Apple.

Harder Questions And Answers

Q *After my computer crashed I was advised to restore Windows XP with the restore disc. After I installed this disc I now have two Windows XP systems running at start-up. I would like to know if I can remove the one which has the problem on it. If so, can you please advise me on how to go about doing this?*

You just delete the folder which the 'defective' version of XP is installed in – by default it's something like C:**windows** or C:**winxp** – this may vary if you chose a different name yourself during installation. You also need to edit a file called **boot.ini** which you'll find on your **C:** drive. This is a hidden system file and if you can't see it, in **My Computer** click **Tools** > **Folder Options** > **View** and check the 'Show hidden files and folders' button and uncheck the 'Hide protected operating system files' button. Open **boot.ini** with Notepad and at the start of the line which refers to the duff version of XP, type **REM** (for REMark) which will disable it being shown on the start-up menu. Save the file and restart. Others who've done this have found that they also need to reinstate the 'system' and 'hidden' properties of the file, in that order, to get it to work.

I've had to reinstall Windows XP twice so far for reasons unrelated to the performance of the operating system itself. However, each time I've had to reactivate it, which is a pain. Is there any way around this?

Assuming you're reinstalling WXP to the same hardware, you can back up the activation status by copying the file **wpa.dbl**, which you'll find in the **system32** folder of your Windows installation folder – you can find it with a document name search. Save it somewhere safe and then, after reinstalling XP, restart the computer in Minimal Safe Mode, find the current **wpa.dbl** file and rename it to **wpa.noact**, then copy your saved version back to the **system32** folder. Reboot and you should find you don't need to reactivate your installation. Note that this only works when you're reinstalling to the same hardware where you've already activated the OS – it's not a way to avoid activation.

My godson has a problem when starting his computer. It has Windows 98 as its operating system, 24 MB of RAM installed, and a 4.3 GB hard drive with plenty of free space. When switching on, the computer gets to a stage when nothing appears to be happening (including the screen not responding or showing anything). When this happens, by switching off and then on, or pressing the reset button, the computer then starts normally and continues to work normally. Shutting down the computer is OK at all times.

There are lots and lots of reasons why your computer may have a problem, and Microsoft has several troubleshooters devoted to working through and solving the problems. Go to support.microsoft.com and have a look at articles Q136337 (for Windows 95) and Q188867 (for Windows 98).

I have a 400 MHz Pentium II computer. It has a 4 GB hard disk which is partitioned as a 2.72 GB C: drive and a 1.28 GB D: drive. The operating system was Windows 98SE but just recently I upgraded to Windows Me. I have a CD-ROM E: drive and

118

*also just recently I had a CD rewriter put in which is the F: drive. The space on my hard drive is running out quickly so I wanted to attempt to reinstall Windows Me on a clean drive and tried to reformat my drives by booting with my start-up disk and then selecting the 'with CD-ROM support' option. Everything seemed OK except I noticed in the list on the screen it said my CD-ROM is F:. I tried to use the command **aformatc:** but all it said was 'Not ready reading drive F'. I cannot get past this.*

Assuming there's no data on either your C: or D: drives, what you want to do is combine them into one drive and use that to run Windows Me (which I have to say, by the by, I don't consider to be a worthwhile upgrade from Windows 98SE at all, but there you go). To do this, you first need to run the fdisk program on your start-up floppy disk. Delete the C: and D: partitions and then create one new partition, which will be C:. Format this using the command **a:format c:** (not the version you have), then install Windows Me. If you want to keep the C: and D: drives separate, don't run fdisk, just the command **a:format c:** – note the space.

You'll find a lot of information on using fdisk at www.fdisk.com/fdisk.

fdisk and format will remove all information on the disks you run them on: nothing will remain.

Our office has about ten PCs on Windows 2000 and an NT4 server. We're thinking of going over to the Small Business Server so that we can use Microsoft Exchange. Good idea? Bad idea? Wait for something better?

I've been a big fan of SBS for some years, and used it here at Chateau Keyboard until fairly recently when I decided I could make better use of the box it ran on. It's definitely best-of-breed for small companies, but the Windows 2000 version is a tad complicated, and Microsoft and I both recommend that you find a specialised, qualified installer to set it up for you.

How can you boot a PC without a physical keyboard attached?

This all depends on what operating system you wish to use. Some, like AIX, are quite happy if the machine on which they run never sees a keyboard; others, like Windows, are completely lost without one. I note from your original question that you're running Windows 2000 which, I'm pretty sure, won't boot up without a keyboard attached to the machine it's running on.

I've been advised that it's best to leave my PC on all the time, but I can remember the problem of memory leak reducing the capability of the PC over time as 'used' memory isn't restored when I close a program. Is this not the case any more?

That depends on what operating system you're using. Windows 95, 98 and Me still suffer from the problem; Windows NT, 2000 and XP are much better. My advice is to re-boot (**Start > Shut Down > Restart**) your Windows 9x machine at least once a day. Windows NT, 2000 and XP machines don't need this.

Application Software

What Do Applications Do?

Applications are the really interesting things on your computer, the programs that allow you to make some use of the pile of metal and glass that sits on your desk and do something interesting with it. Because there are so many different programs available – hundreds of thousands if not millions of them – it's impossible to cover all those you may come across, so this chapter will look at some of the more popular ones you're likely to find have already been installed on your computer and where to go to find ones that may interest you.

Office Productivity Software

These are programs such as word processors, spreadsheets, database programs, presentation software, website creation software, desktop publishing, e-mail and PIM (Personal Information Manager) software. Nowadays the market is dominated by the Microsoft Office suite of programs, various versions of which include different combinations of Word, Excel, Access, PowerPoint, FrontPage, Publisher and Outlook. If you or any of your direct family are involved in education, either as teachers or pupils/students, keep an eye out for the Student version of Office (and Windows) which costs just a fraction of the price of the full product – details via the Microsoft education website at www.microsoft.com/uk/education.

What You May Already Have

Apart from Microsoft Windows, which comes preinstalled on almost all new computers, you're likely to find anything from a couple of feeble games up to entire collections of office productivity software and more on a new computer. Be cautious and don't get sucked in by the promise of software apparently worth more than the actual computer you're buying – nothing is free, and any such 'deals' are likely to comprise outdated software, demonstration versions of games and out-of-date encyclopaedias.

Microsoft Works

Once regarded as the poor relation to Microsoft Office, Works is now a rather respectable collection of software. It used to contain a rather basic word processor, a database and a spreadsheet program. Now, depending on which version you buy (or comes preinstalled on your PC) it will include Microsoft Word, the word processor from the full Microsoft Office Suite, the AutoRoute Express route-finding program, Money, the excellent financial management package, Picture It! Photo Studio, the Encarta encyclopaedia and Works 6.0 database – pretty good value for money and well worth considering if you don't need any of the other applications from Microsoft Office. See works.msn.com for full details.

Microsoft Office

Once there were any number of office productivity suites from companies like WordPerfect, Lotus and Microsoft. Now Microsoft Office has become the default choice for most companies and individuals (but see 'Star Office' below, page 124). It won through partly because it's actually very good, partly because of Microsoft's mighty marketing team and partly because of laziness and stupidity on the part of Microsoft's competitors. The only real question is which version and package of component programs you should go for. You'll find full details of the options available at office.microsoft.com. If you have an older installation of Microsoft Office, the same rules about deciding whether or not to upgrade apply as to when you're thinking about your operating system. Again, Microsoft supports the current version and up to two previous versions, so at the time of writing you can get support (and security patches and bug fixes will be written for) Office XP and Office 2000. Versions before this (e.g. Office 95) are no longer supported so, if your hardware is up to the task of running a new version, think very hard about upgrading. If you already have Office 2000, while there are some nice new features in Office XP the odds are that none of them will be must-haves for you, although you should double-check with the features list on the Office website just in case. If you have Office 97 and your hardware's up to the task, upgrading to Office XP is probably going to be worth the effort and cost.

Other Common Software Packages

Anti-virus Software

Many new computers now come with some sort of anti-virus (AV) software installed. Check very carefully what the package is and update it as soon as possible – preferably the very first time you go online, in fact – from the manufacturer's website. Often such packages are 'last year's model' or limited functionality versions. See Chapter 18 for more details on AV software.

Encyclopaedias

Like the AV software included with new computers, the encyclopaedias which come with them may well be older versions. Again, check to see if any free updates are available online.

Games

Check for updates and patches available online (and remember that if you're going to play the latest games, you'll need a higher-specification PC than you need to run basic office productivity applications).

Software Included With Sound And Video Cards

Often, manufacturers of these types of devices include games to show off the capabilities of their hardware. They may also include software to allow you to adjust many of the controls and settings on the device. Updates for these 'controller' applications are often available online.

Modem Software

Some manufacturers include software for sending faxes or using your computer as a telephone. Personally, I've given up trying to use my PC for faxing – particularly for receiving faxes – having decided that the cost of a cheap standalone fax machine more than covers the grief offered by fax software. That said, many people have a lot of success with such programs, as they do with the software designed to allow you to use your PC to make cheap(er) long-distance telephone calls. The quality of such software is gradually improving but does depend on the quality of your connection to the internet and the general level of 'business' between you and the person you're calling. Again, I prefer to use a standalone telephone to make voice calls.

Alternatives To Microsoft Office

WordPerfect

WordPerfect used to be the most popular word processing software in the world, and it still exists as part of Corel's WordPerfect Office 2002 suite of software. Available in Standard, Professional and Academic versions, the package also includes a similar range of products to Microsoft Office. See www.wordperfect.com for full details.

Star Office

Now owned by the Sun computer company, Star Office has the usual office suite features at a lower price than Microsoft Office but with much of the functionality. See www.staroffice.com.

Open Office

See www.openoffice.org for a free, open-source version of Star Office.

Shareware And Freeware

Shareware is 'try before you buy' software which you're usually permitted to try for something like 30 days, after which you pay for it if you like it enough. Shareware may also have restricted functionality – you may not be able to print or save the files you create, for example, or images may have 'trial version' or similar stamped on them. Freeware is usually completely free, although the authors often ask that you send them something like a postcard or e-mail with feedback on the product. You'll find lots of such software available from many websites, and that many manufacturers offer trial versions of their software. Also, check the websites of the manufacturers of your current software and hardware to see if they offer any free enhancements and additions for download. Three of the best-known and most popular sources of shareware are www.shareware.com, www.download.com and www.tucows.com. Check Mercury Freeware, www.mercury.org.uk for some tested, UK-compatible freeware. The following is a list of the shareware and freeware programs I find most useful and install on all of my computers.

➤ About Time. This will keep your PC's clock accurate to within a few milliseconds a day by synchronising it with online atomic clocks at regular intervals. Written by Paul Lutus, this is 'Careware' – see www.arachnoid.com for details.

➤ AdAware from Lavasoft, www.lavasoftUSA.com, removes 'spyware' applications from your computer. Many programs – probably without you being aware of it – send back information to their creators on your surfing and computer use habits. AdAware stops them doing this and removes any such programs which may have implanted themselves on your computer as you surf the internet.

➤ Adobe Acrobat Reader, invaluable for reading PDF (Portable Document Format) documents (ending with **.pdf**). You may find online documentation and disc-based computer manuals in this format. Download it from www.adobe.com.

➤ Free Agent from Forté, the best program for reading newsgroups on Usenet (see Chapter 12 for more information on this topic). Visit www.forteinc.com to download it.

➤ AVG anti-virus software from Grisoft, www.grisoft.com. See Chapter 18 for more details on this program.

➤ Babelfish from AltaVista, babelfish.altavista.com. Named after the ear-resident fish which translates between all languages in the late, great Douglas Adams's book *The Hitch-Hiker's Guide To The Galaxy*, this little widget can translate between many different languages. It's not perfect but is usually good enough to give you an idea of what someone's going on about.

➤ Chilton Preview, www.geocities.com/SiliconValley/Peaks/8392, replaces the standard **Preview** pane in Microsoft Outlook (not, unfortunately, Outlook Express) with one which doesn't allow HTML (web page) format e-mail messages to be displayed in a dangerous way (some viruses and worms can infect your PC if you just open a web page containing them – see Chapter 18 for more details).

➤ CuteFTP from Globalscape, www.globalscape.com. There are any number of FTP (File Transfer Protocol) programs available. This is the one I prefer.

➤ DigiGuide, www.digiguide.com, the only way real geeks find out what's on TV tonight. DigiGuide not only lists what's on but will keep an eye out for your favourite programs, stars and even types of programs, then tell you in advance when they're on. Excellent.

➤ Infuzer, www.infuzer.com, is a growing community of websites which will put important dates into your Outlook calendar. You can get local weather, public holidays in most countries, rugby match dates and more.

➤ MBSA, the Microsoft Baseline Security Analyzer, www.microsoft.com/technet/security/tools/Tools/mbsahome.asp. This analyses the security settings of Windows 2000 and XP computers (see Chapter 18 for more details).

➤ MusicMatch Jukebox, www.musicmatch.com, for converting CD music to MP3 format to play on your computer.

125

➤ Paint Shop Pro, www.jasc.com – the painting and photo manipulation program that works best for me.

➤ Popcorn from Ultrafunk, www.ultrafunk.com for peering into apparently defective e-mail server inboxes. (NB: Some ISPs won't work with Popcorn, so instead try Mail Washer, www.mailwasher.net.)

➤ SETI screensaver, setiathome.berkeley.edu. There are a number of 'good causes' which ask you to donate the 'downtime' from your PC when you're not using it to their efforts. SETI uses PCs all over the world to analyse signals from outer space for signs of extra-terrestrial life. Hopefully, when we find these ETs, they'll have the secret of non-crashing computers, which is why I support SETI.

➤ TClockEx by Dale Nurden, http://users.iafrica.com/d/da/dalen. Changes the simple time display in your System Tray into something more useful, showing the day and date as well.

➤ WinZip, www.winzip.com. Vital for opening compressed zip format files. Windows XP can handle these files to some extent on its own but WinZip vastly extends its capabilities.

➤ ZoneAlarm, the personal firewall software, www.zonealarm.com (see Chapter 18 for more details).

Educational Software

There are entire books devoted to this topic and there are thousands of different programs available for pre-school to post-university age groups. The British Educational Communications and Technology Agency, BECTA, runs BESD, the BECTA Educational Software Database which allows you to search by various criteria for software covering particular subjects, ages and so on. You'll find it at besd.becta.org.uk.

Questions And Answers

Easy Questions And Answers

*I've tried the **Alt Gr+4** trick to get a Euro symbol, but it doesn't work.*

You may need to install Euro-enabled fonts, then. Go to office.microsoft.com, do a search for euro and download the appropriate bits for your version of Windows. Check the Windows Update site at windowsupdate.microsoft.com too.

Q *Do you know of a self-help user group for Office products? I've only managed to find links to Keen via the Microsoft site, and I really don't want to have to pay their fees.*

A Good help and advice is worth paying for, but you could try Yahoo! Groups – groups.yahoo.com. Also, typing **"Microsoft Office User Group"** (with the quotes around it) brings up about four pages of links on Google, www.google.com.

Q *If there is a way to permanently prevent the Microsoft Office Assistant from popping up, please let me know.*

A Right-click the Assistant then left-click **Options > Options** and then uncheck all the tick boxes. In Office XP you click **Help > Hide the Office Assistant**.

Q *I have folders called **config.msi** containing huge numbers of ***.rbf** files. They seem to be associated with Windows 98 and MS Office setup. Are they essential or can I junk them?*

A These are roll back files used by the relevant program if you want to 'roll back' your installation to an earlier version, e.g. go back to Office 97 from Office 2000. They can, as you've found, take up a lot of room, being, essentially, copies of the original files. You'll also find some ***.rbs** files, roll back script files, which tell the new program how to uninstall itself and reinstate the old one. So if you delete these files you won't be able to go back to the original version of your program. It's your choice.

Q *I have purchased a PIII 800 MHz bundled with MS Works with Word 2000. I would like to install my older copy of Office 97 (I use Outlook a lot). Will this simply overwrite Word 2000 or will I be in a right mess afterwards? Ideally I would like to be left with Office 97 comprising Word 2000 – is this possible?*

A You'd either have a mess or find that the older version of Word wouldn't install, so do this: first, uninstall Works then install Office 97 and then reinstall Works including Word 2000. This should 'upgrade' your older version of Word without causing any problems.

Q *I have recently upgraded from an AMBRA 386 to a Gateway Pentium III with Windows 98 and Office 2000 Small Business. I saved my documents/records which were held on Lotus AmiPro to floppy disk, but when I try to load these to my new computer in Word, the result is a 'strung out' series of odd letters and parts of text.*

127

This is because the widget Word needs to read your AmiPro files isn't installed by default. The AmiPro filter is in the Office Resource Kit on your Office CD. For other file formats, re-run the Office installation disc choosing the 'Custom' option and look for the option to include other file converters during that process.

I bought a computer with a pre-loaded anti-virus program. When I tried to update it the manufacturer said it's an OEM version and updates aren't available. Is this right?

You can only expect what you pay for. Your version of the AV program would have been sold without support or upgrades/updates by the manufacturer to your PC maker – you'll have to buy the full version to do anything more.

I've been used to Word 97 and have just upgraded to 2000, and now every time I create a new document I get a new instance of Word on my toolbar. What am I doing wrong?

Nothing, Word 2000 does this by design. Office XP, the latest version, allows you to choose between this method and the original, where you have to click on the Window menu to switch documents. You can also close down all Word files at once by holding down **Shift** and then clicking **File > Close All**.

Can I open WordStar 4 files in Microsoft Word? When I try I get gibberish at the moment.

Re-run the Word installation program, choosing the 'Custom' option. In there you'll find an option to install different sorts of converters – choose the appropriate one.

Harder Questions And Answers

I have loaded PowerPoint separately from Microsoft Office and it sits in a folder of its own under C:. Everything on it works perfectly except two things; one, I can't run spell check and get the error message, 'PowerPoint can't load the main spelling dictionary. You should run set up and reinstall'. And two, I can only open PPT files through PowerPoint and not through Explorer – I can see them but they have no PPT icon and just won't open. I think this is a file association problem but can't seem to create one.

Microsoft Office programs are extraordinarily fussy about where they're installed. Theoretically, as is offered during the installation process, you can put them anywhere you want. However in practice I and others have found that if you don't put them in the default location many different and strange errors occur – as you're finding. I'd suggest uninstalling PowerPoint from wherever you have it now and then re-running the Office installation to put it into the default location.

On a multi-operating system computer, where do I have to load the program? From Windows 2000 is it possible to access Windows Me programs or vice versa? Do I have to load programs in both operating systems?

You do need to load every program you want to use in each operating system but you can load them into the same location/folder. Say that you have Windows 2000 on your D: drive and Windows Me on the C: drive and that you want to load Office 2000. Start in Me and load it with the default location – usually **C:\program files\office**. When the installation has finished, restart your computer, booting into Windows 2000 this time, and reload Office 2000. This time choose the 'Custom' installation option to make sure that it's put into the same location as before, **C:\program files\office**, and not **D:\program files\office**. This process ensures that each program takes up the least possible amount of hard disk space, but that they're also 'registered' in the individual operating systems so that both versions of Windows know where they are.

As a personal and small business user I am still using Office 95 but have Windows 97 documents, particularly Excel files, sent to me by e-mail which I cannot open. I understood that installing Winzip 7.0 would do the trick but it doesn't. Perhaps I am not applying it properly?

It depends. WinZip will allow you to see what's inside a zipped up archive file, usually ending in **.zip**. If you're being sent Word and Excel documents which have been zipped up, this is your first step to opening them. If you still can't open them, it may be because you don't have the relevant programs installed, in which case you can download viewers for them for free from the Microsoft website via office.microsoft.com. Microsoft also used to offer **Save As** filters for Office 95 which allowed you to save Office 95 documents in Office 97 format – check the Office website for details. You may also find them on the Office 97 installation CD if your correspondent has that and can send you copies.

I wish to reload Office 2000 from the original CDs. However, having started with Office Professional 95, I have Office 97 Upgrade, and Office 2000 Professional Upgrade CDs. Do I need to go back and install the 95 version followed by the two upgrades to ensure everything is installed correctly?

No, you don't need to re-run the entire process. You should just be able to run the Office 2000 installer. It may ask for proof that you're entitled to the upgrade by asking you to put an earlier CD in the drive – the Office 95 CD should do the trick. You may also need to reinstall the WMF graphic filter.

Open **Control Panel > Add/Remove Programs > Office 97**, choose **update** and then the WMF filter on the appropriate installation screen.

Q *I have always been able to copy over my AutoText file from Templates from one computer to another operating on Windows 98. I have upgraded my laptop to Windows 2000 and use Office Professional 2000. I cannot find where to put my AutoText file where it works. There is a file Templates 1033 and Excel solutions but these seem to have nothing to do with this. As I use AutoText a lot this is quite important to me. Can you help please?*

A The AutoText files are stored in a file called **normal.dot**. You can find its location from inside Word by clicking **Tools > Options > File Locations**. Click the **User Templates** line once to select it and then click the **Modify** button – this will make the location of the template files easier to read. Note it down and then close Word. Copy your old **normal.dot** file to this location. There's now also the Save My Settings Wizard available for download from Microsoft via office.microsoft.com which will copy AutoText and many other settings from one machine to another.

Q *I have an Excel spreadsheet which has to be updated on a regular basis. When these amendments (which can be figures or text) are made they need to be incorporated into other spreadsheets. Is there a way that this can be done automatically without the time consuming 'copy and paste special' routine?*

A You need to use a linked object. Arrange the two program windows so you can see the two Excel spreadsheets you want to contain some of the same data. Left-click and drag across the cells you want to copy from the first, then right-click on the border of the area (not the now shaded area itself) and drag the cells to the point where you want them to appear in the second spreadsheet. When you release the mouse button, choose the **Link** option from the pop-up menu. Now go back to the first set of cells and change something in one cell – you'll see it changes immediately you hit **Enter** in the second set of cells too. You can do this with any OLE-enabled program – such as the whole Microsoft Office suite. This means that you could, for example, have a PowerPoint presentation containing an automatically changing 'Monthly report' and 'Monthly results figures' without actually having to open the presentation at all once you'd set the process up.

Q *I have great difficulties in typing complicated maths formulae in Word 2000. Can you please suggest an easier way?*

A Click **Insert > Object > Create New** tab. In the **Object type** box click **Microsoft Equation 3.0** and then **OK**. Build your equation by selecting symbols from the Equation toolbar and typing in your own variables and numbers.

Part 4
The Internet

Nowadays, anyone with access to the internet can find out the answer to virtually any question they can think of. The irony, of course, is that the most popular question is 'How do I get on to the internet?' – and to answer it you need to get on to the internet which would mean you wouldn't need to ask the question in the first place … These chapters will help you drag yourself up by your own bootlaces to get on to the internet and then, once you're there, show you how to cope with the problems of staying online, using your e-mail effectively and how to make best use of the resources available to you, including optimising your online time.

Connecting To The Internet

Just getting connected to the internet in the first place can be a problem. Staying connected can be even more difficult. And then when you sort that out, how do you know you're collecting your e-mails and surfing the web as well and efficiently as possible?

How Does The Connection Work?

The internet is a worldwide collection of computers and computer networks to which anyone can connect if they have the right sort of equipment. Its two main uses are for communication with others, by e-mail, and finding information via the world wide web. Don't confuse the internet with the world wide web – the latter is part of the former. The internet is the physical setup, the wires and computers which connect everything together. The WWW is essentially a graphics- and text-based means of finding information (and lots of other things now, too) on the internet. E-mail is transported across the same wires and computers that transport information on the world wide web.

The best way for an individual to get connected to the internet is via an ISP, an Internet Service Provider. These companies have direct, hard-wired connections to the network of computers that makes up the internet, and you can connect to them via your telephone line. No one organisation, body, government or individual owns or controls the internet. Things are done, largely, by mutual agreement and cooperation, which is great when it works well but is unfortunately easy to abuse (see Chapter 18).

To get connected, then, you need the following:

1   A computer.

2   Software on that computer which will both connect you to the internet and then provide the tools you need to do something useful while you're online – an e-mail program and a web browser are the basics. Luckily, Windows comes with such software built-in and preinstalled.

3   A telephone line.

4   A modem, the device which connects your computer to your ISP via your telephone line. Nowadays, so-called 'broadband' connections such as ADSL (Asynchronous Digital Subscriber Line) and cable modems are also available. These are 'always-on' connections which keep your computer connected permanently to your ISP, something which would cost a lot of money to do with a modem and also would be a lot slower.

5   An account with an ISP.

Getting Connected

When you buy a new computer, the odds are that it will come with at least one, and probably several, CD-ROMs from a selection of ISPs. Even if your computer doesn't come with such discs you can pick them up from just about anywhere now – record stores, book shops, even petrol stations – all offering dozens or hundreds of free hours. So, what criteria should you judge them by?

Reliability

Unfortunately, reliability isn't the easiest thing to judge from the outside so ask friends, colleagues and acquaintances which ISP they use and what they think of them. Websites like ISP review, www.ispreview.co.uk, the UK ISP directory at www.uk-isp-directory.co.uk, the UK ISP users' group at www.ukispusersgroup.co.uk, Net4Nowt at www.net4nowt.com and (for broadband connections) www.broadband-help.com can be useful. Of course, if you don't already have a computer this can be problematical although friends have computers they'd love you to borrow and there are always internet cafés and, increasingly, public libraries where you can use a computer for a few hours at a time, often with some help to get going. Also have a flick through the many magazines devoted to computers and the internet available from all newsagents – there's often a 'comparison test' between various ISPs in one or another of them each month.

Cost

Free trials aside, there are four main ways to pay for your internet connection:

1   Via your telephone bill. ISPs do a deal with British Telecom (or another telephone company) and take a share of what you pay for calling them. This can be an ideal way to test the waters, so to speak, since there are no up-front bills or contracts to sign. Normally the calls are charged at local rates, although it's worth checking with your telephone service provider exactly how much they charge for the specific calls you'll be making. FreeServe, Virgin and others offer this sort of service.

2   An up-front subscription plus the cost of your telephone calls. You pay for the two items separately, hopefully getting better service since you're paying more. Typically, such subscriptions have a one-, three- or six-month duration, although this varies considerably. ClaraNet and Cix offer this sort of service.

3   An up-front payment for an 'all you can dial' ISP service where the price of the subscription includes the cost of all your telephone calls. Usually these are described as 'unlimited' subscriptions but many providers limit the actual number of hours you can be online over a given period, and the number of hours you can stay connected consecutively. For example, some offerings from British Telecom limit you to two hours at any one time and 12 hours in any 24. FreeServe, BT, Virgin, AOL and many others offer this sort of service.

4   ADSL and cable modem services are permanent connections to the internet which, like the 'all you can dial' ISP services, are charged at a fixed rate each month no matter how much you use them. They're usually more expensive than dial-up accounts but you'll have a connection that's up to 10 times faster and permanently connected, too. ADSL and cable modem services aren't available over the entire

country and some more rural areas may never have them – it depends on how far you are from a suitable telephone exchange for ADSL and whether or not a cable TV company has installed its cables in your area for cable modem service.

Once you've chosen your first ISP, the easiest way to set up a connection to it is to insert the CD-ROM they gave or sent you and allow it to run automatically. It will install the software you need and, through prompts and wizards, make the appropriate settings for your connection and e-mail account. NB: Do *not* do this for any subsequent ISPs – see below.

Using More Than One ISP

It may sound daft to have more than one ISP account, but it all goes towards providing a backup for your computing and connectivity. What do you do if your car breaks down? Catch a bus. The same applies to connecting to the internet – you need to know how to still get online when your main means of doing so breaks down. When you start using the internet you won't be relying on it at all, but you could quite quickly come to find that it's your main method of communicating with many of your friends and family. And if you use it for your business you could find that your internet connection has become, to you, one of the industry's favourite buzzword phrases: *mission critical*, i.e. your business can't function without it.

Setting Up A Second Connection

The simplest thing to do is, once you've set up your 'main' internet connection, log on to the website of another ISP which offers 'free' connections for just the price of your telephone call and sign up for an account with them too, adding the connection manually to your PC. Don't, whatever you do, set up a connection from more than one ISP using a free CD – it will certainly overwrite your first ISP's settings and quite possibly neither will work properly. To set up a manual connection in Windows 95, 98 or Me, you open **My Computer** and then **Dial-Up Networking** and double-click the 'Make a new connection' icon. In Windows 2000 open 'Network and Dial-up connections' and double-click 'Make New Connection', and in Windows XP it's the **Network Connections** section of **Control Panel** you open, then click 'Create a new connection' or **File > New Connection**. Whichever version of Windows you have, follow the wizard through, filling in the information given when you registered online with your second ISP. Typically all you'll need is your username and password and the telephone number to call to make a connection. Keep all this information safe – see Chapter 17 for more details. Once you've done this you will find that there are now two connection icons (connectoids) available. If you connect manually to the internet, double-click the one of your choice to go online. If you connect automatically, open **Internet Connections** in **Control Panel** and choose which you want to use on the **Connections** tab (see below, 'Making The Connection' for details on how to choose between manual and automatic connections). This configuration dialog box is also available from within Internet Explorer – click **Tools > Internet Options** to open it.

Downloading Your E-mail From Multiple ISPs

It's a hard concept for many people to grasp, but you *don't* have to be connected to your ISP to collect your e-mails, although you *do* have to be connected to the internet. There's no way for your computer to know that you have e-mails waiting to be collected without being connected to the internet, but it doesn't matter which ISP you use to get online. What you will find is that, in the majority of cases, you can only *send* e-mails via the ISP you've used to connect, not via your 'home' ISP. For example, if you have a holiday home in France you can use a local ISP (find one via www.lesproviders.com, incidentally) to get online and collect your e-mails from your UK ISP. However, you'll find that you get error messages if you try to send e-mail via that UK ISP, and you'll have to change the appropriate e-mail program settings to send via the French ISP. The following is an example using UK provider FreeServe and French provider Wanadoo.

In Outlook Express click **Tools > Accounts**, choose your appropriate e-mail account by left-clicking it once, then click **Properties** and the **Servers** tab. The *only* thing you need to change is the name of the Outgoing Mail (SMTP – Simple Mail Transport Protocol) server. In Figure 10.1 you'll see the e-mail account is configured to both send and receive via FreeServe. Figure 10.2 shows how the outgoing mail (SMTP) server name has been changed to that of Wanadoo, the French ISP.

The reason you need to do this is because ISPs will usually only allow you to send e-mails via their computers if you're actually connected to them via your telephone line. If anyone could use the ISP's computers to send e-mail it would make life much easier for spammers (senders of unwanted e-mails advertising everything you never wanted, from pornography to get-rich quick schemes – see Chapter 18 for details of how to receive less if this bothers you), who could then use any ISP they wanted to send out their rubbish. Some ISPs do offer 'SMTP authentication' which allows you to send e-mail via their servers whether or not you've dialled in to them – ask yours if they offer this facility. If they do, check the 'My server requires authentication' under the **Outgoing Mail Server** section of the dialog box you see in Figures 10.1 and 10.2. You can use the same procedure when connecting via different ISPs at home. If, for some reason, you're finding it hard to get a connection via your primary ISP, connect using the second, backup account you established 'just in case'. Change the setting for the outgoing mail (SMTP) server to that of the backup ISP and you'll be able to send and receive e-mails. You do *not* have to change any other settings in your e-mail program (although in Internet Explorer you'll need to change to the new ISP dial-up connection under **Tools > Internet Options > Connections**) and you don't need to tell your e-mail recipients that they should reply to a different address. As far as they're concerned nothing has changed – they won't know that you're sending your

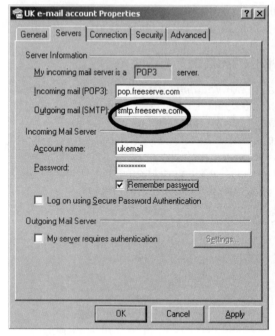

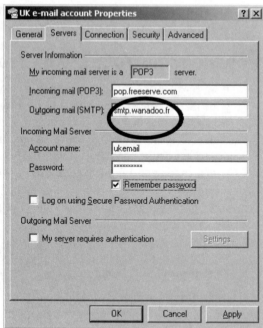

Figure 10.1 *Configuration settings in Outlook Express*

Figure 10.2 *Changing the outgoing mail setting*

e-mails via a different ISP and your e-mail address won't change. They could, if they were technically inclined, view your e-mail's 'headers' and discover the route the message took, but they'd still reply to the same address as normal.

Making The Connection

Once you've set up your internet connection and it works you'll find that there are a number of ways to start it up and do something online. Some programs you start up will connect you when you don't want to be connected; others won't connect just when you wish to go online. Unfortunately if you sometimes want programs to connect automatically and not connect at other times you're going to have to tell them to do that yourself – they're not telepathic, not yet anyway, so you need to decide how to work your connection automation.

Manual Connection

Using Internet Explorer and Outlook Express, do the following. In IE click **Tools > Internet Options > Connections**, click the name of your preferred dial-up connection (if you have more than one) and then click the 'Never dial a connection' box below it.

In OE, click **Tools > Accounts,** click to select the relevant e-mail account (if you have more than one), then click **Properties > Connection,** click to put a tick in the 'Always connect to this account using:' box and then click the drop-down arrow to the right of the box below and choose 'Local Area Network' or 'None' and **OK** your way out. Now, to make a connection you'll need to do so yourself – open **My Computer > Dial-Up Networking (Control Panel > Network and Dial-up connections** in Windows 2000, **Control Panel > Network Connections** in Windows XP) and double-click your connection to start it up. You can put a shortcut to it somewhere more convenient such as your desktop – just right-click and drag it wherever you'd like it to be, release the mouse button and then left-click **Create shortcut here** on the menu which pops up. Now you can double-click this shortcut to connect to the internet and then start the program you want to use online. You will also need to remember to manually disconnect when you've finished online. There should be a small icon which looks like two connected monitors in your System Tray, the area next to the time display. Right-click this and left-click **Disconnect** on the menu which pops up.

Automatic Connection

In Internet Explorer click **Tools > Internet Options > Connections,** click the name of your preferred dial-up connection (if you have more than one) and then click the 'Always dial my default connection' box. Now when you start a program which needs to connect to the internet your dial-up networking connection will automatically start and try to connect to your ISP. You can choose whether dial-up networking goes all the way or asks for your permission, too – right-click the icons in **Dial-Up Networking** and left-click **Properties** on the pop-up menu to see the options. You can choose the same option in Outlook Express, but this means that your internet connection will start up even if you only want to compose a new e-mail or read some old ones, which may be annoying – keep the manual option as in the previous subsection to avoid this. There are further connection options in OE you can adjust. Click **Tools > Options** and on the **General** tab you'll see a **Send/Receive Messages** section. Check the 'Send and receive messages at startup' to do just that, and the 'Check for new messages every' option followed by the number of minutes if you'd like OE to check automatically for messages. You'll also need to choose something appropriate (like your ISP) from the drop-down box below these options under 'If my computer is not connected at this time'.

Choosing A Connection Method

Your first foray online will almost certainly be by using a modem to connect to your ISP via your telephone line, and for 99 per cent of users and in 99 per cent of circumstances, this is absolutely fine. If you find yourself using your internet connection a lot, you may choose one of the various 'unlimited' connections on offer from most ISPs where you pay a fixed fee each month and can connect as much as you like, with your ISP subscription including the cost of your telephone calls. However, there may be circumstances when you find that this method of connecting, while fine for sending and receiving e-mails and surfing most web pages, just isn't fast enough for your needs. If you find yourself downloading a lot of files – music, for example – or accessing a lot of animation-, graphics- or video-heavy web pages then you might want to look at a broadband internet connection. Broadband simply means that you have more bandwidth available for your internet connection – a fatter pipe connecting your computer to your ISP. Think of it by comparing your garden hose to those used by the fire service – dial-up modems equate to garden hoses, broadband connections to fire hoses, with the amount of water coming out of each equal to the amount of data you can receive at once on your PC. Most broadband connections are of the 'always-on' type, where you have a permanent link to your ISP, and there are a number of different types:

1   ISDN. Although not strictly speaking a broadband connection, ISDN (Integrated Services Digital Network) can give you much faster and definitely more reliable connections (in terms of bandwidth) than dial-up modems. The standard ISDN subscription gives you two digital telephone lines, each of which can give you a guaranteed 64 kbits/s (kilobits per second or thousands of bits per second) connection to your ISP. Use both lines at the same time (if your ISP allows this) and you get a guaranteed 128 kbits/s connection, although you may have to pay either for two telephone calls or two ISP subscriptions, depending on the type of contract you have with your ISP.

2   xDSL, usually ADSL or SDSL, Asynchronous or Synchronous Digital Subscriber Lines. ADSL is the most popular version of this in the UK. *Asynchronous* means that the upload and download speeds are different, typically with a speed of 128 kbits/s upstream (from you to your ISP) and 512 kbits/s downstream (from your ISP to you). SDSL gives the same speed in each direction and is much rarer in the UK, mostly for internal political reasons at British Telecom. To connect a computer via ADSL, your ISP (which could be BT or any one of dozens of others reselling their packages) will provide you with either an external box or a card which slots inside your computer. This box connects via your home telephone lines to the BT exchange, but leaves your telephone line free for normal use. There is also another (extremely rare) type of DSL connection, IDSL, which is essentially an always-on ISDN connection giving a 128 kbits/s connection. In theory this has a much wider range than regular DSL services, which are usually only available within three kilometres of a suitable telephone exchange. IDSL should be available, technically, to anyone who can get an ISDN line. But then we'd all like to live in Theory, wouldn't we, since everything always works there?

3   Cable modems come from cable TV providers and use their dedicated networks of wires to connect you to the internet. Speeds and usability are comparable with ADSL systems.

4   Satellite internet connections have been around for longer than both ADSL and cable modems but aren't as popular, mostly because they're more expensive. Monthly subscription prices used typically to be three to five times the cost of an ADSL or cable modem subscription and you also need to spend something like £500 to £1,000 to buy the equipment you need to get connected. Now though, a new generation of cheaper satellite connections is becoming available, with prices closer to ADSL levels. Satellite connections may be bi-directional, where both the upstream and downstream signals between you and your ISP go via the satellite dish you need on the roof to the satellite and then back to the ground, or may use a modem or ISDN connection for the upstream connection from you to your ISP, with the return signal coming via the satellite. This means that while you may get a download speed of between 512 kbits/s and 2 megabits/s, the upload speed will be limited to that of your modem or ISDN connection.

5   Wireless Internet connections have been rare in the UK, due mostly to licensing and political factors which delayed use of the 802.11b WiFi standard for financial gain until the summer of 2002. Now you'll find places like airports, railway stations and even coffee shops offering wireless internet connections to their customers as is becoming increasingly common in the USA, although they're not cheap. You'll need an 802.11b WiFi PC card for your laptop to use such facilities.

6   If you're really hip to the beat, look into WarWalking and WarChalking (www.warchalking.org), the arts respectively of finding open wireless networks (e.g. one in an office complex accessible from the public highway outside the building) and then marking the locality suitably so that others can make use of it too.

Staying Connected

Many people find that their modem dial-up connection to the internet fails and cuts off just when they don't want it to. This can happen for a number of reasons.

1   If the connection is dropped at regular intervals, e.g. 10 minutes after you did something online, open the **Modem** section of **Control Panel (Phone and Modem Options** in Windows 2000 and XP) and check the **Properties** of your modem. Some, by default, are set to disconnect after so many minutes of inactivity. Also, some ISPs will disconnect you if your connection has apparently been idle for more than a specified period of time. If this is a problem you can set another program to check something online at a more frequent intervals – set your e-mail program to check for new e-mails every 10 minutes, for example.

2   Check that there isn't a problem with your modem. The two commonest modem problems are bad cables connecting it to your computer and telephone line, and having either the wrong drivers or drivers which aren't the latest available for it. If you suspect the cables – perhaps if they've been badly kinked or even damaged – see if you can swap them out with someone else's to isolate the problem. For

drivers, visit the modem manufacturer's website and download and install the latest available for your version of Windows.

3   Look in the support sections of your ISP's website and, if they have them, users' discussion forums or newsgroups to see if anyone else is having similar problems. Some ISPs also have 'current status' or similar web pages to notify users of any known problems.

4   Some 'call waiting' and telephone messaging services can cause your internet connection to drop. If you do have such a service which normally changes the dial tone of your line (the tone you hear when you pick up the telephone), turn it off before connecting to the internet.

5   Have your telephone line checked by your telephone service provider. Unfortunately, British Telecom's standard terms and conditions only require that they offer 'voice quality' lines – which work at 9,600 bps (bits per second). Compare this to the potential 56,000 bps V90 modems can work at (although 45–50,000 bps is normally the highest achievable). They may be able to boost the 'gain' of your line but, in some circumstances, two or more lines could be sharing the same physical bit of wire between you and the local exchange or junction box and you may be stuck with a slow connection. Upgrading to an ISDN line may be the only alternative in this case.

6   You can check the speed of your internet connection on various websites: bandwidthplace.com/speedtest and webservices.cnet.com/bandwidth are two such sites.

7   Note, when you connect to the internet your connection dialog box may say that you've connected at 115,200 bps yet your modem only works at a maximum 56,000 bps. This isn't an error and you aren't getting something for nothing: the 115,200 bps figure refers to the speed at which your modem and computer are talking to each other, not the speed at which your modem is talking to your ISP.

8   Remember that the speed with which you connect to and download from websites around the internet will vary enormously. It's not just your connection to your ISP that limits the speed – if many other people are trying to connect to the same website at the same time they all have to share that server's own bandwidth so individual connection speeds may be low, and it won't make any difference what speed modem or ADSL connection you have. General traffic conditions on the internet itself can also have an effect. For example, early evening in the UK coincides with peak afternoon activity on the East Coast of the USA and lunchtime on the West Coast together with early morning traffic in the Far East. With everyone in the UK trying to log on at the same time to check their e-mails after arriving home from work, things can slow down considerably. Normally traffic on the internet is at its lightest early in the morning UK time, around 5-7 a.m., so get up early if you have some large files to download.

9 If your file downloads are constantly being interrupted for unavoidable reasons there are programs which will allow you to resume a download at the point where it was cut off, so if you'd downloaded 6 MB of a 7 MB piece of software you don't need to start all over again. CuteFTP from Globalscape, www.cuteftp.com, and GetRight, www.getright.com, both do this.

10 If it seems to take a long time to connect to your ISP (20–30 seconds is about normal) via a modem, open **Dial-up Networking** in **My Computer**, right-click your connection icon and left-click **Properties** (in Windows 2000 and XP open **Control Panel > Network and Dial-up Connections** or just **Network Connections**). Look on the **Server Types** tab (**Networking** in Windows 2000 and XP) and check that only TCP/IP and nothing else is checked, especially not 'Log on to network' in Windows 95, 98 and Me. You can leave 'Enable software compression' checked.

Disconnecting

If you're paying by the minute for your internet connection the last thing you want to happen is for your line to remain connected when you think it's been hung up. When you close the program(s) which prompted your internet connection (if it's set to start automatically; see above) it should automatically close the connection, or offer to close it if that's the option you've chosen. You can double-check by looking in the System Tray (next to the time display, which is usually in the bottom-right corner of your screen) where, when you're online, you should see a small icon of two linked computers. Right-click this and left-click **Disconnect** to close your internet connection. And if you have an external modem (which I'd highly recommend you do) you can turn it off to make triple sure you've disconnected from the internet and aren't running up your telephone bill.

Connectivity Problems

Sometimes you may think you've made a successful connection to the internet but nothing seems to happen when you try to collect your e-mails or visit a website. There are several things you can check to see whose fault all this is.

1 First, double-check to see that you are connected to your ISP – look in the System Tray for the two connected computers icon and double-click it to open and show your current status.

2 Next, double-check the settings in both **Dial-Up Networking** and in your e-mail program to make sure they're as they're supposed to be.

143

3 If you're definitely connected, open your web browser and try connecting to your ISP's home page. If this doesn't work, there may be a problem with their computer system.

4 If you can connect to your ISP's website, try connecting to others, both in the UK and abroad. Sometimes you may find that, for example, connections to the USA are slow or unavailable but European websites open without any problems. This can be caused by problems with computers in the USA – for example, heavy traffic to one site or group of sites may slow connections to many others which are apparently unrelated as they all share connections.

5 You can check where the problem may lie by running a 'ping' or 'traceroute'. Ping is named after the SONAR system used to find submarines – your computer sends out a small amount of information to a distant machine and waits for it to bounce back, confirming that the second machine is working and connected to the internet. Traceroute does the same thing, but reports back on each computer it passes through on the way to its destination. When you connect to a website on the internet, your connection can pass through many other computers on the way – dozens, sometimes. The connection is 'routed' through each computer on its way, each computer deciding which is the best way to send on the connection to the ultimate destination. To run ping, open a command prompt window (**Start > Programs > Accessories** in Windows 2000 and XP, **Start > Programs > MS-DOS Prompt** in Windows 95, 98 and Me) and type, **ping www.microsoft.com** and hit **Enter**. You should see something similar to Figure 10.3. To run traceroute, open a command prompt window and type **tracert www.microsoft.com** and hit **Enter** (you can replace www.microsoft.com with any website address, domain name or even a numerical IP address if you wish).

Figure 10.3 shows a traceroute failing to reach its destination, timing out after step 13. The details may look complicated, but all that's happening on each line in turn is that your computer is connecting to the next computer in the chain on the way towards www.microsoft.com and sending back details of how long it takes to get to that computer. So, on line 13, it takes 2282, 437 and 1422 milliseconds to reach the computer called pos7-0.mprl1.seal.us.mfnx.net. Sometimes computers have more sensible and obvious names, but the essential thing to take from this is that your attempt to connect to www.microsoft.com is leaving your computer and getting out past your ISP and onto the internet where something else is causing the problem – so, you know that you don't need to do anything apart from wait until whatever is causing the problem is fixed. Ping, as in Figure 10.4, is a 'quick' version of this – it shows that there's a problem of some kind between your computer and www.microsoft.com; traceroute can tell you more about where that problem lies.

```
Command Prompt                                                    _ □ ×

C:\>tracert www.microsoft.com

Tracing route to www.microsoft.akadns.net [207.46.230.219]
over a maximum of 30 hops:

   1     *          *          *       Request timed out.
   2     *          *          *       Request timed out.
   3     *       2484 ms    2641 ms    access12-loh-P3-0.router.aol.com [195.93.52.49]

   4    485 ms    234 ms     234 ms    pop5-loh-P2-0.atdn.net [66.185.146.89]
   5    250 ms    234 ms     219 ms    bb1-loh-P0-3.atdn.net [66.185.146.81]
   6    281 ms    265 ms     250 ms    pop2-loh-P0-0.atdn.net [66.185.136.242]
   7    234 ms    235 ms     234 ms    pos7-0.er1a.lhr4.uk.mfnx.net [213.161.69.153]
   8   1250 ms   1453 ms    1438 ms    so-3-3-0.cr2.lhr4.uk.mfnx.net [208.184.231.129]

   9     *          *          *       Request timed out.
  10   2484 ms    360 ms     297 ms    so-7-0-0.cr2.lga1.us.mfnx.net [64.125.31.182]
  11    297 ms    328 ms     297 ms    so-1-0-0.cr1.lga1.us.mfnx.net [208.185.0.233]
  12    375 ms   1672 ms     391 ms    so-5-1-0.cr2.sea1.us.mfnx.net [216.200.127.66]
  13   2282 ms    437 ms    1422 ms    pos7-0.mpr1.sea1.us.mfnx.net [208.185.175.181]
  14     *          *          *       Request timed out.
  15     *          *          *       Request timed out.
  16     *          *          *       Request timed out.
  17     *          *          *       Request timed out.
  18     *          *          *       Request timed out.
  19     *          *          *       Request timed out.
  20     *          *          *       Request timed out.
  21     *          *          *       Request timed out.
  22     *          *          *       Request timed out.
  23     *          *          *       Request timed out.
  24     *          *          *       Request timed out.
  25     *          *          *       Request timed out.
  26     *          *          *       Request timed out.
  27     *          *          *       Request timed out.
  28     *          *          *       Request timed out.
  29     *          *          *       Request timed out.
  30     *          *          *       Request timed out.

Trace complete.

C:\>
```

Figure 10.3 Running traceroute

```
Command Prompt                                                    _ □ ×

C:\>ping www.microsoft.com

Pinging www.microsoft.akadns.net [207.46.230.219] with 32 bytes of data:

Request timed out.
Request timed out.
Request timed out.
Request timed out.

Ping statistics for 207.46.230.219:
    Packets: Sent = 4, Received = 0, Lost = 4 (100% loss),
Approximate round trip times in milli-seconds:
    Minimum = 0ms, Maximum = 0ms, Average = 0ms

C:\>_
```

Figure 10.4 Pinging Microsoft

Choosing Software For The Internet

Most of the software mentioned in this chapter comes from Microsoft, since it's included with the Windows operating system. But there are alternatives to all of their programs. These are some of the most popular ones:

1   Netscape (previously Netscape Navigator). This was the first widely used web browser, but now it's been eclipsed in popularity and, in my opinion, usability by Microsoft's Internet Explorer. You'll find it at browsers.netscape.com/browsers/main.tmpl. Netscape also includes an e-mail program plus Netscape composer, a web page creation program.

2   Opera, another web browser, available from www.opera.com. Also includes an e-mail program.

Questions And Answers

Easy Questions And Answers

 My old Apple PowerBook 1400CS laptop computer had a Village Modem PC card whose instruction leaflet warned against using it on a digital switchboard (meaning a switchboard within a building, not a digital telephone company exchange). The warning was that the card could be destroyed and the computer with it. I thought this was quirky, but I have now bought a new iBook laptop with a built-in modem. When I phoned up the Apple helpline to check, they said this modem too should not be used via a digital switchboard because it might, in effect, 'blow up'! Can this be true? It seems odd in a world where hotel and office switchboards are increasingly likely to be digital that laptop computers' modems are not compatible.

 It is indeed true that regular modems won't work on digital telephone lines such as those used by hotels. They carry a higher current which can damage your modem's circuitry. However, there are a couple of solutions. First, check with your hotel that they don't offer analogue telephone lines which your modem can use – many offer two lines in rooms, one for the voice line and the second for your computer modem. Second, you can buy an adapter which will convert your analogue modem to work with the digital line. TeleAdapt sells such a device; its website is at www.teleadapt.com. It also has details of the IBM digital line tester – it'll check if you're not sure whether or not the line in your room is digital.

 I can't read the text on some web pages as it's too small – can I do anything?

If you're using Internet Explorer click **View** > **Text Size** and choose a larger size. Note, this doesn't work on all web pages – some page designers think they know better than you what size text you should be looking at. If this is important to you, click **Tools** > **Internet Options** > **General** > **Accessibility** and check the 'Ignore font styles specified on Web pages' and 'Ignore font sizes specified on Web pages' options. You can also choose to ignore specified colours, too. Click **OK** then click the **Fonts** button and choose fonts which suit you, then click **OK** twice.

ADSL sounds just what we need. But does it work with a standard modem? I'm thinking of a new machine – iMac or PC. Will the modems incorporated in these machines work with ADSL? Or do you need some other gadget?

You'll need a new widget (slightly different to a gadget – gadgets can be useless, widgets are always useful). The good news is that BT or whoever you sign up with will provide it.

After some ill-advised tinkering I now get a small window headed 'Pre-Dial Terminal' whenever my dial-up window appears – how do I get rid of it?

Open **Dial-up Networking**, right-click your connection, and left-click **Properties** > **Configure** > **Options**.

Harder Questions And Answers

I wanted to start afresh and so converted to FAT32 and formatted my C: drive. After reloading all my software and reconnecting to the internet I found that whenever I want to reconnect to the web I can only go through the dial-up networking facility – if I try and use IE6 all I get is an error page. How can I get back the connect box when I click IE or a favourite?

In IE click **Tools** > **Internet Options** > **Connections** and check that it's set to dial your ISP of choice on demand. Now when you try to open a web page it should connect as you wish.

I am using my internet connection through dial-up. My problem is that whenever the power goes off it disconnects automatically and does not connect until the power comes back on. My UPS is working properly. Is there a problem in the UPS or the telephone line or the dial-up settings? I use Windows Me.

At a guess I'd say you're using an external modem which, when the power goes off, stops working and hence the line is dropped. Try plugging the modem into your UPS (Uninterruptible Power Supply) and it should keep the

147

connection going. If that's not the problem it could be the telephone system which is also losing power, although usually it's kept going by backup generators – and, in any case, may not be suffering from the same power cut as you if it's not in the same area. If you already have UPS its battery may be wearing out or failing, and in any case if you have the same sort of rat's nest of wires that I do in my office there could be interference between them.

Chapter 11

E-mail

In This Chapter

➤ Sending and receiving e-mail

➤ Choosing an e-mail address

➤ Opening attachments

➤ Address books

➤ E-mail software

Sending And Receiving E-mail

Most e-mail problems are due either to problems with connectivity, as described in Chapter 10, or incorrect addressing. The computers which send e-mail around the internet are not very clever: they take everything you say quite literally. If you were trying to send me an e-mail to help@drkeyboard.net, it wouldn't get to me if you got any of this address wrong. You can't type help@drkeyboard, for example – unlike human postmen and women, e-mail computers won't look at that and think, 'Oh, they mean help@drkeyboard.net – I'll send it there'. Instead, something with a name like MAILER-DAEMON will send you a stern reply saying that your attempt to send the e-mail has failed. So check and recheck the e-mail addresses you type. Sometimes people even mistype their own e-mail addresses so that even though you've clicked **Reply** in your e-mail program, the mail bounces back. If this happens to you, examine very carefully the address to which you've sent the e-mail. Double-click on the message to open it and right-click the name/address and left-click **Properties** (in Microsoft Outlook and Outlook Express) to see its details. Common mistakes include putting a space somewhere in the address (e-mail addresses won't work with a space in them), mis-spellings of names or domains (e.g. typing **btInternet** instead of **btInternet.co.uk**) or not typing the full address (e.g. completely missing out **btInternet.com** and typing just the first portion of the address, the user's name) or missing out the @ symbol.

Choosing An E-Mail Address

When you sign up with an ISP, the end of your address will probably be settled by them – @freeserve.net, @virgin.net and so on – you get to choose the part before that. However, if you have a common name you may find that bill@ and mary@ are already taken on most ISPs, and you'll be offered something like bill65@ or mary432@ instead. Think carefully about what you choose since you could be stuck with that address for a while – the problem with an e-mail address is that, once you start publicising it, people will use it and eventually it will prove almost impossible to change it or give it up. Some ISPs offer a forwarding service whereby they'll forward your e-mail to another address if you change to a different company, but most don't. You could also opt for a permanent 'free' address from, for example, Hotmail (www.hotmail.com) or Yahoo! (www.yahoo.co.uk or www.yahoo.com) but many such services are now either starting to charge or getting out of the business altogether. You could also buy your own domain name (e.g. **yourfamilyname.com**) and use a forwarding service from the company selling the name to forward e-mails to your current ISP.

Opening Attachments

First, *never* open any e-mail attachments that you're not expecting to receive and which aren't specifically mentioned and/or described in the e-mail – even if they're from your best friend, a member of your family or anyone else you would normally trust. Virus writers now are getting very clever at sending out messages (or, worse, getting 'infected' computers to send messages) which look very innocent and as if they're from someone you know and trust. See Chapter 18 for more details on this.

Once you're absolutely, definitely positive that the attachment is safe, in Outlook and Outlook Express you'll see either a paperclip symbol at the top of the message preview pane (the area bottom-right of the program where you read the message) or an icon at the bottom of the preview pane representing the attachment. If you see a paperclip, left-click it and then click **Save Attachments**. Click the **Browse** button and put the attachment somewhere you can find it again. If you see the icon at the bottom of the preview pane, right-click it and left-click **Save As**, again putting it somewhere you can find it again. Now go to the folder where you've saved the attachment (I have one on my Desktop called **Suspect**) and scan it with your anti-virus software, just to be extra-sure. Norton Anti-Virus and AVG from Grisoft (detailed in Chapter 18) add the option to scan for viruses to the right-click menu, i.e. you right-click the saved attachment and left-click **Scan** from the pop-up menu.

Now you know the file is safe, you can open it. If it's a file type for a program you already have installed on your computer, double-clicking it will open it in the appropriate program. So, Word documents will open in Microsoft Word and Excel spreadsheets in Microsoft Excel. Images will open in whatever image editor you have installed – I use and recommend Paint Shop Pro from JASC, www.jasc.com. There's also a very good freeware image editor called IrfanView, www.irfanview.com. And Microsoft provides free viewers for most of its Office suite of programs; download them from the Office Update website at www.microsoft.com/office/downloads/default.asp. If you're sent an attachment for a more specialised program, you'll either need to get hold of a copy of it yourself or ask if it can be sent in a more common format accessible by other programs. For example, word processors can save their files in plain text or Rich Text Format (RTF) and, of course, if you're just sending text then do so in a regular, plain-text e-mail instead of clogging up the internet with gigantic files (see 'Netiquette', Chapter 12, page 166). Also, some versions of Windows are shipped with a program called Quick View which allows you to 'look inside' some files to give you an idea of their content. Right-click the file name and, if it's installed, you'll see a Quick View item on the menu which pops up. It's now available as a standalone program from JASC as Quick View Plus, www.jasc.com.

The other essential you'll need for many file attachments is an unzipping program. Any file – a program, a document, a picture, anything – can be 'zipped up' to compress it and make it smaller, thus making it quicker to send and receive across the internet. Windows XP now has built-in handling for zipped files (which usually end with **.zip**) but you'll find that WinZip, www.winzip.com and PKZip, www.pkzip.com are more versatile and useful.

Address Books

Having been a journalist for more than two decades I've become very used to always keeping names, addresses, telephone numbers and, now, e-mail addresses. All decent e-mail software has a built-in address book where you can store the addresses of those whom you e-mail regularly, and you should get used to using it. The address books in both Outlook and Outlook Express can be accessed by clicking the open book symbol on their toolbars (see Figure 11.1) and you add someone's details by either clicking the **New Entry** button or clicking **File > New Entry** (in Outlook Express you click **File > New Contact**).

Figure 11.1 The Address Book icon in Outlook

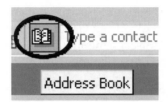

The easiest way to add the e-mail address of someone who's sent you an e-mail is to double-click the message to open it and then right-click their name. Now left-click **Add to Contacts** and it will be added to your address book, with a **New contact** form opening to allow you to confirm the details you've added and insert more information such as street address and telephone numbers.

To insert an address into a new e-mail, click the **To** button (see Figures 11.2 and 11.3) and the address book will open.

Figure 11.2 Inserting an address into a new e-mail (Outlook)

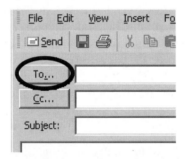

Figure 11.3 Inserting an address into a new e-mail (Outlook Express)

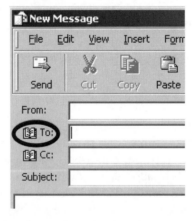

Select the name of the person you wish to send the message to from the list on the left by clicking it with your left mouse button, and then click the **To** button in the centre column. You can choose to send a copy to someone else by clicking the **Cc** (carbon copy) button, or send a 'blind copy' by clicking the **Bcc** button. Blind copies are sent without the main recipient (people in the **To** box) knowing you've sent a copy to anyone – they will be able to see anyone you've **cc**-ed the message to.

152

E-mail Software

Apart from Outlook Express (included with Internet Explorer) and the e-mail programs with the Netscape and Opera web browsers (see Chapter 10), other e-mail programs include:

1   Eudora, www.eudora.com. This is a very versatile and useful program, probably more versatile than Outlook Express. It comes in three different versions: sponsored, in which you get full functionality in return for being presented with adverts; paid, in which you get the full program after paying for it; and light mode which is free of ads and free to you but has fewer features.

2   Pegasus Mail, www.pmail.com. Pegasus is probably the oldest e-mail program around but it's still going strong and being updated regularly. It's also completely free.

3   Popcorn, available from www.ultrafunk.com. Ultrafunk has stopped developing Popcorn now, but the final version – 1.20 – is extremely useful and works in all versions of Windows. It's a tiny program – around 100 KB (that's kilobytes, not megabytes), small enough to be carried around on a floppy disk. Its most outstanding feature is the ability to examine just the 'headers' of e-mails as they sit on your e-mail server at your ISP. This means that if your e-mail is taking a long time to download, you can use Popcorn to examine the messages waiting for you, and see if one of them is particularly large or has a large attachment. You can delete such messages from within Popcorn, freeing up your e-mail inbox. And as it will fit on a floppy disk, you can take it with you and run it on other computers to collect your e-mails while you're away from home.

Questions And Answers

Easy Questions And Answers

When I e-mail some people and they're not in I get an 'Out of office' reply. How can I set one up for myself from home?

If you have a permanent internet connection you could do this with most e-mail programs – use the 'Rules' facility to automatically reply to all messages in the way you want after setting it to check for new mails at regular intervals. However, this relies on you leaving your computer on all the time *and* it not falling over while you're away, which may be problematical with Windows 9x or Me. You'll have better luck with this using Windows 2000 or XP. If you're on a dial-up connection you'll find it's probably impractical, especially if you don't have an unlimited-type connection and you have to pay by the minute.

If this is the case (and you might prefer it anyway) check with your ISP to see if they offer such a service.

I am unable to receive e-mails – the connection window shows 'Receiving 1 of 3 messages' but nothing happens.

You don't say what e-mail program you're using but I note that you're actually using Windows 98 with Microsoft Internet Explorer 5.5, so I'll hazard a guess that you're using Outlook Express. Whatever, I'd guess that you're trying to download one very large e-mail message (probably an attachment of some kind) and, although it appears that nothing is happening it's just taking a long time to arrive. In the area of your Taskbar next to the time display you'll see an icon of two small computers connected to each other. Double-click this to open it and you'll see if you're actually receiving data. You can use a small e-mail program called Popcorn to look just at the 'headers' of your e-mail – who sent it, when, and the subject line – and to see if there are any attachments and what size they are, and delete the entire message without downloading it. You'll find it at www.ultrafunk.com.

I have been receiving e-mail intended for someone who isn't me at a domain name I own – in the format joebloggs@domain.com (where Joe Bloggs is not the real name nor mine). How is it technically possible for this to happen? Is there a connection between e-mail addresses and websites?

You're a little confused about what exactly a **Domain Name** is. It is the **domain.com** portion of the address above and can relate to e-mail addresses, web sites and more. E-mail addresses will take the form **name@domain.com**, websites **http://www.domain.com** and so on. In other words, you own anything to do with that name – hence the description 'domain' name: you own the entire domain. And because you own the name the company hosting it for you have presumably set things up so that any e-mails sent to anyone at that domain name are actually forwarded to you. So you'll get johndoe@domain.com, joebloggs@domain.com, anyoneatall@domain.com ... you get the idea. You may wish to reply to whoever's sending you these e-mails to explain that no one of that name is known to you, but you should also be aware that this may be a trick by a spammer (sender of unsolicited commercial e-mails). In this case, replying may just confirm that they have a live human at the end of the e-mail address and you'll get even more unwanted e-mails.

How can I look up someone's e-mail address?

Unfortunately there's no central location like the white or yellow pages which lists everyone's e-mail addresses. You can try sites like www.411.com and www.emailaddresses.com/email_lookup_large.htm which may help, but the most reliable way to find someone's e-mail address is still to ask them.

Is it possible to back up my Outlook Express e-mails?

Yes. In fact you should adopt a decent strategy for keeping copies of all your e-mail messages. See Chapter 17.

I have recently upgraded to Outlook Express version 5 from a previous version. When opening Outlook Express the dial-up connection box comes up OK and I am able to get online. However, it does not disconnect after sending and receiving. I have to disconnect. Under **Tools > Options > Connections** *the box for hang-up after sending and receiving is ticked. When clicking on send and receive again, if offline, an error message comes up saying that an error occurred while establishing the dial-up network connection. It does not present the dial-up connection box. I am not able to make a connection through Outlook Express and have to get online through Internet Explorer. Once online I am then able to send and receive. I would like the connection to hang up after sending and receiving and to be able to get the dial-up connection box when clicking on send and receive when offline.*

Check that the preferred internet connection is the same in **Tools > Options > Connections** in Outlook Express and under **Tools > Internet Options > Connections** in Internet Explorer. If they're different you can experience the symptoms you describe.

Harder Questions And Answers

I am able to receive e-mails but can only send them through a website. Every time I try to send a message through Outlook I receive the following message: 'The connection to the server has failed. Account 'pop.{ispname}.net', server 'smtp.{ispname}.net', Protocol SMTP, Port 25, secure (SSL). No, socket error 10060 Error number 0X800CCC0E.' and the recipient does not get the e-mail. I do not understand a lot of the technical terms and cannot find the answer in the manuals.

Error 10060 is actually a timeout error. Look in **Tools > Accounts > Properties > Advanced** and move the **Server Timeouts** slider over to the right as far as possible. However, what I suspect is actually happening is that you're trying to send your e-mails via an ISP (Internet Service Provider) other than the one you're using to connect to the internet. Almost all ISPs will only allow you to send e-mail via them if you've actually dialled into their system, as a security measure to stop the sending of spam (unwanted commercial e-mails). Check with whoever you use to connect to the internet what the correct settings are for their SMTP/e-mail sending computer and then enter the details in **Tools > Accounts > Properties > Servers**.

I keep getting the error message 'The instruction @ '0x77f536f7' referenced memory @ 0x007f4d18'. The memory could not be "written". Click **OK** *to terminate the program' headed 'MSIMN Application error' after shutting down Outlook Express. When I joined my new ISP it installed another Outlook Express 6 on my computer. Could this have anything to do with it?*

Outlook Express suffers from any number of such problems, with many different causes. For example, if you have McAfee Personal Firewall installed, Microsoft KnowledgeBase article Q297225 applies. You can read it at support.microsoft.com. The list goes on – and goes on so far that Microsoft has now set up a dedicated Outlook Express support centre at support.microsoft.com/default.aspx?scid=fh;en-us;oex. I also recommend Tom C. Koch's very good page dedicated to Outlook Express at www.tomsterdam.com.

Now You're Online

Optimising Your Internet Connection

There are a few things you can do to speed up your life online. In particular, some of the default settings in Internet Explorer are less than optimal.

1   Change the size and location of your temporary internet files. Internet Explorer keeps a copy of recently visited web pages on your local hard disk. When you visit any website, IE first looks in this 'cache' of files to see if you've visited it before. If you have, it compares the version stored locally with the online version. If nothing has changed, it loads the copy from your local hard disk. If there are changes it downloads the online version of the page. By default, this cache is set to a huge size, a percentage of the total size of your hard disk and, while it may

initially sound attractive to have a large cache – local versions of pages load much, much more quickly than those which have to be downloaded over the internet – having too large a cache can actually slow your Internet Explorer to a crawl, or even make it fall over completely. Unless you have lots of pages set to be available offline, the optimum size for IE's cache seems to be around 50 MB. You adjust it by clicking **Tools > Internet Options** and, on the **General** tab of IE, you'll see a **Temporary Internet files** section. Click the **Settings** button and change the size to 50 MB.

2   On the dialog box to change the size of your IE cache you'll also see a button marked **Move Folder**. This allows you to put the temporary internet files cache elsewhere on your computer, and if you have more than one hard disk you can speed things up a little by moving them to a different disk to the one on which IE is installed. NB: if you have one physical hard disk split up into two or more 'logical' partitions, moving the cache to a different partition won't speed things up and may even slow things down a little.

Downloading, Saving And Installing Programs From The Internet

This can cause enormous problems for some people, particularly grasping the concept of 'downloading'. All it means is that you're copying a file from somewhere out on the internet to your local computer. And the larger the file you're copying, the longer it will take to copy. The most popular way to transfer files used to be by FTP, File Transfer Protocol, and this is still used a lot. If you find you're using this a lot you should invest in a specialist FTP program – CuteFTP from Globalscape, www.cuteftp.com, is what I use and recommend. But generally most people will be happy using their web browser to download files. This section tells you how to do it.

First, find something to download. This might be a piece of software you want to try out before you buy it – shareware – or an update to something you already have installed on your computer. The principles are the same, and I'll use the example here of updating drivers for a SoundBlaster sound card from Creative. The card is made by Creative, the documentation which came with the card tells me, and Creative's website is at www.creative.com so I open that site in my browser. There I see a link to 'Support', which sounds likely (Figure 12.1) and hovering the mouse pointer over it drops down a menu to select the region I'm in.

The next page has a link to 'Download Drivers' (Figure 12.2) – this is what I'm looking for. Clicking on that link takes me to a page where I tell Creative what card I have, which operating system I use and what language I speak. It's important to get all these things correct – in particular, the model of card and version of Windows are very important. Trying to install drivers for a different version of Windows will almost certainly fail. You can see in Figure 12.3 that I've chosen my card – the Sound Blaster

158

Figure 12.1 Support drop-down menu

Figure 12.2 Download Drivers link

Live! Platinum 5.1 – Windows 2000 and English. There are also options on this page, if you're not sure what model you have, to type in your card's model number if you know it.

To the right of these boxes is a **Search** button – clicking that brings me to the final page where I can download the file. You'll see in Figure 12.4 details confirming the card model, the operating system, the language and its size. This 8.85 MB file will, it is estimated, take about 31 minutes to download using a standard 56k modem.

Clicking **Download** (bottom-right, Figure 12.4) takes me first to a page to read and agree with the 'EULA', the end-user license agreement, and then pops up a dialog box asking whether I want to open the file from its current location or save it. Choose the 'save' option and you'll see a dialog box like the one in Figure 12.5.

Don't accept the default location to save the file: put it somewhere you can find it again and in a folder with a sensible name. I keep a folder on a separate hard disk called **Downloads** with a folder under that called **Creative** and one more below that called **Live 51** (Figure 12.6).

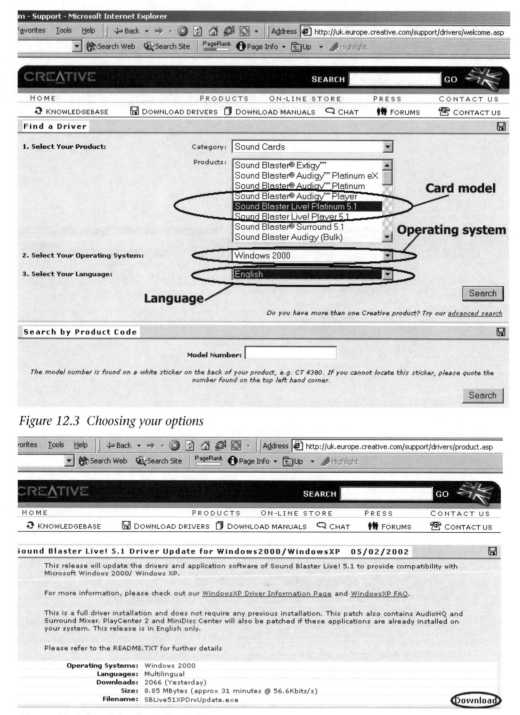

Figure 12.3 Choosing your options

Figure 12.4 Download confirmation screen

Figure 12.5 Save As dialog

Figure 12.6 Choose a sensible location for your file

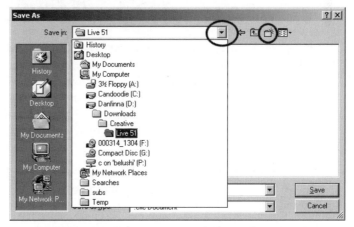

You navigate to new locations in this dialog box by clicking the downwards-pointing arrow to the right of the **Save in**: box and make new sub-folders inside the one where you currently find yourself by clicking the **Create new folder** icon to the right of this (both circled in Figure 12.6). The left-pointing and upwards-pointing arrows between them take you, respectively, back to the previous folder you were viewing and one folder 'up' in the nested hierarchy. When you're satisfied with the location for saving the downloaded file, click the **Save** button bottom-right and wait for the download to finish. When it does, you'll see a dialog box like Figure 12.7.

If you plan to work with the file or program later, click **Close**. To install the new driver now, click **Open** and follow the instructions on your screen to install the software. This procedure varies from manufacturer to manufacturer, but whichever system is used the important thing is to *always read everything on the screen*. Many, many mistakes are made by people who assume they just need to click **OK** to each screen that pops up – but this can lead to you deleting files you'd rather have kept, or worse. In particular, heed recommendations to close running programs, especially anti-virus software.

Figure 12.7 Download dialog

In this case, the driver is an executable file – it ends with **.exe** – and is what's called a 'self-extracting archive'. This means that, once it's started to run, it knows itself what it wants to do. Sometimes, though, you'll download files which end with **.zip**. To work with these you first need to download or install a program like WinZip or PKZip (see earlier in this chapter). With one of these installed, when you click **Open** it will take over decompressing the file. If you have WinZip installed you'll see a dialog box like Figure 12.8.

With later versions of WinZip (this image is from version 8.1) you can double left-click on the **Setup.exe** file and the installation program will run from inside WinZip. You should also look for any instructions inside the zipped file – here there's a file called

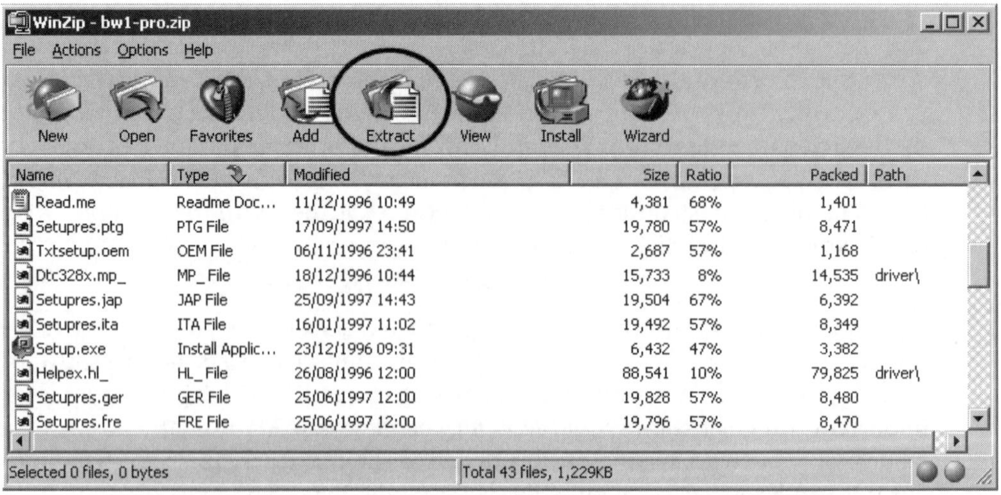

Figure 12.8 Decompressing with WinZip

Read.me. Double left-click it to see what instructions it may contain.

You can also click the **Extract** button (circled), which will, as its name implies, extract all the individual files from inside the zipped archive. As before, unzip these files to a location you can find again. Then you can run the installation program by double-clicking the appropriate file – check the Read.me file for details of which one it is: it's usually called something obvious like **install.exe** or **setup.exe**. Occasionally, you may find that your download consists of a single file ending with the extension **.inf**. These are 'information' files which contain a driver file for a piece of hardware. You install them by right clicking then left-clicking **Install** on the menu which pops up.

Netiquette

As more and more of us crowd on to the internet – thousands a day – the levels of politeness online seem to be declining, so here are a few pointers.

1   First, you need to realise that no one is in absolute charge of what goes on on the internet – it's self-regulating and there's no one body to complain to when you're upset about something.

2   When you're sending an e-mail it's easy to sound off and click **Send** without reviewing what you've said. Would you say it in person? Would you even say it in a printed letter? Review what you've written before firing it off, or you may end up coming across as outstandingly rude. If you really can't help yourself, look at Eudora, www.eudora.com, which includes a 'language minder' to warn if you're going over the top. If you do feel angry at something you've received, hang on to your reply for a few hours or overnight and then read it again before sending it.

3   Don't write anything – in e-mails, in chat rooms, in newsgroups or on message boards – ALL IN CAPS. It looks like you're SHOUTING.

4   If you're intending to post to a newsgroup or message board, 'lurk' for a while and read what's been said before you ask your question. The odds are it's a FAQ, a Frequently Asked Question, a list of which will either be posted regularly or be available somewhere on a website. On message boards, look to see if there's a forum or set of guidelines on how to use the place. If it has one, use the search engine to see if your question has already been answered.

5   If you must have a .sig file, a signature which is automatically appended to your e-mails and newsgroup postings, try to keep it to a minimum – four lines is about right. If you have a huge disclaimer at the end of your e-mails which you don't put on printed letters, you'll instantly be marked as pretty sad and, personally, I really doubt their legal effectiveness since I'm not sure you can impose contractual conditions on someone without their consent.

6   No one is in overall control of the internet and, while there may be consumer or

other organisations you can complain to in some countries, in general you need to be on your guard about who you do business with.

7 Don't even think of sending spam – unwanted and unsolicited commercial e-mails advertising your product or ideas. You'll just get all your internet accounts cancelled and make yourself a lot of enemies.

8 If someone asks you to remove them from your 'Everyone I know' list, your 'jokes' list or anything else, do it straight away.

9 Don't forward warnings about viruses without checking their veracity first – look at the 'Virus and Security Warnings' forum at www.drkeyboard.net for a guide on how to check whether something's a hoax.

10 Don't forward chain letters, even if they appear to be in a good cause. They're often hoaxes and a good source of e-mail addresses for spammers.

11 Use plain text format as your standard e-mail format; many people either can't or won't read or open HTML-format mails because of the security risk they pose. They also waste bandwidth (the carrying capacity for information) on the internet in general and take longer to send and receive.

Chatting

Chatting is sometimes called Instant Messaging, although the two are not strictly the same thing. You can often do both with the same program and switch back and forth between the two. Chat/IM programs include AOL Instant Messenger (www.aol.co.uk/aim), Microsoft MSN Messenger (which comes preinstalled in Windows XP, or you can download it from messenger.microsoft.com) and ICQ (www.icq.com). Yahoo! (www.yahoo.com), Excite (www.excite.com) and others also offer chat and/or instant messenger facilities. However, at the time of writing (late Spring 2002) most of these different applications won't inter-operate, i.e. you can't send a message from AIM to someone using MSN Messenger or vice versa. There are some IM programs like Jabber, www.jabber.com, that do work – or try to work – across the different systems but, for whatever reason, these efforts are often blocked by the administrators of those other systems.

Whichever system you end up using, the principle is the same; you can type messages back and forth with friends in 'real time', i.e. you can read their messages as they type and they can read yours. Some systems allow you to speak using a microphone and speakers attached to your computer; others allow the use of webcams to give videoconferencing.

Chat rooms work on the same principle but they allow many people to chat together at once. Some IM software, like AIM, allows you to switch between instant messages between two people and chatting in a group.

IM and chat software can be problematical to set up, particularly if you're in an office behind a firewall. Many IM programs know about firewalls and the help files will give you details on how to adjust your firewall, e.g. ZoneAlarm (see Chapter 18 for details) to allow you to use them.

Message Boards

Also called bulletin boards (even though, strictly speaking, the two are different), these allow users to post a message for others to read and reply to. You'll see an example of one I run at www.drkeyboard.net.

Newsgroups

The newsgroups on Usenet are one of the oldest parts of the internet, dating back to well before the world wide web was invented. You need software called a newsreader to access them, and most ISPs run a news server which gives access to the groups from all over the world. There are now something over 30,000 different groups covering every topic imaginable.

A newsgroup is a worldwide version of the bulletin board at work or outside your local post office, but with one very important exception: you can reply to any message which anyone 'posts' in a newsgroup, and anyone who wants to can then reply to your reply. This process makes up what's called a 'threaded discussion' – the messages are presented to you in the order in which they were posted so you can follow a topic as it progresses from the original question through, possibly, many dozens of levels.

You'll find that Outlook Express includes a newsreader program – click **Tools > Accounts > Add > News** and follow the wizard through. Personally I use Agent from Forte, the paid-for version of the excellent Free Agent program – you can download it from www.forteinc.com. Once you've installed it, Free Agent will ask you for a few details like your e-mail address and the address of your news server. This is a computer usually run by your ISP which keeps an up-to-date copy of all the messages posted to all the newsgroups in which its subscribers are interested. The news server's address should be in the documentation provided by your ISP – it will be something like news.yourisp.co.uk.

You may sometimes find that you've subscribed to a newsgroup which appears to be empty but which fills up with messages a day or so later. This is because, with so many tens of thousands of groups available, your ISP won't automatically download all of them all of the time. Usually, however, its news server will be set to start this process once a subscriber asks for it, and from then on you'll get all the new messages. However, be aware that because the Usenet system works on a series of many thousands of servers all over the world it can take a little while – usually less than a few hours but sometimes a day or so – for your question to percolate all the way around the world and for all those who subscribe to the newsgroup to see it.

When you've connected to the internet your newsreader program will download a list of all the newsgroups, and then you can 'subscribe' to those in which you're interested. Be warned – it can be tempting to subscribe to dozens of these at first but you'll soon find it difficult to keep up if more than a few are very active – some newsgroups can attract hundreds, even thousands, of new messages a day. Start off with a few which really interest you to start with, and then see how it goes.

The usual rules of 'netiquette' – how to be polite on the internet – apply even more strictly on Usenet. Read the FAQ (Frequently Asked Questions) list in any newsgroup before asking a question, and spend at least a few days reading what others have written before you dive in and make a fool of yourself. Of course, some know-it-all 'old hand' will be very quick to jump in and tell you, rightly or wrongly, that you are a fool and have no business being there. Ignore them and don't, whatever you do, get involved in a 'flame war' with increasingly rude exchanges from each side, which tend to drag in everyone else around too.

Questions And Answers

Easy Questions And Answers

Just recently my FreeServe Internet Explorer comes up with some awful chat page rather than my regular FreeServe homepage. This also seems to initiate other web pages, which I also do not want. How can I get back to having the good old FreeServe homepage and none of this junk?

Go to the page you want to have as the start page. Then click **Tools > Internet Options** and click the **Use Current** button.

Can I save web pages to read them offline?

If you use Microsoft Internet Explorer just click **File > Save As** when you find a page you'd like to read later, then put it somewhere you can find it again on your hard disk. If you like to read, say, a newspaper site every day you can set your computer to automatically make it available offline for you – in IE click **Favorites > Add to Favorites** and check the 'Make available offline' box, then click the **Customize** button to set how many links you want to be followed and saved from that page. This means that if you're on the front page of a site and you set the link depth to 1, each link on the front page will be saved on to your computer. If you set the link depth to 2, each link from the front page and then each link from each subsequent page will be saved. You can follow the wizard through to set this to be done at a certain time each day.

Can I turn off pictures in Internet Explorer to speed things up a bit?

 Sure, click **Tools > Internet Options > Advanced**, scroll down to the **Multimedia** section and uncheck anything you don't want to see or hear.

 The windows from some internet sites do not fit my computer screen – I have tried my computer and the screen size is the minimum it can be (800 × 640, I think).

 Do you mean that the websites are too large or too small for your computer? 800 × 600 (not 640) is a fairly standard size for screens and website resolutions – although the better sites work to ensure that they fit all screen resolutions, rather than being 'optimised' (designer-speak for 'I'm too lazy to work at this one') for a single resolution. There are some sites which require horizontal scrolling, and many which require vertical scrolling – we just have to put up with this, I'm afraid, until Darwinism weeds out the lazier designers.

 Is there a way of selectively removing recently visited websites from the drop-down history list in Internet Explorer?

 No, you can only delete the whole lot – click **Tools > Internet Options** and then the **Clear History** button under the **History** section of the **General** tab.

 I would welcome your advice on the reason why I am continually being disconnected from the internet after I have only been connected for some 5 to 10 minutes. Is there some way in which I can set time limits before disconnection takes place?

 There are quite a few potential reasons why this might be happening: noise on your phone line; an incoming call sending a 'Call waiting' signal; a short timeout set in your internet connection program; and more.

Harder Questions And Answers

 In Outlook Express, whenever I want to read messages offline and switch from one newsgroup to another I get the error message, 'Unknown error has occurred'. Can you tell me how to configure OE so that I eliminate this annoying problem?

This is probably being caused because you've told Outlook Express that you're connecting to the internet via your LAN (Local Area Network) when in fact you've made a dial-up connection. In Internet Explorer, click **Tools > Internet Options > Connections** and select your dial-up ISP connection as the default connection method.

Part 5
Improvements And Modifications

Just getting a computer up and running can be a real achievement, but then you'll want to start printing things, connecting it to other computers in the house, write letters, start working with digital pictures and more. This section of the book covers all the sorts of things that go wrong with all these processes, how to make a few small changes to the way you do things which will save you minutes or hours every day and how little upgrades can go a long way towards making your computing life much easier and richer.

Connecting To A Network

Networking is, when it works, an excellent way for two or more computer users to communicate. But some of the concepts and practicalities aren't easy to understand, and for many computer users with just one PC it's not that relevant. So this chapter gives a brief overview of the technologies and capabilities concerned and then points you to more in-depth features and tutorials online where you'll find step-by-step instructions and help.

Why Would I Want A Network?

The simple answer is, to save money. If you have two computers, networking them together means that they can share one printer, one internet connection, one place to store all your data.

Networks used to be only for big companies with specialised staffs of experienced administrators. Now, if you have a couple of PCs, you can buy a kit from many computer shops which will network them together for less than £50 and take you less than an hour to set up.

That said, networking computers can be fraught with problems and, in particular, can possibly leave your computers open to attack from outside if one or both machines is connected to the internet, and there are precautions to take before connecting PCs together.

The main purposes of networks are to allow users to share resources such as printers or your internet connection and to allow them to easily exchange information and swap files.

If you have only one line connecting you to the internet – whether it's a telephone line or a broadband connection – it makes sense to share it among all the computers in the office/at home. Similarly, it makes sense to share expensive peripherals like a printer. This chapters covers the principles of setting up a simple home network, where to find detailed instructions on what to do and some simple precautions to take.

What Do I Need?

1   Network hardware, which can be either network cards in your PCs joined together with wires, or network cards which connect to each other 'wirelessly' using radio signals.

2   Network software. All the software you need comes included with Microsoft Windows already – you don't need to buy anything extra.

How Networks Work

There are a number of different ways to refer to the type of network you use. There's the physical 'topology', the way the wires all connect together – and is that physical connection actually a bit of wire or do you have a wireless network? – then there's the choice of Ethernet or, well, Fast Ethernet these days; and what protocols would Sir like with that? TCP/IP is rapidly becoming the most popular but others exist and may be more appropriate in some circumstances.

The choices can be confusing and it's not difficult to get lost in the terminology so first, a few definitions.

The Hardware Connections

Wired Networks

1 On a peer-to-peer or 'bus' network, sometimes known as a 'daisy-chain' network, each computer on a network is connected to those either side of it – 'peer' means that all computers are equal. So if you had three computers A, B and C, you would connect A to B and B to C. This is the cheapest kind of network but has problems with some configurations – if computer B breaks down (or just isn't turned on), A and C may not be able to communicate. However, in the peer-to-peer system called 10base2 the 'middle' computer can be disconnected from the 'daisy-chain' while still allowing those on either side to continue communicating so long as you don't break the cable connections. This is now quite rare and you may not find any NICs (Network Interface Cards) which support it.

2 Networks that use hubs, switches and routers are sometimes known as 'star topology' networks because they can be thought of as having the hub in the centre with the networked machines radiating out like the rays of light from a star. These devices come in a variety of shapes, sizes and 'speeds', but essentially they all sit at the centre of your network and all computers are connected to them. This is a slightly more expensive option than the peer-to-peer network, and they're not essential if you have only a few computers but can make life much easier, especially if you plan on adding more.

3 Each computer also needs a 'network card', usually an add-in card (see Chapter 4) which allows you to connect to the network. You can now also buy USB network connectors which means you don't need to open up your PC at all – just plug a box into a free USB socket and plug the network cables into that box.

4 Wires come in different 'categories', usually abbreviated to just CAT. The commonest is CAT 5, and you can buy cables of appropriate lengths for your situation. Cables can have different types of connectors at the end. The commonest are now RJ45 plugs, which look like square telephone plugs. You may also come across BNC (Bayonet Neill-Concelman, the people who invented the BNC connector), which looks a little like a TV aerial plug. BNC connectors are used in 'peer-to-peer' networks of two PCs or more.

Wireless Networks

Like it says on the tin, these are networks which have no wires connecting the PCs. These networks still require that each PC has a network card – a wireless card in this case – and they can work with and without wireless 'hubs', normally called 'base stations'. This is a maturing technology and prices are coming down, but you'll still pay something like five times more for a wireless network than a conventional 'wired' installation.

The Software Connections

Ethernet is the standard type of network used today. You may see something called 'Token Ring' in a few offices, but only very rarely now.

The Basics

The Ethernet networking protocol was developed in the mid-1970s. At the time there were a number of other ways to network computers but over the years Ethernet has become the most popular. Just as VHS video recorders aren't the best way to make video tapes, Ethernet is not necessarily the best way to connect PCs but it works and it's now very cheap compared to the alternatives. Certainly for home and small business networks, it's easily good enough.

Speed

Network speeds are measured in megabits per second. The cheapest kind of network cards and hubs/switches work at 10 Mbps, with 100 Mbps rapidly becoming the default standard. Most network cards can work at both speeds and are usually designated '10/100 Mbps' cards. Many hubs and switches can work at both speeds, with there being a slight price premium for 100 and 10/100 Mbps models. If you can afford it, it's worth opting for the dual-speed or high-speed models. 100 Mbps Ethernet is often called Fast Ethernet. There are two faster speeds now, Gigabit (1000 Mbps) and 10 Gigabit (10,000 Mbps) Ethernet. Some PCs are starting to appear with Gigabit Ethernet network cards which also work at 10 and 100 Mbps.

Wireless Ethernet

There are a number of versions of the wireless networking standard, including 802.11a, 802.11b (also now called 'WiFi') and 802.11h. The WiFi 802.11b standard was the first to be established and works at a maximum speed of 11 Mbps, although this varies greatly depending on how far away you are from the base station or other PC using a wireless network card. Next came 802.11a, which works at up to 54 Mbps but isn't certified for use in the UK and Europe because of potential conflicts with other devices using the same wireless frequencies. Instead, in Europe the 54 Mbps standard will be 802.11h, due to be certified by the end of 2002. It incorporates everything in the 802.11a standard and adds on a few extras required by the regulatory authorities here. You may see 802.11a equipment for sale but you'd be advised to avoid it, since you're liable to prosecution for using an unlicensed wireless device.

Network Protocols

1   TCP/IP. Transmission Control Protocol/Internet Protocol is what the Internet runs on and is rapidly becoming the commonest way to run all kinds of other networks, too.

2 NETBIOS, the Network Basic Input/Output System allows applications on PCs to communicate with other computers on the network. It can't be the only protocol on a network since it doesn't support 'routing' – direction of traffic on a network – so works in conjunction with, for example, TCP.

3 NetBEUI, the NETBIOS Extended User Interface, is a development of the NETBIOS standard.

4 Others. The list does tend to go on a little. For all practical purposes, the first three network protocols listed here are the main ones you'll come across. In some office environments you may see something called IPX/SPX, the Netware protocol from Novell.

Setting Up A Network

The commonest options are 'all in a box' kits. Setting up a network can become very complicated if you let the process run away from you. If you're setting up a network between two computers all you need are two network cards and a bit of wire called a 'crossover cable'. One step up from this would be to include a hub, which connects to each PC using a 'patch cable'. Buying a hub means that you can add further computers to the network simply by installing a network card and buying one extra cable, and it also makes removing computers from the network much simpler – if you have a peer-to-peer network, removing any PC from the middle of the chain means that those either side of the 'break' can't communicate without you re-routing the wires.

Try to keep network cables away from other cables, particularly electrical cables, which can cause interference. There's an upper limit of 100 metres for Ethernet cables without additional hardware 'repeaters'.

The range of wireless networks is reduced by thick walls and metal objects – don't site your wireless base station behind a metal filing cabinet, for example. You should also read and implement the security measures offered by your particular wireless network, otherwise someone outside the building with a laptop and a wireless card could access it.

Setting Up Your PC

All versions of Windows offer useful information in their help files to guide you through the basics of setting up a network, and there are a lot of websites devoted to this task (see the 'Further Information' section at the end of this chapter for details). These are the basics for all versions of Windows which you'll find in the **Network** section of **Control Panel** or by just right-clicking the **Network Neighborhood** icon on your Desktop.

1   Give your computer a name. This sounds easy but there are two bitterly divided camps which use completely different naming schemas. The first, sensible camp gives each computer a name so that, when you connect to it over the network, you can identify it and what it does easily – 'NewYorkEmailServer' would be an example from the 'sensible' camp. The not-so-sensible camp names its networked computers after favourite characters from cartoons, Star Wars movies or the Star Trek TV series, or after some favourite personalities. The computers at Chateau Keyboard are named after characters played by the late, great John Belushi in his various TV and film appearances. So the computer I'm writing this on is called Vito, after his *Saturday Night Live* impersonation of Marlon Brando playing Vito Corleoni in *The Godfather*, and my laptop's named Jake after his character in *The Blues Brothers*. I like computers with character.

2   Set up a workgroup. All the computers you want to connect together should be members of the same workgroup, i.e. the group of computers which work together. Posher networks use domains, but stick with a workgroup to start with.

3   Add the TCP/IP protocol to your PC if it's not already installed. You will also need to set up an IP address and a subnet mask and set a 'default gateway' – see the links at the end of the chapter for more information on doing this.

4   Decide what file and printer sharing you want and add the 'Client for Microsoft Networks'. 'Client' in this case is a small piece of software which allows computers on a network to talk to each other and share information (this may already exist on your PC). Then set up File and Print Sharing – this is where security considerations come into play. You'll find that you can share both printers and files, and that there's an option to have individual passwords for each. The problem is that if you don't set a password, anyone on the internet could, in theory, connect to your machine and delve through your files. With some types of broadband internet connections, particularly cable modems, you might even find that you can browse the computers of your neighbours if they have this set up wrongly. So, opt for passwords for files and then only share across your internal network those files and folders which have to be shared – don't automatically share your entire hard disk. You can also set the level of sharing – you can make it so that folders are read-only, i.e. those elsewhere on the network can read files but not delete or change them. This can be useful to prevent the kids changing or reading files you don't want them getting into. You 'share' folders by right-clicking them in **My Computer** or Windows Explorer and left-clicking the **Sharing** option.

What You Actually Need To Buy To Connect Two Computers

I'd strongly recommend buying a 'network in a box' kit with two 10/100 network cards and a 10/100 hub or switch, joining them together with appropriate lengths of

CAT 5 RJ45 cables. This is a well-proven method of starting a network and allows for plenty of future expansion. You can buy four- or eight-port hubs (some have even more ports but models with more than eight tend to be very expensive for home/small office use) for very reasonable prices now, under £50 for four-port models.

Connect them with the TCP/IP networking protocol. You may find that the 'network in a box' kit includes a CD with software to run on each machine on the network, which will smooth the path.

Security Considerations

Be careful when you set up Internet Connection Sharing if you also share printers and, particularly, folders on your computers – it's easy to do this in a way which leaves these open to the rest of the world as well as those you intended to give access to.

Run firewall software such as ZoneAlarm or BlackICE on all machines. See Chapter 18 for more details.

You *must* run anti-virus software on all connected PCs, not just the 'gateway' machine which actually connects to the internet. See Chapter 18 for more details.

Further Information

1   How Stuff Works, howstuffworks.com has a useful step-by-step tutorial on basic networking at www.howstuffworks.com/home-network.htm, although it's a little light on installing the software in Windows.

2   Home PC Network, www.homepcnetwork.com has a number of very useful 'How to' tutorials covering all aspects of wired and wireless networks, including sharing an internet connection.

3   Home Net Help has a series of home networking tutorials at www.homenethelp. com/home-network.asp.

4   Practically Networked, www.practicallynetworked.com, covers many areas, particularly sharing an internet connection and wireless networking.

5   CERT, the Computer Emergency Response Team Coordination Center, has a very thorough overview of Home Network Security at www.cert.org/tech_tips/home_networks.html.

Questions And Answers

Easy Questions And Answers

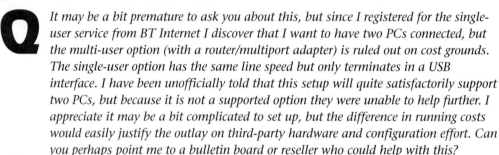

It may be a bit premature to ask you about this, but since I registered for the single-user service from BT Internet I discover that I want to have two PCs connected, but the multi-user option (with a router/multiport adapter) is ruled out on cost grounds. The single-user option has the same line speed but only terminates in a USB interface. I have been unofficially told that this setup will quite satisfactorily support two PCs, but because it is not a supported option they were unable to help further. I appreciate it may be a bit complicated to set up, but the difference in running costs would easily justify the outlay on third-party hardware and configuration effort. Can you perhaps point me to a bulletin board or reseller who could help with this?

BT used to specifically ban this idea, now they say they just 'don't support' it which probably means that, if your connection fails for any reason, they'll blame you and your home-brewed connection sharing. You can set up the connection using, for example, Internet Connection Sharing (ICS), which comes with Windows 98SE and later versions of Windows and usually works quite well in a Windows-only network. There are also a number of hardware devices specifically designed to facilitate the sharing of an internet connection – have a look at the links in the 'Further Information' section earlier in this chapter and the offerings from companies like LinkSys, Belkin and, if you're rich, Cisco.

I've heard about a 'crossover' cable to connect two computers – I thought you needed a hub for this?

I'd recommend a hub anyway as it allows a network to expand, but if you'll only ever connect two machines then a crossover cable will do the trick. Although externally it looks the same, this is different to the sort of cable you use to connect to a hub.

Harder Questions And Answers

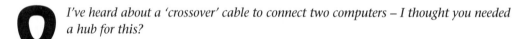

*I have two machines networked together to share my cable modem. I am using Windows 98SE Internet Connection Sharing. The PC that connects to the internet is running Windows XP, the second PC Windows 98SE. On booting up the Windows 98 machine I always get the prompt for the Windows network password. I haven't set a password and I always just click **OK**. Every time I reboot the 98 machine it always asks for this password again. Is there any way of stopping the 98 machine asking for a password every time? I have disabled password caching in the system policy editor, but it still asks for this network password.*

Download and install the TweakUI applet – you'll find it at www.mercury.org.uk. Unzip it and right-click the **inf** file then left-click **Install**. You'll find a **TweakUI** item in **Control Panel** afterwards – look on the **Logon** tab and you'll see you can automate the process.

I see Windows 2000 has a facility to alter drive letters. How does it work ? Do I alter the DVD (currently D:) to L: to put all the HD partitions in a row then alter them all back one letter so the DVD eventually ends up as K:? What implications does this have for my network?

Apart from drive C: you can change the drive letters in Windows 2000 to anything you want. The only potential problems are if a program is installed on one and you change the letter, or if it's looking to a particular drive letter for some data or a temporary file. The same applies to the network: any mapped drives will need re-mapping after you change the letters.

Could you please explain to me what IP addresses are and how they work?

Computers understand numbers rather than words, and every computer connected to the internet has a numeric IP address in the form XXX.XXX.XXX.XXX where XXX is a number between 0 and 255. This gives a theoretical maximum of 4,294,967,296 computers which can be connected to the network at any one time. In practice the actual number is much lower because whole ranges of numbers are 'reserved' as 'private' – all those beginning with a 10, for example, instantly excluding 167,772,160 numbers. When you connect to the internet via your ISP you will usually be assigned a 'dynamic' IP address – right now, the computer I'm typing this on has the number 172.182.167.81, one of the many assigned to AOL – the ISP I use to connect to the internet. When I disconnect from the internet that number will go back into the pool of numbers used for AOL dial-up connections and will soon be reassigned to someone else. Next time I connect, I'll get a different number. When I connect to a website, such as www.chateaukeyboard.com, it has a fixed IP address – 212.53.93.237. So when I type **www.chateaukeyboard.com** into my web browser's address bar, it looks to what's called a DNS computer, a Domain Name Server, which contains a lookup table of domain names like chateaukeyboard.com. It converts the easy-to-remember name into the numeric IP address and then connects me to the computer with that address, which then sends back the web page I want to my numeric IP address, which is, currently, 172.182.167.81. (This, incidentally, can account for many of the 'false alarms' received by those using firewall software such as ZoneAlarm or BlackICE – when I hang up my internet connection there may still be some outstanding

messages heading across the internet to my assigned IP address which are
then picked up by whoever is next assigned that number.)

 *Is it possible to use one set of Outlook Express files across a network? Sometimes I
use a laptop in another room in the house and would like to be able to check my e-
mails on it, and at the moment am having to physically copy the set of OE files
across the network, which is a bit tedious. The laptop is connected permanently to
the network via a wireless network card.*

 This has been a personal bugbear for me too for ages and ages. If you try to
select a network location as the **Store Folder** in OE (click **Tools > Option >
Maintenance** and click the button), the **OK** button is greyed out and you
apparently can't use it. However, I've just discovered that the **Store Folder** is a
simple registry setting which you can change as you wish. On the network
machine which currently can't use the network OE files, close OE and then
click **Start > Run** and type **Regedit** then click **OK** to start the registry editor.
Before changing anything, click **Registry > Export Registry File** and save a
copy somewhere safe. Now, click **Edit > Find** and type in the current location
of that computer's OE files (check the 'Match whole string only' box) then
click **Find Next**. On my Windows 2000 machine it turned up at
HKEY_CURRENT_USER/Identities/{long number e.g. D4001374-0E8B-XXXX-
XXXXXXXXXXXX}/Software/Microsoft/Outlook Express/5.0/Store Root, but
may be different for you. Right-click **Store Root** on the right and left-click
Modify. Type the network location in the **Value data:** box, e.g. **n:\oe** and
click **OK**. Now open OE and it should be using the network OE file store. You
should only have OE open on one machine at a time – it appears to work
with both machines accessing the file store at the same time, but it's a bit of a
recipe for problems trying to manipulate them from two locations. As an
alternative, safer method of achieving the same end, copy the OE folders
across once between machines and then configure one or both PCs to leave a
copy of e-mails on the e-mail server for a set period of time (under **Tools >
Accounts > Properties > Advanced**), say five days. Then when you download
e-mails on each PC you'll always get all the e-mails sent to you. You can
ensure that the **Sent** folders are synchronised either by sending a Bcc copy to
yourself each time or by copying the **Sent Items** folder between machines
regularly.

 *I've installed the Microsoft Critical Updates Notification but it seems to have ordered
my computer to connect to the internet every five minutes. What's going on?*

The problem occurs on networked computers with any sort of always-on or dial-on-demand connection to the internet. It checks for an update to 'vital' bits of software as soon as you turn the machine on. If it can't make a connection it keeps trying every five minutes (hence the five-minute interval set in Program Scheduler). If it does make a connection and finds nothing needs updating it resets its own, internal timer (not the one you see in Program Scheduler) to check again in 24 hours. If it does find an update, it pops up a dialog box asking what you want to do. You can ask it to remind you later, which it will do in 24 hours, or look at the update. This whole behaviour is only really a problem on networks where you have some sort of router set to dial the internet on a metered telephone or ISDN line, when it will be running up your phone bill by calling every 24 hours – and that includes computers using Windows 98's or 2000's Internet Connection Sharing facility. When the dialog box is on-screen, Critical Updates Notification will not go online again until one of the options is checked – so if you reboot your PC just before leaving the office on Friday evening the dialog box will remain on-screen until Monday morning but it won't dial up again. You can uninstall Critical Updates Notification either by using the **Add/Remove Programs** applet in **Control Panel** or, if it's not there, by going to the Windows Update website (windowsupdate.microsoft.com) and clicking the **Show Installed Updates** button. You'll see the Critical Updates Notification option displayed with an **uninstall** button next to it. Click this to remove the program. Finally, you'll be able to see whether or not your PC has this 'problem' by checking in Program Scheduler – it'll have a Critical Updates Notification item which apparently takes place every five minutes. Critical Updates Notification doesn't work on Windows NT and, if you do manage to install it somehow (it won't be presented as an option on the Windows Update site so you'll have to work at this one) Microsoft says it won't support it. If you are having particular problems with this software, drop me a line at help@drkeyboard.com and I'll put you in touch directly with the Microsoft support team.

*My home PC is Windows Me and my laptop is Windows 2000. I have network cards and a hub. Unfortunately the two computers very rarely recognise each other. Sometimes they do but then they disconnect and are back to not being able to find the other one! I have been told it is about using the correct protocols in **Network in Control Panel**. Which one(s) should be there?*

TCP/IP is the main one, and NetBEUI if that doesn't do the trick. Run the troubleshooters on networking in the help files on both computers – they're actually quite good. Also, doing a search for the computer by name may turn the connection back on.

Additional Storage

A Brief History Of Removable Storage For PCs

There used to be a time when you were *always* short of storage space on your PC. Back in the olden days (any time before the end of the last century, basically) we used to assiduously reclaim every spare kilobyte on our hard disks and eye hungrily such devices as Iomega's Zip drive which, when it was launched in the mid-90s held a *hundred megabytes* of data. Remember, this was back when a top-of-the-range hard disk would hold something less than 500 MB, so being able to get an entire hard disk on to five removable disks was a real achievement.

Then Iomega launched the removable Jaz drive which held an entire gigabyte on one removable cartridge, at a time when internal 1 GB hard disks weren't that common or cheap. Once you'd splashed out a few hundred pounds for the drive itself, the cartridges were about a third of the price of a new 1 GB hard disk.

There are now millions of original Zip and Jaz drives in use. Other systems have come and gone – the LS120 drive still exists here and there – but it's Iomega's products that have largely stood the test of time, and now the company is promoting its 20–160 GB removable hard disks and Peerless drives.

Now, hard disks are so large that we don't need additional storage as much as we used to, although removable devices are becoming popular as a way of backing up these ever-larger hard disks. This is a brief listing of the alternatives and the pros and cons of each.

CD And DVD Drives And Writers

Also known as 'optical media' since they're written and read using optical lasers, the great advantage of CD-ROM drives (read-only drives which can't write CDs) is that they're now ubiquitous – just about all new PCs come fitted with one as standard. And if they don't have a CD drive they'll probably have a DVD or CD writer of some kind, drives which are all capable of reading a standard CD-ROM. This means that if you have a CD writer you can be fairly confident that other computers will be able to read the discs you produce without any problems – although if you're going to rely on this as a way to transfer data between drives do check first that discs written by one PC can be read in the other. CD-R (write-once then read-only CDs, which you can save information to once only, then the disc is 'closed' to saving new information once you've finished the writing session) discs are very cheap, as little as 10 pence or less if you buy them in bulk. CD-RW (write-many, read-many) CDs are more expensive but can be reused over and over again. Older CD-ROM drives may have trouble reading CD-R or CD-RW discs, however, so watch this if you're intending to send discs to someone with a PC more than a few years old. DVD writers are both more expensive for the drive themselves and for the blank discs, although they do hold considerably more information than a CD. There's also still a question over which specific DVD recording format will become the industry standard – see Chapter 17 for more information. The downside to CD (and DVD) discs as a means of extra storage for your PC is the slow access speeds – it takes a considerable amount of time both to create the disc and then to read the information back, orders of magnitude slower than hard disks. Although Windows XP now allows you to simply drag-and-drop files on to a properly formatted CD-RW disk, effectively treating it like another hard disk, in practice this is still a slow process for anything other than backups and archiving data. Both CD and DVD drives are really too slow to run programs, for example.

Zip, Jaz, Peerless And Other Removable Magnetic Media (Including Removable Hard Disk Caddies)

Iomega has had the removable hard disk and hard disk-type cartridge market to itself for a while, although some other manufacturers are now starting to make inroads with external hard disks, particularly in the Firewire marketplace. Expect to see many USB 2.0 external hard disks for sale soon, too – these will be cheaper than Firewire devices (Intel owns the USB standard but, unlike Apple which owns the Firewire standard, doesn't charge a royalty to anyone for using it). Zip and Jaz disks have capacities (250 MB and 2GB) which, nowadays, look small compared to other devices, such as Iomega's Peerless removable hard disk unit which can hold 20 GB and against external Firewire and other hard disks, which can be as large as the biggest hard disks available, currently approaching 200 GB. The downside to the Iomega range is that you need to have a 'reader' device for the various cartridges at each end, unlike the external hard disks, which can simply be plugged into each machine they need to access, assuming they have the relevant ports free (they usually use USB or parallel – printer – ports, or occasionally serial ports). Even if you're carrying the 'reader' between machines you'll still need to install the drivers for the device at each end.

Hard disk 'caddies' are slot-in units which can hold a hard disk of more or less any capacity. With a caddy 'holder' in two computers, this allows you to carry the contents of a whole hard disk between them. Caddies are inexpensive – in the order of £20 – but don't offer much protection against shock to their contents when they're being transported. Also, unless you opt for the much more expensive 'hot-swappable' devices your PC has to be turned off before swapping caddies, and some PCs have difficulties booting up from such a hard disk.

Tapes And Backup Devices

Tape drives can be internal or external and are much, much slower than removable media like Zip disks and CDs. While tapes can, potentially, hold many gigabytes of data and the total amount available to you is limited only by the number of tapes you buy, access to an individual file on a specific tape will be slow (even when you've found the relevant tape), so don't consider them for anything other than archiving old files or regular backups. See Chapter 17 for more details.

Network Storage

If you have more than one PC there are a number of advantages to networking them together, including the ability to share large hard disks. So if, for example, you have an older machine with a single small hard disk you could use that to run Windows and

185

the software you use and keep all your data files on a newer machine with a larger hard disk with capacity to spare. See Chapter 13 for more information.

Online Storage

The idea of keeping files backed up online isn't new, and it can be useful to have copies of important documents you're working on in a place you can access from anywhere – companies like Net Store, www.netstore.com come well recommended. However, unless you have a fast internet connection it's not viable to use an online storage system as a way to add additional storage to your PC, but if you do look at this option consider the privacy options very carefully and make sure whichever company you use is thoroughly reputable.

Questions And Answers

Easy Questions And Answers

Q *On trying to back up to Zip, it always tells me that the disk is not formatted, so I attempt to format it. All the Zip drive does is clunk and click loudly, but nothing actually happens. If I try to view files on the Zip drive in Windows Explorer, it tells me this drive is not accessible. If my memory serves me correctly this has been since Windows 98 was installed, but I may be wrong.*

A It sounds as though your Zip drive is suffering the infamous 'Click of Death', which can actually be caused by a number of faults. Get in touch with Iomega (www.iomega.com) or your vendor and have your machine and disk(s) looked over. You'll also find a 'Click of Death' test program on Steve Gibson's website at Gibson Research, grc.com.

Q *I have recently installed a USB Iomega Zip 250 unit. Within days I discovered that I am unable to eject the disk either via software, using the manual eject button, or (power off) using the emergency eject procedure mentioned in the Iomega documentation. The unit is working fine in all respects except that I am unable to remove the (250 MB) disk.*

A There's an excellent troubleshooter for this on the Iomega support website at www.iomega.com/support/index.html – have a browse through it for the answers.

Q *I'm about to start working in two different offices on a regular basis, still for the same company but where there's no network connection between the two. I'll need a computer in the second office to run Microsoft Windows with fairly simple accounting and tax programs, and Microsoft Office. Am I better off taking an old*

186

one from here, which will have to be upgraded for a modem, USB and probably other bits, or buying a new one for the second office? I am thinking of buying an external CD-RW for backing up and carrying data from one location to the other, and perhaps some music. I am not seriously considering a laptop, apart from the expense and the weight, because I need a numeric keyboard for accounting and a decent screen.

With laptops you can usually plug in a full-size keyboard and regular monitor so, effectively, it would function like a regular desktop, especially if you invest in 'docking stations' which allow you to slide your laptop into a single connector and automatically make connections to your other peripherals. You could have a monitor and keyboard in each location and just carry the laptop. It sounds as though your 'old' machine will need a fair amount spending on it – you may be better off starting from scratch or, as I say, going for a laptop. Otherwise a CD-RW would transfer the files but the discs can be difficult to read in older CD drives, or sometimes in any machine other than the one which created them – you'd be better off with the write-once CD-R discs, which can only be used once but which are much, much cheaper and more reliable. These also have the advantage of providing 'generational' archives – once written, the information stays the same, unlike with a rewritable disc where you may overwrite older versions of a file with a new version with the same name. CD-Rs mean you can go back and see a version of a file from the past. You could also go for a removable disk like the Iomega Zip and Jaz products, or even a removable hard disk.

187

Chapter 15

Speeding Up
Your Computer

In This Chapter

➤ Why your once-fast computer is slowing down

➤ Simple things to do to speed it up again

➤ Getting best value for money from hardware and software upgrades

Why Your Once-fast Computer Is Slowing Down

That blazingly-fast, Super-Duper Multi-Megahertz machine you bought perhaps only a few months ago will, surprisingly quickly, start to feel as though someone's poured treacle inside it. It will happen gradually but one day you'll realise that it takes ages to start up now, that files and programs take longer to open and, well, it just seems *slower* somehow.

That's because it *is* slower. Your hard disk has filled up with rubbish, you load lots of unnecessary programs into its memory every time you start it up and, what's worse, you were seduced by the sales-talk when you bought it into buying more megahertz (or gigahertz) for your CPU instead of spending your cash more wisely.

Of course your new PC felt fast when you first started using it. If it was your first ever computer then you had nothing to compare it with. If it replaced an older one, then it's bound to have a newer, faster specification – not many people go looking for slower computers when they buy a new one. And then, of course, there's the spend factor – you have to justify spending hundreds or thousands of pounds to yourself so *of course* it's faster. If it wasn't faster then you'd be stupid, and no one wants to admit that.

So what can you do? The temptation may be, once you've finished complaining, to throw some money at the problem – upgrade that computer, add a faster CPU, more memory, another hard disk or a newer video card. And, sometimes, such upgrades can have a worthwhile effect.

But before you start splashing out on the hardware there are some simple things you can do to recover at least some of that old sensation of speed.

Simple Things To Do To Speed It Up Again

1   Clean out the fluff. Take this one literally – it means cleaning out the dust bunnies which collect inside your PC. If you feel up to it, open up your PC case and – gently – remove the accumulated dust, especially around the case and CPU fans. If you're at all doubtful about this, get someone who knows what they're doing to clean it out for you. The problem with dust is that it can cause your PC to overheat, thus slowing it down.

2   Remove temporary files. Windows and many programs running under it are notorious for creating many temporary files to store versions of themselves and other data while running. Word, for example, usually creates one copy of each document you work on from which it can restore the data should your computer crash, and also creates an 'image' version of any document you try to print. All these temporary files are supposed to be removed when you close Windows but if for some reason your PC hasn't been shut down correctly, these temporary files will be left cluttering up your hard disk. Over time they can take up a considerable amount of hard disk space and interfere with the proper functioning of your computer. First, do a search (click **Start > Search**) for ***.tmp** and delete all the files you find. You may receive an error message that some files cannot be deleted as they are in use – don't worry if you do, this is normal, just delete the other files. Next, search for **temp** to locate any directories of temporary files. Again delete their contents as above.

3   Move log and temporary files to another disk. If you have two hard disks (but not if you have one hard disk partitioned – divided up – with two or more drive letters), it can give something of an improvement in performance to move temporary files to a different hard disk from the one where your applications are stored. It allows, in simple terms, one hard disk to concentrate on running the program and the other to concentrate on storing the temporary files. If you have Windows 95, 98 or Me you need to edit the **autoexec.bat** file you'll find on your

C: drive. The easiest way to get to it is to click **Start > Run** and then type **sysedit** and click **OK** or hit **Enter**. You'll see a window open containing four files, including **autoexec.bat**. Select this one and type at the top of it the following two lines, exactly as here and each on a line of their own: **set temp=d:\temp** and **set tmp=d:\temp** (where **d:** is your second hard disk). Close Sysedit, saving your changes, and restart your computer. In Windows 2000 and XP open the **System** applet in **Control Panel**. On the **Advanced** tab click the **Environment Variables** button and in the top window change the default location for **temp** and **tmp** to **d:\temp** (where **d:** is your second hard disk). You'll need to actually create a folder called '**temp**' on this hard disk, too. Now scroll down the lower window, **System Variables** to change the same settings. **OK** your way out of the dialog boxes and reboot your computer when prompted to do so.

4   Move the swapfile. Windows runs programs in RAM, Random Access Memory. Typically your computer will have 32, 64, 128 MB or more. When it runs out of actual RAM Windows will start to use a portion of your hard disk as 'virtual' RAM, which may sound clever – and, in a way, it is. But your hard disk is much, much slower than RAM – many orders of magnitude slower – so it's preferable to have as much RAM as possible (up to certain limits – see later in this chapter). Like your temporary files, it's worth moving your swapfile to your second hard disk, should you have one. In Windows 95, 98 and Me you do this by opening the **System** applet in **Control Panel**, then clicking the **Virtual memory** button on the **Advanced** tab. Check the 'Let me specify my own virtual memory settings' radio button. Choose your second hard disk from the drop-down list and then type in a figure equivalent to 1.5–2.5 times the amount of physical RAM you have on your computer (use larger numbers for smaller amounts of RAM up to 128 MB) in both the Minimum and Maximum boxes, **OK** your way out and reboot your computer, ignoring the warnings about not letting Windows manage virtual memory any more (you really do know best this time). In Windows 2000 and XP look on the **Advanced** tab of the **System Properties** applet as in point 3 above and click the **Performance Options** button (under XP click the **Settings** button under the **Performance** section then the **Advanced** tab). Make sure the 'Applications' radio button is checked and then click the **Change** button under **Virtual memory**. You want to both change the size of the swapfile to be fixed and move it to your second hard disk here. Calculate the size by multiplying the physical amount of RAM you have by 1.5–2.5 – use larger swapfiles (also called 'paging' files) for smaller amounts of RAM. Select your second hard disk and type this figure into both the 'Initial size' and 'Maximum size' boxes. This will fix the size of the paging file and stop Windows growing and shrinking it as it goes along. Also on the **Visual Effects** tab of the **Performance Options** dialog in Windows XP, uncheck all the options for a 'Custom' option to improve performance.

5   Check what programs are running. First, keep an eye on programs you install which insist on running all the time; things like Real Jukebox will put a little icon

191

in your System Tray (next to the date and time) and say they're keeping an eye out for something to do. Open all these things up and hunt around for the way to turn them off, so they only run when you want them to. Leave things like your anti-virus program running, but widgets like the Jukebox can be left until you want music. And second, don't try running too many programs at once – if something's sitting on your Taskbar and you aren't using it, close it down and free up a few resources.

6   Delete old applications. It's tempting when you find a new piece of software – perhaps some shareware or freeware you've found on the internet – to install it and play with it a little. But if you then find you don't really like, want or need it, do you always remember to uninstall it? Perhaps not, so start with the **Add/Remove Programs** utility in **Control Panel** and look through the list of installed programs, removing those you no longer need or which you don't use. Look through the **Start > Programs** list for those programs you don't use which have their own uninstall options.

7   Clean out the registry. Before Windows 95 came along, all important information, personalisations and program details were kept in initialisation or INI files (ending with **.ini**). Then came the Registry, a humungous file where even the brave often fear to tread. I say this not to be funny but to warn you – messing up your Registry can seriously damage your Windows installation, even perhaps forcing a complete reinstall, so if you're not confident about these sorts of things, skip this step and move along.

The first thing to do is to back up your Registry so you can restore it if you make a mistake.

Open it up by clicking **Start > Run** and typing **regedit** in the dialog box and clicking **OK**. Then click **Registry > Export Registry** and save a copy somewhere safe – choose the 'All' option under Range at the bottom. To 'clean' the Registry of stray entries from, for example, programs you've uninstalled but which have failed to remove their Registry entries, the best option is to use a small program from Microsoft called Regclean – although they're strangely shy about publicising it themselves (possibly through fear of the harm messing up the Registry can do). There are any number of places to download this program – just do a Google search for it, and read the instructions carefully before using it. The biggest difference you'll probably notice after using Regclean is in the start-up time for your PC – Windows has to read through the entire Registry when it starts up, which can be a time-consuming process. NB: The latest version of Regclean, 4.1a, is *not* compatible with Windows Me or XP – it *only* works with Windows 95, 98, 98SE, NT3.51, NT4 and Windows 2000. *Don't* use it with Me or XP.

8   Update applications and drivers. As well as fixing bugs and adding features, new drivers often 'optimise' the performance of the relevant hardware. For example, the manufacturer of your computer's video card may have found a way to make better use of the memory on its hardware to speed up the display of images on your monitor screen.

Getting Best Value For Money From Hardware And Software Upgrades

Of course, even the most expert mechanic can only keep an old banger going for so long. At some point you have to bite the bullet, pull out your wallet and spend some money. But you may be surprised to learn how little money – certainly in comparison to the cost of buying your new computer in the first place – you may have to spend to gain a worthwhile improvement in performance.

Where's Your System's 'Choke Point'?

Try to work out which component is holding back the rest of your machine – the CPU, the RAM, the hard disk, the video card or something else. There are a number of utilities which will show you how much memory you're using and how busy your CPU is – in Windows NT, 2000 and XP hold down **Ctrl** and **Shift** and hit the **Esc** key to bring up the Windows Task Manager. In Windows 9x I use the TClock applet (available from www.mercury.org.uk), which, as well as vastly improving the time display, includes the ability to show CPU and memory usage. Using these you can see that, for example, if your memory is constantly fully utilised you should think about adding more RAM.

1   CPU. Most PCs these days are sold on the 'megahertz value' – the speed of the CPU. Nowadays there are Intel Pentium 4 and AMD Athlon processors of 2 GHz and more, which sounds impressive but in fact isn't as useful as the marketing divisions of both companies would have you believe. Certainly for most purposes the processors at the bottom of their ranges – down at 1 GHz or less – can cope admirably with running Windows XP, Microsoft Office, web surfing, e-mail and such regular tasks. Fast processors are useful if you're editing video files or large digital images but don't make much difference when you're word processing or web surfing. So, unless your CPU runs at less than 400 MHz I wouldn't even consider upgrading it – and, in any case, designs change so much and so quickly that you'd probably also need to upgrade your PC's motherboard, too, and possibly the RAM at the same time. The minimum processor speed recommended for Windows XP is 300 MHz (see www.microsoft.com/windowsxp/ pro/evaluation/sysreqs.asp).

193

2   RAM. Windows has become more and more memory hungry as it's evolved. Windows 95 was, theoretically at least, happy with 8 MB of memory, although 16 MB was a likely recommendation. Now the recommendation for Windows XP is a minimum of 128 MB, and I'd recommend at least double this, 256 MB.

3   Hard disk. The amount of information we stored on our PCs remained fairly small for a long time, then along came music, image and video files which suddenly were crying out for gigabyte after gigabyte of hard disk space. Now the smallest hard disk you can buy is around 20 GB, with new machines being routinely fitted with 40 or 80 GB models. 160 GB HDs are available, and 500 GB disks are not far away. They're also getting much, much cheaper in cost-per-megabyte terms, and you'll find a 40 or even 80 GB disk for under £100 now. The minimum recommended for Windows XP is 1.5 GB of free hard disk space. If your current hard disk is more than half full, it's worth thinking about adding a second one (which would also allow you to use the tips about moving various files to a second hard disk earlier in this chapter), the largest you can reasonably afford without having to sell any children.

4   Video card. If your display will accommodate at least 16-bit colour and an appropriate number of pixels for your screen size (see Chapter 5 for details) and you don't want to play any games which demand the latest, greatest video cards around then, unless you like spending money, your video card is adequate. If you do want to play the latest, greatest games then reach for your wallet.

Cost-effective Hardware Upgrades

1   Upgrade the RAM first. In terms of performance bang for your upgrade buck, doubling the amount of RAM inside your PC is the single most effective thing you can do if you have 128 MB or less. You do start to run into the law of diminishing performance returns for Windows 95 and 98 between 128 and 256 MB of RAM, unless you're editing huge video or image files. In any case, if you are editing this sort of file you'd be much better served running Windows 2000 or XP, which can handle large amounts of memory much better than the Windows 9x family.

2   If you already have a minimum of 128 MB of RAM, think about adding a larger hard disk. This will allow you to run two hard disks, with the new one becoming your primary disk (since it will almost certainly be faster than your original disk) and your old one being used to store data and temporary files as detailed earlier in this chapter.

3   Once you've upgraded the RAM and hard disk, think – but think very, very carefully indeed first – about upgrading the CPU. Both Intel and AMD change the configuration of their CPUs once or twice a year and the odds are that those

available now won't fit motherboards more than 18 months old, possibly less. So upgrading the CPU would mean at least also changing the motherboard, which, in turn, could mean also changing all the RAM if your old memory isn't compatible. Generally I advise against upgrading CPUs.

4 Input and output devices. The monitor is the part of the computer you look at most, and a good quality monitor will outlive just about all computers. Buy a decent quality 19" monitor now – even top brands are available for under £300 now. The same applies to keyboards and mice. Those which come with most standard PC systems are the cheapest the manufacturer could find, so spend a while looking for decent ones. Personally I prefer the Microsoft ergonomic (banana-shaped) keyboards and optical mice (the ones with red lights underneath instead of balls).

Software Upgrades

Is it worth moving from version X to version X.1 of a given software program? Well, that depends. For example, if you're currently using Office 95 or 97, I'd say it's worth upgrading to Office XP. Having said that, whichever version of whatever program you're using and considering upgrading, look carefully at the new features and facilities offered by the latest version and make sure that you can really use them. While I use Office XP and find its new features useful, I'm currently two generations behind the latest version of Paint Shop Pro, the picture editing program I use. This is because, although I can use the features Word and FrontPage offer in their XP incarnations I have no use for the new editing features offered in Paint Shop Pro version 7 over the version 5 I have.

You can get 'bug fixes' for free. Check regularly with the manufacturers of your software to see if they have any bug fixes or upgrades on offer on their websites. As with hardware drivers, these can often speed up the running of your PC. Many have e-mail notification programs which will tell you when new and/or improved versions are available.

You can also find free upgrades to Windows and other Microsoft software: windowsupdate.microsoft.com is the place to find product updates for Microsoft Windows; office.microsoft.com/productupdates/mainCatalog.aspx the place for updates and additions to Microsoft Office. You can also browse the Office site via office.microsoft.com – it often has a wealth of updates, additions and improvements to many Office programs and is well worth a regular visit.

Regular Checkups

There are a number of routines you should run regularly on your computer.

1 Scheduling defrags and/or scandisks. These will run unattended and/or while

you're doing something else in Windows 2000 and XP, but in Windows 9x they will both fail if you have *any* other software running at all. The easiest remedy here is to restart your computer in Safe Mode – when it's starting up hit the **F8** key as soon as you see the white-on-black 'Starting Windows …' message. Disk defragmenter is necessary because, particularly in Windows 9x, the way files are stored on your hard disk can dramatically slow its performance. Think of the hard disk as a giant spiral like an old vinyl record. When you save a file, Windows looks along the spiral and saves that file in the first blank spot it comes to. If you then delete that file, the space becomes available again and Windows will reuse it for the next file it saves. However, if the second file is bigger than the first, only part of it will go into that space – the rest of the file will go into the next available spot, and so on. After a few weeks or month, files will be 'fragmented' into many small parts spread across your hard disk. Disk Defragmenter (find it under **Start > Programs > Accessories > System Tools**) gathers up all these file fragments and puts them back together in one place on your hard disk, reducing the amount of time it takes to read it.

2   Software which will check your system out for you. Conscientious though you may be, it's easy to miss updates to the plethora of programs you'll soon have installed on that shiny new PC. BigFix (www.bigfix.com) will scan through your hard disk and point to locations where you can find and download updates for much of the sofware on your PC, including virus definition files, Microsoft security updates and more.

3   Websites which will ceck out your machine for you. PC Pitstop, www.pcpitstop.com has been checking PCs online for some years now and can offer some handy hints.

4   See if your software packages can automatically check for themselves if they're up to date. Programs like ZoneAlarm and Norton Anti-Virus will check whenever you're online or at regular intervals to see if new versions are available, so check your software to see if it offers this facility.

Questions And Answers

Easy Questions And Answers

 I have something which I believe is classified as a 'Win modem', which I've been told can slow my computer up no end. Is this true?

Win modems are cheap versions of regular modems which rely on your computer's CPU to do most of the work they should be doing themselves. If you have a modern, fast computer it won't be too problematical, but if not then it can slow things down. Manufacturers install them to save – literally – just a few pounds. If you have one and think your web surfing speed is slow, splash out on a 'proper' new modem; external ones are best.

Since last month, for apparently no reason, my defragmenting (which I always do at least every week) has now refused to go beyond 10 per cent. The PC does seem to have become slower and more unreliable (Windows 98 now crashes every day, at least two or three times). I have already scanned my hard disk and have updated my Norton Anti-Virus regularly and am pretty sure that I don't have any viruses. Any advice please?

Restart your computer in Safe Mode – when it starts up, hit the **F8** key as soon as you see the 'Starting Windows …' message and choose from the options. Now run Disk Defragmenter. You can also achieve the same end by holding down **Ctrl** and **Alt** and hitting **Del** in your regular Windows and turning off everything except for Systray and Explorer, then running Disk Defragmenter. The problem is that another program is accessing your hard disk and Disk Defragmenter thinks the contents of it have changed so it wants to start all over again. Check the results from your machine carefully to see if it's marking an increasing number of 'bad blocks' on your hard disk, which could be indicative of a failure.

*Some programs, particularly web utilities like RealPlayer, AOL Chat, McAfee Virus Scan etc., when downloaded from the web and installed by clicking on the compressed file, install themselves to be auto-started at boot-up. They appear in the Taskbar status window and can be 'exited'. However, what I want to do is remove them from whatever directory or registry key where they are listed for auto-start. I cannot find how to do this. Windows Help thinks that it tells you, but it simply points back to the **Start** button. These tasks are very annoying as they slow down execution noticeably even when not in direct use. I want to be able to decide when they run, not have them run automatically.*

What the Help files are pointing to is how to remove programs from the **Startup** menu – right-click **Start**, left-click **Open**, open **Programs** and then **Startup** and delete the offending program. All those you mention have internal options to stop them running on start-up – investigate their own help files and menus for details. You'd be advised to leave your anti-virus scanner running, though – that way it will protect you from virus infections.

My Windows 98SE machine seems to slow down throughout the day. What can I do about this?

 Windows loads and unloads programs and files from RAM as you work. In theory when you close a program or document it is removed from memory but Windows 9x isn't always as efficient at this as you might hope and bits get left behind. Eventually your RAM gets clogged up to the point where Windows starts using the swapfile on your hard disk instead of RAM, considerably slowing everything it does. The only way to clear this that definitely works is to reboot your computer – there are 'memory managers' on the market that claim to do this for you but most are just snake-oil.

 Microsoft Word seems to be taking longer and longer to open files I've previously worked on, and some are huge.

 Click **Tools > Options > Save** and uncheck the 'Allow fast saves' option. If enabled, this means that Word sticks your changes to the document at the top of the previous version when it saves, rather than going through and removing older bits and replacing them with your changes. As a result the file can become huge, as you've found.

 A few weeks ago a friend informed us that he had intercepted a Melissa virus in an e-mail attachment we had sent him. We had been unaware of the virus and at his suggestion bought Norton SystemWorks Version 3.0 which apparently eliminated our virus. Since then the whole system seems to have slowed considerably and Norton Crash Guard interrupts quite frequently to tell us that it has intercepted a crash in OleMainThreadWndName. I am offered two options to click: 'Terminate', which closes Windows down and restarts it, or 'Revive', which brings up a message saying 'No save action detected', and I can then click 'Close'. Either action allows me then to continue with what I was busy with when the original crash warning occurred. I was not aware that I had a program called 'OleMainThreadWndName' and I do not know what these crash warning messages mean. Can you please help? What should I be doing?

 While there are those who like programs like Crash Guard, I'm not one of them. I think they use up too many system resources like RAM (Random Access Memory) and hard disk space to start with. They occupy your computer's CPU (Central Processor Unit – the chip, such as a Pentium III, which is the 'brains' of your machine) with pointless tasks, and so on. And, in my experience, they can't actually prevent your machine crashing anyway, so they're pointless. You're better off uninstalling this portion of the program and keeping the anti-virus protection, as well as running Disk Defragmenter and ScanDisk at regular intervals, instead.

I have an Intel Celeron 400 Windows 98 system with 64 MB of RAM. What's the most cost-effective upgrade: a faster processor or more memory?

RAM without a doubt. Slot in another 64 MB and you'll notice an immediate difference. Personally, next up I'd spend money on a larger, faster hard disk rather than a processor – 400 MHz sounds slow in terms of today's gigahertz-plus screamers but, in real terms, it's good enough for most tasks like word processing, web surfing and so on.

Please don't say bin it! Old yes! For no obvious reason this 486 machine with 64 MB of RAM has slowed down to about a 2400 bps speed with IE5. The 850 MB hard disk is partitioned to C: = 500 MB, D: = 350 MB. C: has around 70 MB free, not fragmented, no viruses although the software is six months old. I haven't installed anything lately, no apparent interrupt conflicts and I'm at my wits' end. Could it be the battery? The system time falls behind – would this have any effect? I'm not too keen on reinstalling when I don't know what has happened. I have had Windows 95 on here for, say, nine months, maybe less, moved swap file to D: to no avail.

If you were talking about a horse and I were John Wayne, we'd probably take it out the back and put it out of its misery. Your machine is right on the limits for running current software, in particular in terms of the free hard disk space you have – lots of programs, particularly Internet Explorer 5, make lots of temporary files which will slow things right down. Check the settings for your temporary internet files (**Tools > Internet Options > General** and then the **Settings** button under **Temporary Internet Files**). There are lots of other options too so, as ever, pop on over to www.drkeyboard.net if you're still stuck after trying this.

I have had my Windows 95 computer for just over two years. It seems to have slowed down substantially although I have plenty of RAM and about 5 GB free on the hard disk. I have been told that it is advisable to format the hard disk and reinput everything every 6 to 12 months. Is this correct? If so, how do I go about it? I assume that I restart in DOS mode and then enter format C but this will presumably mean that I have no DOS files and therefore will be unable to input Windows.

There are lots of reasons why your computer may be slowing down. First, you undoubtedly have lots more software installed now than you did two years ago and run more of it at the same time – this will inevitably slow it up. Check in the System Tray to see what applications you have running there and turn off any unnecessary ones. Run ScanDisk and Disk Defragmenter (you may need to restart your computer in Safe Mode to get these to work properly – hit **F8** as soon as you see the 'Starting Windows …' message). Next, clear out your temporary files folder – it may be in **c:\windows\temp** or elsewhere – you can find it by searching for ***.tmp** (the ***** means 'look for any file ending in **.tmp**). Delete anything created before the last time you started your computer. Also, if you use Internet Explorer click **Tools** > **Internet Options** > **General** and under the **Temporary Internet Files** section click **Settings** and change the amount of disk space used to 25 MB – anything larger than this and your computer will spend ages checking through thousands of pages stored on your local machine every time you go online. Finally, yes, reinstalling everything can be a good way to clear out junk – but it means making absolutely, definitely sure that you have all your data stored safely elsewhere. This includes any word processing files, e-mails, pictures, downloads and so on. Personally I always store such things on a separate hard disk (or partition on the disk if there's only one physical hard disk on the machine) so that reinstalling software doesn't lose the files I've created. Come on over to the message board at www.drkeyboard.net where we can discuss this in greater depth.

 Is it correct that having a picture on my computer Desktop will slow it down?

 Yes, strange though it may sound, the picture on your Desktop is permanently stored in the RAM of your computer while it's turned on, leaving less room for programs to run. The same applies to Active Desktop items which can hog memory. And if you must use wallpaper, don't use the 'Stretch' option which can take up even more RAM.

 I've been told that because I use about 700 fonts on my computer it will be slower – is this true?

 Blimey, 700? Yes, having lots of extra fonts will slow your PC, especially when it comes to loading Windows – it has to load each font in turn.

 I keep losing things on my Desktop when one icon slips behind another. How can I stop this?

 The more things you have on your Desktop, the slower your computer will run. Try putting things into just a few organisational folders on the Desktop and save things in them, rather than directly on the Desktop itself.

 When typing in Word 97 my machine slows right down and eventually grinds to a complete halt. Why?

Try installing the Office Service Pack Two, which you can download from office.microsoft.com.

I have lost the 'Find Fast' program from my computer. Where and how do I restore it?

Good grief, why on earth do you want that piece of rubbish? Anyway, it's part of your Microsoft Office package – reinstall that (choose the 'Custom' option) and you'll be returned to your nice, slow PC straight away. Those who would like to turn it off and regain some of their PC's previous speed will find it in **Control Panel** – set all update intervals to zero and delete all indexes.

*Whenever I try to tidy up my folders, either in Explorer or just by moving about within **My Documents**, everything goes painfully slowly. I have noted over the years your comments re. Find Fast and have never had it enabled. What can you suggest?*

Do you regularly run Disk Defragmenter and ScanDisk? The symptoms you describe are those of a hard disk gradually cluttering up with bits of files, other bits of half-deleted files and so on.

I have a Pentium 75 computer which is hopelessly out of date and slow. Although we have doubled up to 16 MB of RAM, the speed of the machine is too limiting for meaningful work. Is there any company that will do me a trade in for it? Would the manufacturer be interested?

You will have trouble finding anyone interested in buying your machine now, unfortunately. Buy a new one and network it to the old one so two people can work at the same time.

Harder Questions And Answers

My computer runs slowly and complains it's 'out of resources' yet there's loads of free RAM. What's going on?

I'm guessing you're running Windows 95, 98 or Me, which has what's called 'resource heaps' where it keeps track of what it's doing. These are limited in size no matter how much memory you have. Either close down some applications or restart your computer. Windows 9x is particularly prone to this problem; Windows 2000 and XP are much better at managing memory.

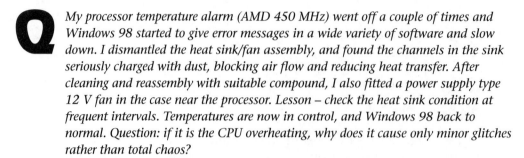

My processor temperature alarm (AMD 450 MHz) went off a couple of times and Windows 98 started to give error messages in a wide variety of software and slow down. I dismantled the heat sink/fan assembly, and found the channels in the sink seriously charged with dust, blocking air flow and reducing heat transfer. After cleaning and reassembly with suitable compound, I also fitted a power supply type 12 V fan in the case near the processor. Lesson – check the heat sink condition at frequent intervals. Temperatures are now in control, and Windows 98 back to normal. Question: if it is the CPU overheating, why does it cause only minor glitches rather than total chaos?

The glitches will vary from minor to major depending on what the CPU's doing at the time of the error, but there's a chance they'd get worse over time if the CPU were to be damaged. Windows 9x manages your CPU less well than Windows NT or 2000, but there's a free widget called CPUIdle (www.cpuidle.de) which will fix things. Basically, when your computer's idling it slows your processor down, thereby keeping it cooler than if it runs at full throttle like it would be doing under Windows 9x.

My hard disk is divided into two partitions, C: and D:. C: has filled up, and the computer has slowed down. D: is relatively empty. The biggest programme on C: is Office 95. If I delete it from C: and reinstall it on D: it will solve my hard disk space problem. But will all my existing Office 95 related files which live on both C: and D: (letters in Word, spreadsheets in Excel etc.) still be able to open and work normally as before even though Office 95 has moved from C: to D:?

In a word, yes. The way to ensure this is to use the options inside Word, Excel and so on to tell the programs where the files are located – you'll find it under **Tools > Options > File Locations**. Do back up your settings before the remove/replace, though – see Chapter 17 for details of the 'Save my settings' wizard.

I have a 600 Mhz Pentium III, with 128 MB of RAM running Windows 98. If I added another 128 MB of RAM would I notice any improvement?

That all rather depends on what you want to do. If you're word processing, web surfing and e-mailing then 128 MB is enough under Windows 98. Indeed, you run into a fairly high wall of diminishing returns at this point with any version of Windows 9x – the speed improvements you get above this point are drastically less than leading up to this point. Indeed, the difference between 64 and 128 MB isn't huge – certainly nowhere near as large as the difference when upgrading from 32 to 64 MB. However, if your work involves manipulating large files such as big spreadsheets or images then you will see an improvement if you add the extra memory. If the size of the file you're working on exceeds the amount of free RAM, the system will be forced to 'page' it from your hard disk, loading segments from it as it goes along and this is orders of magnitude slower than working with a file in RAM. That said, if you are working with large files like this you'd be doing yourself a big favour by upgrading to Windows 2000 or Windows XP which has much, much better file and memory handling systems – Windows 9x is based on the now ancient DOS system and it really creaks with large loads.

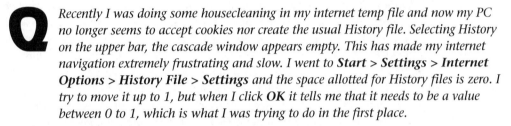

*Recently I was doing some housecleaning in my internet temp file and now my PC no longer seems to accept cookies nor create the usual History file. Selecting History on the upper bar, the cascade window appears empty. This has made my internet navigation extremely frustrating and slow. I went to **Start** > **Settings** > **Internet Options** > **History File** > **Settings** and the space allotted for History files is zero. I try to move it up to 1, but when I click **OK** it tells me that it needs to be a value between 0 to 1, which is what I was trying to do in the first place.*

I don't think you're looking in the right place. If in IE 5.01, which I gather you're using, you click **Tools** > **Internet Options** and then the **General** tab, you set the number of days worth of pages visited in the **History** folder at the bottom of that pane – the 'Days to keep pages in history' scrolling number box. If you've clicked a **Settings** button on this dialog tab you're adjusting the amount of space allocated to temporary internet files, an amount of disk space in megabytes allocated to this purpose. If you've set this to zero you will indeed have problems. Try setting it to something like 100 MB.

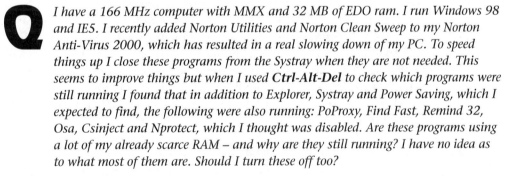

*I have a 166 MHz computer with MMX and 32 MB of EDO ram. I run Windows 98 and IE5. I recently added Norton Utilities and Norton Clean Sweep to my Norton Anti-Virus 2000, which has resulted in a real slowing down of my PC. To speed things up I close these programs from the Systray when they are not needed. This seems to improve things but when I used **Ctrl-Alt-Del** to check which programs were still running I found that in addition to Explorer, Systray and Power Saving, which I expected to find, the following were also running: PoProxy, Find Fast, Remind 32, Osa, Csinject and Nprotect, which I thought was disabled. Are these programs using a lot of my already scarce RAM – and why are they still running? I have no idea as to what most of them are. Should I turn these off too?*

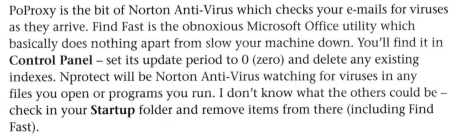

PoProxy is the bit of Norton Anti-Virus which checks your e-mails for viruses as they arrive. Find Fast is the obnoxious Microsoft Office utility which basically does nothing apart from slow your machine down. You'll find it in **Control Panel** – set its update period to 0 (zero) and delete any existing indexes. Nprotect will be Norton Anti-Virus watching for viruses in any files you open or programs you run. I don't know what the others could be – check in your **Startup** folder and remove items from there (including Find Fast).

I would like to improve the performance of my PC, which I recently 'inherited' from a friend and consequently do not have a lot of (any) paperwork detailing its specifications. However, I have managed to ascertain the following. It's made by Carrera, 3 years old, a Pentium II 300 processor, 64 MB RAM, and a 33 something modem. Oh, and it has a Matrox Millennium II card (PC came with NT4 on it). It has a brilliant Nokia 447E, swell sound card and speakers and I use it almost exclusively for e-mail and playing Hearts/similar online. I recently installed Microsoft Flight Simulator 2000 on it, but quickly uninstalled it as watching paint dry would have been more exciting; dreadfully slow. Well-meaning friends say I should immediately buy and install 256 MB of RAM and get a 56K modem and I will reach Nirvana. Can it really be as simple as that? Is the processor completely innocent? Don't even ask me what a motherboard is. I suspect the video card is 2D? I feel I have reached the zenith of my IT skills in finding out the above info and, as I prefer Dim Sum to DIMM/SIMM, will shortly be placing the tower onto the counter of my local PC doctor for treatment. He is, however, surely unlikely to say I only need the memory increased for £50 if he can wheedle out much more from me, right? Or am I being grossly unfair? My budget to improve this gothic monstrosity is £250–£300.

For your budget I'd do two things: bump up the RAM as far as possible, perhaps even to 512 MB if your motherboard will support it (since you're using Windows NT4 it'll be able to make proper use of this extra memory). That'll cost you under 50 quid, probably, at current prices – click on the Crucial advert at www.drkeyboard.net to find out just how cheap it is (I get a small cut from Crucial if you use this link, it doesn't cost you anything, and they do make some of the best quality RAM around). Next, I note that you have a 4 GB hard disk – stick a big new one in, you'll get something like 40–60 GB for a hundred quid. Finally, think about a video card, although unless you have an AGP socket it won't be easy to find one and, for 2D work your Matrox is pretty good anyway. Spend something on a 56k external modem or, if you can, on a broadband (xDSL/cable modem) connection or, failing that, ISDN.

I have a Celeron 700 PC with 64 MB of RAM and a 10 GB hard disk running Windows 98. It seems to run very slowly. What basic things can I do to speed it up?

In terms of hardware your CPU – the Celeron – is well up to most modern software, unless you're a game-playing nut. Assuming you just want to run basic productivity applications like a word processor, surf the web, send and receive e-mails and so on, the single most productive hardware upgrade you can perform is to add more RAM. It's very cheap at the moment and I'd advise adding as much as you can afford – an extra 64 MB is the minimum you should add. Windows 9x will struggle to do anything very sensible with whatever you install over 128 MB and 256 MB is a practical upper limit, but the latest version of Windows, XP, will gobble it up. You should also run Disk Defragmenter – you'll find it under **Accessories** on your **Programs** menu – at regular intervals. Weekly is good. In Internet Explorer click **Tools > Internet Options > General** and then the **Settings** button under **Temporary Internet Files**. Change the amount of space they take up to between 25 and 50 MB – any more and IE will take ages looking through old pages before loading a new version. If you have a second hard disk, move the temporary internet files to it rather than your main hard disk. You can do the same for the regular temp file stores that Windows uses by adding the lines **set temp=d:\temp** and **set tmp=d:\temp** to your **autoexec.bat** file. You can get to it by clicking **Start > Run** and typing **sysedit** and hitting **Enter**. Reboot. Also, click **Start > Search > Files and Folders** and look for ***.tmp** and **temp** to find your existing temporary files folders. Delete everything in the old ones (everything created before the last time you turned your computer on). Finally, I can heartily recommend Dave Farquhar's book *Optimizing Windows* (www.drkeyboard.com/books/books/windows9x.htm).

Chapter 16

Managing Disks And Files

In This Chapter

➤ How to organise your files and put them where you want them

➤ Which application for what kind of files?

➤ Formatting and partitioning your hard disk

➤ Moving files, folders and applications

➤ Missing files

➤ Keeping your data and disks in tip-top condition

How To Organise Your Files And Put Them Where You Want Them

By default, most Windows programs store documents and files you create either in their own store or in the **My Documents** folder you'll find on your computer hard disk. To those who designed the programs, putting, say, your new pictures in **C:\program files\application manufacturer name\application name\data** or, worse, something like **C:\Documents and Settings\username\Local Settings\Application Data\Identities\{D4001374-0E8B-47C8-81C6-8123456789EA}\application manufacturer name\application name\data** makes complete sense. And, if all you do is click **File > Open** and there your files are, you may never know that your files are stored in the computing equivalent of Never-Never Land. But if you want to do something like edit a photograph from your digital camera – whose software stores its downloaded pictures in one gibberish-laden location – with your picture editor – which has another gibberish location – and then put it on to your website with your website editor which thinks all your files are in the **My Documents** folder, you'll soon get tired of all this nonsense.

What you need is a *hierarchical filing system* – one which follows a set hierarchy of *nested folders*. Think of it as looking like the root system of the tree. Here's an example of how it might work: at the top is a single folder called **My Documents**. Open that up and below it you could have folders called, for example, **Letters**, **Invoices**, **Diary**. Below the **Letters** folder are three folders called **2001**, **2002** and **2003** representing the years in which the letters are written. Below each of the year dates are folders called **Bank**, **Lawyer**, **Mum**, **Other**, representing the people to whom you most often write. Figure 16.1 shows how this might look (note also that the document in the **Bank** folder has a name that will make sense a year from now, too).

The 'path' to this folder is **C:\My Documents\Letters\2002\Bank** – it's a letter written in 2002 to your bank, as shown by the 'Address' line, and you can see how the folders 'nest' under the 'Folders' column to the left. Figure 16.2 shows another example.

In Figure 16.2, you can see that the item concerned is in **C:\My Documents\Diary\2002**. Below it in the list of folders to the left you can see the **Invoices** and **Letters** items. The small plus symbol (+) next to **Letters** indicates that there are more folders below it – clicking the plus sign shows that there's one called **2002** and, below that, another called **Bank** as in Figure 16.1. Clicking the minus (-) symbol next to any entry 'shrinks' all the folders currently expanded out back under the folder above it,

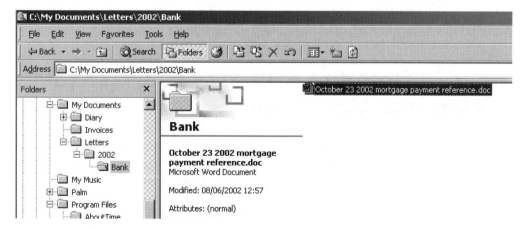

Figure 16.1 Hierarchical filing system

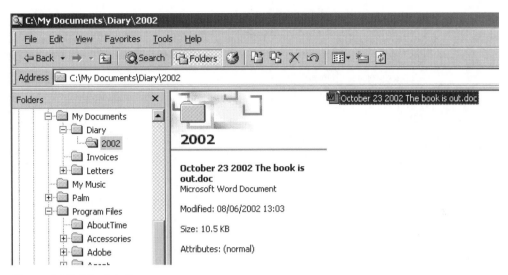

Figure 16.2 File details

and the minus symbol becomes a plus. As you can see, there's no plus or minus symbol next to the **Invoices** folder – this means that there are no folders 'nested' inside the Invoices folder, although there could be documents in that folder. Click on the folder name on the left to see its contents, as in Figure 16.2 – I've clicked on the **2002** folder below **Diary** to see that there's a file in it called **October 23 2002 The book is out.doc**. The additional information below the large folder icon and the name **2002** in the right-hand pane appears when you click on an individual file name. This tells you the type of document – it's a Microsoft Word Document – the date and time it was modified, its size and its attributes: (**normal**) appears when it's not a Hidden or System file. So, you can see that I created this item for my diary at three minutes past 1 p.m. on the 8th of June 2002 in Figure 16.2.

I created these folders by opening the **My Documents** folder on my desktop and then clicking **File > New > Folder**. This creates a new folder under the **My Documents** top-level folder called **New Folder**. Look closely at the folder you've just created – unlike any other folders in **My Documents**, you'll see that its name is in white letters on a blue background and the whole name is in a black-bordered box. Start typing a new name for the folder and you'll see that your typing immediately deletes the whole name **New Folder** and replaces it with what you're typing. You can also rename any existing folders by right-clicking them and then left-clicking **Rename**. To open your newly created and newly renamed folder just double-click it. You can create another folder here in the same way and continue to create the folder hierarchy.

If you're already inside a program and find that you want to put a document into a specific folder, click **File > Save** and 'navigate' your way to the appropriate location. You do this using the options available in the **Save As** dialog box which pops up when

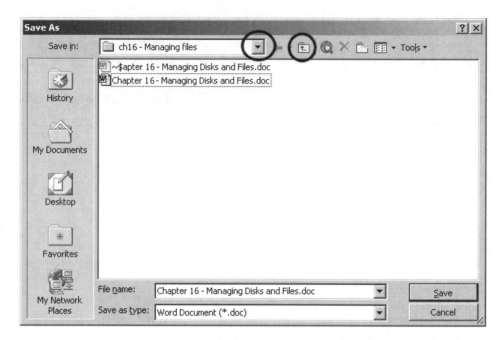

Figure 16.3 **Save As** *dialog box*

you click either the **Save** icon on the toolbar or **File > Save** on the menu at the top of the program window (see Figure 16.3). Some programs like Microsoft Word allow you to change the default location (in Word you click **Tools > Options > File Locations**, click the **Documents** line to select it then click the **Modify** button).

Figure 16.3 shows that I'm saving a document called **Chapter 12 – Managing Disks and Files.doc** in a folder called **ch12 – Managing files** (the version of the file above it beginning with the tilde (~) symbol is the auto-recover version automatically created by Microsoft Word – if your computer crashes, when you restart Word it will find this file and open it so you don't lose any information). This is where I want to save the file so just clicking **Save** is all I need to do.

If I wanted to put the file into a different location, I'd navigate there by clicking either on the downwards-pointing arrow to the right of the **Save in:** box or the upwards-pointing arrow just to its right. The down arrow drops down a hierarchical listing showing the current folder's location (see Figure 16.4). Clicking the up arrow moves one folder 'up' in the hierarchy, in this case to a folder called **Troubleshooting book** – clicking it again from that folder would move up one more level to a folder called **Writing**.

In Figure 16.4 you can see the **My Documents** folder on your Desktop – click on that once and the **My Documents** folder will open in the dialog box. Double-click the folder where you want to put the document and keep on doing so until you get down

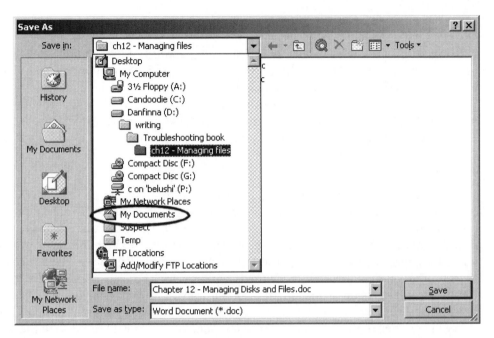

Figure 16.4 ***Save As*** *dialog box: drop-down list*

to the level you want, type a name for the file in the **File name** box and then click **Save**. Remember, if you go down a level too far you can click the up arrow. Also, in later versions of Windows you'll see that the **Save** dialog box has a blue 'back' arrow like the one you see in Internet Explorer (once you've been to more than one folder using other navigation methods) – click this to go back to the previous folder you were in. This blue arrow has a small down-arrow of its own immediately to its right. Click this and you'll see a list of all the folders you've been through to get to your current location – click one to go straight to it.

You can also perform regular file maintenance procedures in the **Save** dialog box – right-click any file name to see the options – so that you can, for example, rename or delete a file or group of files or folders.

To the right of the up arrow in this dialog box you'll see a 'Search the web' icon – click this to go to Internet Explorer's standard 'Search' page; a 'New folder' icon – click this to create a new folder inside the current folder, then rename it as described earlier; a 'Views' icon which allows you to select whether you see large or small icons, a file listing, other information about the files and so on; and a 'Tools' menu – click this to see further options for the file or folders you're dealing with.

Which Application For What Kind Of Files?

A 'file type' is a file of a particular kind. For example, most of the pictures you see on the internet are files of the type JPEG (Joint Photographic Experts Group – files will end with the letters **.jpg**) or GIF (Graphic Interchange Format – files ending with **.gif**). You can tell what type a file is by looking at the three letters at the end of the file's name, although by default Windows turns this 'file extension' off, which isn't very helpful. To be able to see file extensions, open **My Computer** and click **Tools > Folder Options > View** and uncheck the 'Hide file extensions for known file types' box, then click **OK**.

Most of the time, most files will open in the application in which you expect to see them. Most of the time. But, occasionally you'll install a new program and find that it's decided that it should be opening your files for you. This most often happens with painting, drawing and picture editing programs – they tend to grab for themselves all image files, regardless of what you wanted to happen in the first place. To change the program that opens a file, right-click the file's name and then left-click **Open With > Choose Program**, scroll down the list of files until you find the program you want, check the 'Always use this program to open these files' box (if you want to make this change permanent), then click **OK**. If the program you want isn't listed click the **Other** button and locate the program.

You can use the **Open with** option to open files in a different program temporarily – just don't check the 'Always use…' option. This can be useful if you receive, say, a document which you suspect may actually be a virus – try opening with Notepad to see if that gives you any clues about the document's provenance. If it's a Microsoft Word document, open it with WordPad (on the **Start > (All) Programs > Accessories** menu) as it's better able to cope with the extra formatting codes Word creates.

Formatting And Partitioning Your Hard Disk

The hard disk is the part of your computer's hardware where your programs and data are stored. It keeps the information safe even when your PC is turned off (unlike RAM, which is where programs run – when you turn off your PC you lose everything in RAM). Most new computers come with just one hard disk, and these days it's likely to be at least 40 GB or more – probably plenty of room to store everything you'll need for a while.

There are advantages to having more than one hard disk, however. You can put temporary files on the second disk to speed up your computer (see Chapter 15), for example, plus your data files – the files that you create yourself. The advantage of doing this is that if your computer crashes badly and you need to reinstall Windows (not an uncommon occurrence), you can happily reformat your hard disk without worrying about losing any of your data (but see Chapter 17 for more information on preserving your data before attempting this).

Even if you only have one hard disk, it can be divided up into separate 'partitions' which, to Windows, appear to be different drives, each with their own letter – so, in **My Computer** you might see your main hard disk as C:, your CD-ROM drive as D: and your second hard disk partition as E:. Note, this lettering scheme may not happen automatically – depending on how your CD drives and hard disks are connected, this order may change. You can change the order via the **Disk Drives** section of Device Manager in **Control Panel > System**(**> Hardware**).

If you're installing Windows on a new machine you'll have the opportunity, with Windows XP, to create and format these partitions during the installation process. You could choose to make a 20 GB hard disk into two partitions of 10 GB each, for example, and then install Windows on the first, C:, partition and then tell all your programs to use the D: partition to store the files you create. In Windows 9x you need to create these partitions using a DOS program called fdisk, which you'll find on the boot 3.5" floppy disk that comes with the Windows CD.

Fdisk is a very powerful program – *do not* use it on a computer which has data on it you want to keep. If you erase a partition or hard disk using fdisk, you will *not* ordinarily be able to recover the information without specialised software. If you are in any doubt at all, don't use fdisk.

Also during the Windows XP installation process you'll get the chance to decide whether to use the FAT16, FAT32 or NTFS filing system for your disc. FAT stands for File Allocation Table. FAT16 was used in DOS and early versions of Windows 9x, FAT32 in Windows 98 and Me. NTFS (New Technology File System) is used in Windows NT, 2000 and XP. Which to choose? If you're using exclusively Windows XP on your computer, choose NTFS. If you're dual-booting with an earlier version of Windows 9x use FAT32 (or FAT16 if it's Windows 95). NTFS has more advanced features which give more security and encryption options than either FAT16 or FAT32. It's also more reliable and much less likely to get into a mess if you have to reboot without shutting Windows down properly (so you can wave goodbye to those irritating messages when you start up that Windows is checking your hard disk because you didn't close down properly). Don't worry if you're connecting computers over a network which have mixed FAT and NTFS filing systems – while a Windows 9x computer can't read an NTFS disk on its own computer it can do so over a network.

If you've installed Windows XP already and decide that you'd like to convert your hard disk to the NTFS format to take advantage of its extra features there is a 'convert' utility – check XP's help files for details.

213

If you want to change the size of partitions on any Windows computer after installing the OS, you need a third-party application like Partition Magic by PowerQuest, www.partitionmagic.com.

Moving Files, Folders And Applications

By default the **My Documents** folder on your computer's Desktop is on your C: drive. You can change its location by right-clicking it and then left-clicking **Properties** and changing its location in the **Target** box. When you've typed a new location, Windows will move the files it contains to the new location – so, if you typed **D:** all your document files will move to the topmost level of your D: drive.

You may need to tell other applications that their files have moved – check each program's help files for details on how to change the default file location. You'll also need to change this in each 'Profile' you have if more than one person uses the computer and each user has their own logon user name.

Missing Files

If you can't find a file, use the Windows Search feature to find it – click **Start > Search** and type in the file's name. You can also type some of the words you know it contains in the search dialog box if you can't remember the file's name, and you can search either your entire computer or just specific locations.

Keeping Your Data And Disks In Tip-Top Condition

Chapter 15 contains advice on cleaning out temporary files. There are other maintenance tasks you should perform, too.

ScanDisk

ScanDisk, under **Start > (All)Programs > Accessories > System Tools**, looks across your hard disk(s) for corrupt, damaged and misplaced files. Run this about once a week, using the 'Thorough' option to also check your entire hard disk's surface. If it starts to report lots of damaged files and 'bad sectors' this could be a sign that your hard disk is wearing out and may be about to fail. Under Windows 95, 98 and Me, ScanDisk usually fails after scanning a few per cent of the hard disk. This is because it cannot run while any other program is running. If this happens, close down *all* other programs, including those in the System Tray (next to the time display on your Taskbar). Press **Ctrl-Alt-Del** to bring up a list of other programs that are running and close all except Systray and Explorer, then run ScanDisk. You may also persuade ScanDisk to run if you restart your computer in Safe Mode (press the **F8** key on start-up). This unfortunately means that you can't schedule ScanDisk to run overnight – the best option is to set it running when you've finished work for the day.

Disk Defragmenter

Disk Defragmenter is under **Start** > **(All)Programs** > **Accessories** > **System Tools**. Think of your hard disk as being like a record with a long spiral on it where the files are saved. When Windows saves a file on to your hard disk, it puts it into the first space it finds on that 'spiral'. If you then delete that file, the space is left blank. Then when you next save a file it will take up the space left by the first file – but, if it's larger than the first one, only part goes into that space and the rest goes into the next available space. Repeat this a few hundred times with all the temporary files Windows creates and the files on your disk will soon be 'fragmented' with parts of them scattered all across the disk. Disk Defragmenter gathers up all these fragmented file parts and re-sorts them, putting whole files back together again and thus speeding up your computer a little – now it can read all of a file at once instead of hunting backwards and forwards for many little bits of it. Like ScanDisk, however, Disk Defragmenter in Windows 9x cannot tolerate running when any other program is also active, so see above for instructions on how to give it exclusive access to your computer.

Disk Cleanup

Disk Cleanup (in later versions of Windows only) will scan through your hard disk finding temporary files and other unwanted items and show you a table of how much disk space you can recover. To find it open **My Computer**, right-click your hard disk, left-click **Properties** and then click the **Disk Cleanup** button next to the pie chart of your hard disk's usage. You can also access ScanDisk and Disk Defragmenter from this dialog box, on the **Tools** tab.

NB: ScanDisk and Disk Defragmenter may or may not run normally in Windows 2000 and XP while you're doing other things. You may receive a message saying that they cannot run as they require 'exclusive access' to your hard disk and offering to schedule them to run next time you restart your computer.

Questions And Answers

Is there any way to restore files accidentally deleted from a SmartMedia card? I'm using a Fujipix 4900 with a mini USB link and Windows Me – Christmas has accidentally been erased.

There are a few programs which might help. If your card slots into a reader on your computer and you see it as a regular drive in **My Computer**, right-click it and choose **Properties** and run ScanDisk over it, which may cure the problem. Also you could give it a once-over with Norton Utilities, if you have it. If not, try DataRescue, www.datarescue.com/photorescue/purchase.htm, where you can download a demo version of the software to see if it might help. In all situations like this where you've accidentally deleted a file it's very important *not* to save any more files to the disk/card/whatever as they'll overwrite any remnants of the missing ones.

*What are all these files on my hard disk which end in **.chk**?*

They're saved fragments of other files found by ScanDisk. Open them with something like Notepad and delete if you wish.

Part 6
Security And Avoiding Trouble

Hackers, viruses, worms – they're all 'out there' somewhere waiting to attack your computer. This section of the book covers both dealing with potential threats from the outside world and how to set up your computer and the data and information you create so that when – not if – something goes wrong, you'll be ready and prepared for it. A little thought now will make the task of restoring your crashed, burned, hacked and pillaged computer back to its showroom condition as easy and painless as possible. This is the section of the book that allows you to say smug things to your friends like, 'So what sort of back-up strategy do you use then? I favour the grandfather, father, son model myself'. There are more questions at the end of each chapter which I've answered over the years which will help you to narrow down solutions to your own problems.

Backups And Archiving

This chapter, while it includes some 'troubleshooting backups' advice, is really about how to prepare for the terrible day when, after working your way through all the advice elsewhere in this book, you arrive at the conclusion that it's time to start all over again, scraping everything back down to bare metal and reinstalling it from scratch.

It cannot be stressed enough that you need to back up your important data and files for the day *when* something goes wrong – it's not a question of 'if', because hardware/software failure is an absolute certainty: even more so than death and taxes. If you use your computer for e-mailing a few friends and a little light web surfing, you may not have anything you consider valuable on it. But if you rely in any way at all on the information stored inside it – contacts (e.g. your e-mail address book), business information, even your collection of recipes – you should consider how long it would take to put it right if it was all suddenly taken away from you, for any reason whatsoever.

Backup Programs

The most obvious backup program to use with Windows is the one which comes with Windows itself. You'll usually find it under **Start > Programs > Accessories > System Tools**, unless you have the Home Edition of Windows XP which makes you hunt the program down on the original CD and install it manually. You'll find it in the **valuadd** folder.

Unfortunately for many users, each edition of Backup is not often compatible with the ones in earlier versions of Windows. This means that a set of backup data made in, say, Windows 98 can't be restored using the Backup program in Windows XP – and vice versa. Effectively, you can only use Backup to restore data to the version of Windows in which it was created. Normally this isn't a problem, but it can create difficulties when upgrading from one version of Windows to another if you want to start with a fresh installation and copy over just your data to the new setup.

This means either backing up your data manually or turning to a third-party program to do so. Here, I'll list the essential data and its normal locations you should be backing up, whether you do so manually or use some automated process to do so.

What To Back Up

1   Any documents you create – letters, invoices, spreadsheets, diary. It helps tremendously here if you keep all your documents organised and, preferably, on a separate hard disk or drive letter to your programs and Windows.

   a   If you have a chance when you buy a new machine, buy it with, say, two 40 GB hard disks instead of one 80 GB disk – even a 40 and a 20 GB setup is preferable. This allows you to install Windows and your programs on one disk and keep the other purely for data, making reinstallations and moving to a new system much, much easier in the long term.

   b   If you only have one hard disk, try organising it into two 'partitions' – although you only have one physical hard disk, it can be divided up into any number of apparently separate disks, each with their own drive letter. This arrangement would allow you to keep Windows and your programs on C: and data on D:, and if you needed to reformat C: your data would still be safe on D:. However, if your system arrives already set up, you may not have this option initially. While it's possible to repartition your existing, single hard disk into two or more 'logical drives' yourself, it involves either completely starting from scratch and reformatting your hard disk and reinstalling everything, or using third-party software to do the job, and it is probably something beginners won't want to become involved with.

c   Whether you have one disk or two, consider organising your documents logically, e.g. have a main folder called **Writing** and then sub-folders below that for **Letters, Invoices, Diary** and so on. You could even organise sub-folders below these called, for example, **1999, 2000, 2001** and so on, or **Letters to bank, Letters to landlord** and so on. This not only makes finding things easier later on, it makes your backup process easier too – whatever method you use to back things up, you need only tell it to back up the **Writing** folder and all its sub-folders, instead of hunting up and down your hard disk for those important data folders. Give files sensible names while you're at it, too – **Letter to bank re. overdraft extension May 1 2002.doc**, for example, not just **bank.doc**, which turns out to be one of several dozen with similar names when you go looking for it in a year's time.

2   E-mails – sent and received.

a   If you use Microsoft Outlook, by default your e-mails are stored in one large file called a PST, Personal folder STorage – do a search on your computer for files ending in PST (search for ***.pst**) and you'll find the location of yours. As well as your messages this contains your contacts, to-do lists, diary and other information you've typed into Outlook yourself. There's also a lot of information in the directory **C:\Documents and Settings*username* >\Application Data\Microsoft\Outlook** (where **<*username* >** is your logon name for your computer) in Windows NT, 2000 and XP, or **C:\Windows\Local Settings\Application Data\Microsoft\Outlook** in Windows 98 and Me in the following files:

i   **.dat** – Personalised menu and view settings

ii   **.fav** – Personalised Outlook Bar shortcuts

iii   **.inf** – Default program settings

iv   **.nick** – Outlook nicknames (user mail settings)

v   **.rwz** – E-mail rules

vi   **OutlPrnt** – Print styles

vii   **.rtf, .txt, .html** – User signatures (in **\Microsoft\Signatures**), stationery (in **\Microsoft\Stationery**), dictionary

viii   **.oft** – Templates (under **\Application Data\Microsoft\Templates**)

ix   **.reg** – Registry settings

221

b   If you use Outlook Express, your e-mails are stored in files ending with the letters DBX, e.g. **inbox.dbx** which contains everything currently in your Inbox. The simplest way to keep track of them is to click **Tools > Options > Maintenance > Store Folder** and put all Outlook Express folders somewhere sensible, such as on a separate hard disk, or at least where you can find them to copy them onto a CD-R or CD-RW disk. Backing up other elements of OE is even more complicated than Outlook, but luckily there's the excellent Tomsterdam website run by Tom Koch, www.tomsterdam.com with complete descriptions of what to back up and how at www.tomsterdam.com/insideOE/backup/bu_full.htm.

c   Luckily, there are a couple of programs designed to help you through the maze of backing up Outlook and Outlook Express. AJ Systems, www.ajsystems.com, makes Express Assist for backing up OE and Outback Plus for Outlook. It also has a program for Eudora backups called BackDora. All will safeguard your e-mails, address books and more – even your lists of bookmarks and Favorites from your web browser.

3   Address/contact book – e-mail addresses, telephone numbers, snail mail addresses. You may have a Windows address book (a file ending with **.wab**), a Personal Address book (ending in **.pab**), a Contacts folder (in Microsoft Outlook) and any number of others from various other programs.

4   Personalised settings for programs – personalised dictionaries (what you get when you spell-check a document and choose **Add to dictionary** when the spell-checker comes across a word it doesn't know) and changes to the toolbar itself.

a   In Microsoft Office, the personalised dictionary file is called **custom.dic** by default (you can add in and create other ones yourself if, for example, you need to use lots of legal or engineering terms).

b   The easiest way to back up Microsoft Office if you have Office 2000 or later is to use the Save My Settings wizard which you can download via office.microsoft.com/downloads. Depending on which version of Office you have, the wizard allows you to save your Office personalisations either online or on your local computer in a ***.ops** file.

5   Web browser bookmarks/Favorites. You can save your Internet Explorer Favorites and Cookies by clicking **File > Import and Export** and following the wizard's guidance. In Netscape, click **Bookmarks > Manage Bookmarks > File > Import bookmarks** (or **Export bookmarks**).

6   Your ISP settings. This is the information you need to connect to the internet via your Internet Service Provider. Open **My Computer** and then **Dial-up Networking** (**Start > Settings > Network and Dialup Connections** or **Start > Control Panel > Network Connections** in Windows 2000 and Windows XP) and

note down your username, dial-up telephone number and other settings. Your password will be shown only as a row of asterisks, thus: ************. This does *not* mean that your password is ************: Windows replaces the actual password here (and elsewhere) with asterisks to prevent others discovering it. You'll need to check your original ISP documentation for this password and you should keep this information with your regular backups.

7   Files you download, including updates for your installed hardware drivers, program updates, widgets, gadgets, pictures, documents and general internet trivia. Don't delete these downloaded installation files once you've run them in case you need to reinstall your PC's software – keep them somewhere safe. And file them as you do your documents. Have a folder called **Downloads** and then sub-folders called, for example, **Matrox** and below that **G550** if that's the make and model of your graphics card. This way, when you need to reinstall that widget you won't be wondering whether it's the file called **w2k_533.exe** or the one called **Q301625_W2K_SP3_x86_en.EXE** that you need.

Keep Track Of What You've Done

It may sound obvious and make complete sense that you'd remember what hardware and software you've installed on your computer, but in practice most people can't remember what they've done and when they did it. More importantly, a program you install today may not have any immediate untoward effects until some time later when you run another, unrelated program which promptly falls over for no apparent reason.

1   It's well worth the effort to note down somewhere you can find it again the details of what you install and when – a notebook in a drawer beside your PC is fine. A file stored on your PC itself isn't so worthwhile – it's only any good as long as your machine is working, and if you need to read the note about what it was that you installed that made it fall over in the first place you're going to be out of luck.

a   Windows Me and XP now include a 'Roll back' function which allows you to set 'System Restore' points. This means that you can undo any changes made to the computer system without affecting the data you've created (e-mails, spreadsheets, letters and so on) – but there's still no substitute for keeping a note yourself of what you've done.

b   A 'daybook' or journal of some kind – even just a stack of notes on the backs of used sheets of paper can hold everything you do – just remember to date them at the top and add some sort of heading to help looking through them.

2   Work out exactly what's in your computer.

a   When you buy a new computer, keep a copy of the order form, delivery note and any other information which came with it. This will be useful when people like me ask questions like, 'How big is the hard disk?' or 'What kind of CPU does it have?'

b   If you upgrade your computer at all, keep a similar note about what you do or have done to it.

c   You can get a 'quick and dirty' view of your PC's specification by opening the **System** section of **Control Panel** by double-clicking on it and looking on the **General** tab. This will tell you what version of Windows you're running and any service packs which have been installed (for Windows NT, 2000 and XP), to whom it's registered, what type of processor (CPU) it has and how much RAM (Random Access Memory) is fitted.

d   Inside the **System** section of **Control Panel** is also **Device Manager** (under the **Hardware** tab in Windows 2000 and XP) which will give you a full run-down on all the installed hardware. It will also tell you about any immediate problems with the various components.

e   You'll find a list of installed software under **Add/Remove Programs** in **Control Panel**. NB: Older (16-bit for the technical) programs may not be listed here or even on the **Start > Programs** menu – you'll have to trawl through the hard disk itself (open **My Computer** and double-click the C: drive in most instances) to find them.

What To Back It Up Onto

1   Tape. This is the most 'professional' and expensive way to back up your data. It involves a dedicated tape drive using one of a variety of tape formats and generations of tapes to take full and intermediate backups of your data. Tape capacities haven't kept pace with hard disk capacity over the past few years and you'll need an expensive setup to fully back up an 80 GB hard disk. It can be a very reliable way to back up systems, but tapes do wear out and need replacing at regular intervals. Popular with users of tapes is the 'grandfather, father, son' generational backup method which allows you to keep older versions of your data without requiring hundreds of tapes.

2   A second hard disk – built-in, removable or over a network. This is a reliable system which gives quickest access to backed-up data. Hard disks are liable to failure, albeit at longer intervals than most other storage media.

3   Writable or rewritable CDs or DVDs. The most permanent, long-term storage method, with CDs and DVDs being capable of lasting for 10–20 years or more. These are also eminently transportable backups, with almost all PCs now having at least a CD-ROM drive capable of reading CDs. Buy good-quality, branded disks for

224

the best performance and follow the manufacturer's recommendations for looking after them carefully for best results.

4   High-capacity removable disks, e.g. Iomega Zip or Peerless. Disks of whatever capacity with sliding doors giving access to the interior like Zips are a cause for concern for long-term or regularly-changing storage, since the admittance of dust to the interior will cause them to fail more quickly than sealed units like hard disks.

5   Standard 1.44 MB floppy disks. These are the very worst option – both low capacity and most prone to data loss and corruption. You *will* lose data stored on floppy disks sooner or later – guaranteed.

Backup Methods

'Regular' Backup

This means making one copy of absolutely everything on your hard disk – programs, data, the lot – and then making subsequent 'incremental' backups of just those things which have changed. This is how the Windows backup program works, copying the information to tape or disk. Files that have been backed up have their 'archive bit' set to show that it's been backed up. When the file is changed or a new one is created, its 'archive bit' is set to show that it needs backing up. You can see if the archive bit is set on a file by right-clicking it in Windows Explorer or **My Computer** and left-clicking **Properties** – if the **Archive** box is checked, the file has changed since the last time it was backed up (in later Windows versions you need to click the **Advanced** button at the bottom-right of the **Properties** dialog box to check this). The advantage of this method is that it can be scheduled to run when you're not using your computer, e.g. overnight; automation means you're more likely to have an up-to-date backup than relying on doing it manually. The disadvantages are that tape drives and media can be expensive; floppy disk-based backups can require hundreds, if not thousands, of disks, making them an impractical proposition.

Disk Cloning

This makes an exact copy of a hard disk, including the operating system, registry, programs, data, configuration files, absolutely everything. This is useful if you have a 'perfect' working configuration for your PC which you then save somewhere safe so that, when your machine blows up, you can restore this perfect version and carry on. It's useful if you (a) install lots of trial software (e.g. beta-test versions) and (b) can store your important personal data on another hard disk. The process of restoring the cloned hard disk will wipe out everything that you've created since making the clone. The advantages are that it is probably the quickest way of getting a system up and running again, and it can be a good way to migrate to a new hard disk or new system.

225

The disadvantages are that it only restores the system to the point when the clone was made, and restoring to a different machine may be problematical if there are large differences in hardware.

Manual Backups

This means manually copying the data you create and any important system configuration files to a safe place. This relies on you having the original media – floppy disks, CDs, DVDs – for your software and knowing exactly what it is you need to back up to get back to where you are now.

System Restore

Third-party versions of this have been available for a while, and Microsoft introduced it in Windows Me and it features in Windows XP, too. This combines features from disk cloning and regular backup programs by taking regular 'snapshots' of your hard disk and allowing you to take snapshots yourself. This means that you could 'snapshot' your hard disk before installing some software you suspect may give problems and, if it doesn't work out, restore the system back to its starting point before the new software messed things up. The advantages are that it can be useful for wiping out mistakes and can be set to work in the background. The disadvantages are that it can take up huge amounts of hard disk space and system resources; if the hard disk with the system and the snapshots is one and the same, its failure will lose everything plus the backups if you're relying solely on them. Use of this feature in Windows Me and XP is well documented in the Windows Help files.

Backup Software

1   For 'regular' backups: Windows Backup; Dantz Retrospect, www.dantz.com; Veritas, www.veritas.com (a range of products available).

2   For 'cloning' backups: Drive Image, www.powerquest.com/driveimage; Norton Ghost, www.symantec.com/sabu/ghost/ghost_personal; Roxio Take Two, www.roxio.com/en/products/ecdc (comes with Easy CD Creator 5.1 and later).

3   Manual backups: WinZip, winzip.com, and PKZip, www.pkzip.com, will compress files and folders into more manageable sizes.

4   System restore: Windows System Restore in Me and XP; Roxio Go Back, www.roxio.com/en/products/goback/index.html.

Backup Strategies

Even more important than working out what to back up and what to back it up onto is setting up a backup system which will keep your files safe and provoke minimum interruption to you and your life and/or business when it does all go wrong. This means that, as well as taking backups, you need to work out how often you need to do so and what you're then going to do with the backed up data, i.e. where you're going to store the tapes or disks the backup process produces. Work through the process in the following steps:

1   How much of your work, data and files can you afford to lose? If the answer is 'none', then you need to back it all up constantly to a place where you could instantly and immediately carry on with your next keystroke without anyone noticing a difference. While this sort of option is available, it's not cheap to do or easy to implement, involving complicated technologies like disk-mirroring and leased lines. It's more likely you'd want to work along something like the following lines: as you create documents in, say, Microsoft Office have the AutoRecover function set to save your typing and other inputs at regular intervals. By default this is set to 10 minutes, but modern PCs can easily cope with setting this to as little as one minute (**Tools > Options > Save in Word**). This means that if your PC crashes, the most you could lose would be a minute's worth of typing. For programs that don't have auto-save options you need to remember the maxim: Back up early and often. Don't, whatever you do, type something for an hour or two without saving it unless you're prepared to lose it all.

2   Once you've determined how often you're saving information locally to your hard disk (*never* to a floppy disk as your first-line file-saving strategy), the next step is to work out how frequently you need to back up that hard disk. Now, hard disk failures are measured in tens, if not hundreds, of thousands, of hours 'MTBF' – Mean Time Between Failure. Which, when you work it out, means at least several years of average usage before it falls over. However, the key word here is 'Mean' – i.e. some disks fail after a few hours; some are still going millions of hours later. The odds are that yours will last several years, but you never know and so it makes sense to copy the data off elsewhere at regular intervals – again, based on the notion of how long it would take you to recreate everything since your backup – and how much that process would cost. If you have Windows 2000 or XP you can use its Synchronization Manager to keep copies of any or all of your documents on two or more machines – you'll find full details of how it works in the Windows help files. Otherwise, think of using a second hard disk, a removable large capacity floppy disk such as an Iomega Zip disk, a writable or rewritable CD or even, as a last resort, 1.44 MB 3.5" floppy disks (preferably a couple of duplicate sets if you're relying on floppies).

3   So, you've organised backing up what you're working on right now, you've

organised backing up the work you did today, now you need to work on backing up the information you created this week/month and storing it somewhere safe for when your home/office is burgled and the backups are stolen along with your computer. If you're a posh, rich business you'll employ a company which collects your backup tapes each day and stores them in a bomb-proof shelter deep in the heart of the Rocky Mountains. If you're a regular mortal, try arranging with a friend to swap backup disks/tapes with them at regular intervals – once a week or once a month, again based on how long it would take you to recreate the information on those backup disks.

4   Online backup. I categorise 'online backup' all on its own as it combines many of the elements from other backup strategies and methodologies. The basic premise is that your essential information is copied off your PC to a safe location via your internet connection, and you can decide what's copied and how often the process takes place. The process isn't necessarily cheap and it relies on you having a fast, always-on internet connection to be efficient. It will work with slow dial-up connections but the amount of data you can transfer may be more limited. There are dozens, if not hundreds, of companies offering this service now – do a Google search for **Online backup** and you'll see for yourself. The worry with this process is that, if you rely on it and the company offering the service goes bust, how do you get your data back? You'll also want to look carefully into the reliability and trustworthiness of any company you trust with your data.

Questions And Answers

I hope to keep my data and programs secure (as does everyone, I suppose) and I wondered if it is possible for me (or a specialist) to fit a second hard drive in preference to a Zip drive or CD rewriter? What are the pros and cons?

Fitting a hard disk is relatively simple – turn the machine off, open the case, slot the drive into a spare place in the chassis, connect up the data and power cables and away you go (paying due attention to whether you want it to be a master or slave drive and on the same channel as your original drive or, preferably, on the second IDE channel). It will perform backups very quickly indeed, orders of magnitude faster than tape or a CD writer. However, where hard disks fall down is in the case of 'what to do when the house is burning down' – being fixed into the case of your PC, they're less than portable and get-at-able. In this case Zips and CDs are much better. Also, you can send them 'off-site' too – send a backup CD or Zip drive to a friend and keep a copy of his in your house, so you're both covered in the worst-case scenario. Personally I now prefer writable CDs to Zip disks, because of their cheapness and ubiquity of machines which can read them. Don't forget hard disk caddies, too – these allow you to slot hard disks in and out of your PC at will (usually when it's turned off, unless you've got loads of money).

I have purchased a new machine running Windows 98. My old machine was running Windows 3.11. I tried to use backup diskettes made on the old machine to restore on the new but they seem to be incompatible with the Windows 98 software. Is there any way around this problem?

The Backup program in Windows 9x can't restore files from earlier versions of Backup – you have to use the **Restore.exe** or **Msbackup.exe** programs which you'll find on your Windows CD-ROM. First, read the **Lfnbk.txt** file in the **Admin\ Apptools\Lfnback** folder on the Windows CD-ROM. The **Restore.exe** program is for backups made with MS-DOS 5.0 and is in the **Other\Oldmsdos** folder. To restore backups created with the backup programs included with MS-DOS 6.x (which includes those made with Windows 3.xx), use the **Msbackup.exe** program in the **Other\Oldmsdos\ Msbackup** folder on the Windows CD-ROM. Run it by copying all the files from the folder to a folder on your hard disk, then double-click the **Msbackup.exe** file in Windows Explorer to start it. Details on restoring files are in its help files.

How can I put a shortcut for the Backup on my desktop on my computer using Windows 95?

Right-click **Start**, left-click **Open**, double-click **Programs** > **Accessories** > **System Tools**, right-click and hold **Backup**, drag it to the desktop, let go and left-click **Create shortcut here**.

For reasons for which I won't bother you I recently had to do a clean install of Windows 98. I thought that I'd backed up all my data before doing this – indeed, I had apart from all my Outlook Express e-mail addresses. I have managed to get most of these back by various means but I wonder whether you can let me know how these addresses are stored in case I have to do it again? Incidentally, I was surprised how much extra hard disk space I found after doing this – must have been a lot of clutter.

Have a look at Express Assist (www.ajsystems.com/oexhome.html), which has been recommended to me recently along with A J System's version of the same program for backing up Microsoft Outlook. There is a free Microsoft Backup add-in for Outlook (available via office.microsoft.com/downloads), but not for Outlook Express. Express Assist (and the Outlook version, called Outback Plus) will back up not only your mail folders and/or allow you to synchronise the OE/Outlook message folders on two machines, it'll also save the message rules in both programs and in Outlook save your signature files, your address book and remind you to perform the backup at regular intervals. The programs will also save your Internet Explorer Favorites and cookies files. Very useful.

229

Q *A few years ago I bought a McAfee virus program and it came with an extremely useful backup program whereby you could schedule automatic backups after a set period of no activity. However, it only dealt with filenames of 8.3 as in DOS. I am now after the equivalent which will cope with longer filenames and McAfee has said that it does not plan to bring out a version. Do you know of any program that will do this?*

A If you're using Windows, you'll find a Backup program is included with it (somewhere on the **Start > Programs > Accessories** menu). If you have a later version of Windows 9x or the 'Plus' pack installed, you'll also have the Scheduler program (look around the same menu) which will allow you to set the backup to run whenever you like.

Q *I have a program on my system which a friend has loaded on and I would like to make a copy, although I don't have access to the original CD. I was hoping to make a copy straight from my computer but have no idea where to start and was hoping you could help? The CD-ROM is a brand new CD-recordable made by Philips if that helps.*

A The fact that you don't have access to the original CD and that the program was installed by a friend indicates that what you have here is a 'pirate' version of the program – i.e. one which you haven't paid for. If it's your friend's program and they're using it on their computer, you are almost certainly breaking the law by using it on your machine at the same time. If this isn't the case and you've simply lost the CD, what you actually want to do is make a backup of your software in case something goes wrong. The regular backup software which comes with Windows probably won't recognise your CD for backup purposes, but check what came with the drive to see if anything was included. Check out the utilities available from www.cd-tools.com.

Q *Is there an easy way to save old folders from Outlook Express on a floppy so that I can access them via Outlook Express if I need to look something up? Surely there's some logical way to 'store' messages. I know one could use Windows Explorer to copy out the subdirectory, then re-copy it back in to access it, but that seems a long work-around. One would think **File > Export** would be for this purpose, but sadly it only dead-ends into MS Exchange or MS Outlook.*

A You're right that the **File > Export** option in Outlook Express is rather limited. However, you can do as you suggest – save the relevant folder (or even individual OE folders such as your Inbox by copying all the files which end in **.dbx** in your OE folder) to a disk. You shouldn't, however, be keeping *any* important files *only* on a floppy disk – they're much, much less reliable than your hard disk, so use them just for backup purposes, if that. Personally I only ever use them now for transferring files. In the latest versions of OE you can move the actual folders themselves off your main (usually C:) drive to another hard disk from within OE (click **Tools** > **Options** > **Maintenance** > **Store Folder**) which means that if your main disk suffers a crash you'll still have your mail folders kept safe.

Q *Is it possible to run Microsoft Backup to a CD-RW? I have tried but after leaving it running overnight it still had not processed any data onto CD although it showed files going across. Any ideas please, or software which will run Backup to CD.*

A Since you used the form on my website to ask your question, I know that you also have Adaptec's CD-writing software – use this. There are rumours that future versions of Microsoft's Backup program will support CD writers, but the current ones don't, even the one in Windows XP.

Q *I have set Task Scheduler to run automatic backups but it won't run automatically. I have checked that VB Scripting Host is installed, which I believe is required, but it won't run. I am using MS Backup and it runs fine manually. Any bright ideas or have I just missed something obvious?*

A You're missing the obvious: Microsoft Backup won't run unattended, at least in any version earlier than Windows 2000 – the version of Backup which comes free with Windows 98 requires you to be there to click buttons and start the backup job. What you'll find is that Scheduler will start the Backup program but not the job itself. Which isn't much use, I'm afraid. Still, if you think that's bad, wait until you read the official Microsoft 'resolution' for this problem: 'To resolve this issue, upgrade to a backup program that supports completely unattended backup jobs.' So now you know.

Q *I've noticed in a few of your mailings and recently on your message board (www.drkeyboard.net) that you advise against keeping files on floppy disks. Yet dating back to the days when I used an Amstrad 8256 I've kept everything on floppy disks and not lost a single word. Surely if the hard disk on my new computer crashes I will lose everything? Whereas if I lose the information on a floppy disk, I only lose that disk's worth of data?*

A You're correct as far as you go. What you haven't realised is that you are in fact orders of magnitude more likely to suffer a floppy disk 'crash' than one on your hard disk – and, if you haven't lost anything going right back to the days of the 8256 then you've been very, very lucky indeed. Floppy disks are fine for backing up the data on your hard disk, although these days I'd advise writing a CD-R or CD-RW disc instead. If you do use floppies for backups, make several copies of the same data on several different disks. Since floppies readily allow dust in through their sliding covers, and can be subject to passing magnetic fields affecting the disks inside the plastic casings, they are inherently unsafe.

I am looking for a foolproof method for comprehensive data backup and instant disaster recovery for my laptop. My wish is for <1 GB of external memory – Pocket Drive PCMCIA H/D or similar that is small and will conveniently connect with my laptop, and then using some clever software, copy my complete drive so that in an emergency I can boot from that medium with all my programs, data, settings and drivers intact. PowerQuest Drive Space 5 appears to only act with CD formats. Dantz Retrospect Express Backup seems a little more hopeful but I need confirmation. I would have thought most laptop users would welcome a complete hardware/software package they can plug in and forget. I've already lost all my data in a complete hard drive failure and a stall during Windows boot-up, which after trying other options, necessitated a format and reinstall.

I've installed Configsafe Complete Recovery V4.0 from Unosoft which backs up all the system essentials but on the same hard drive. Norton Anti-Virus 2001 surprised me recently during a regular update by asking to create a new rescue disk. It recognised I had a Zip drive connected and proceeded to copy Windows to a Zip disk and data to a floppy to make the arrangement bootable before successfully testing the system. It was very slow and not ideal for copying programs, data and drivers.

You could just partition your hard disk into two and use the second partition to keep your data and, if you wished, a copy of the first hard disk – Norton Ghost is the application I use for this purpose. It makes an exact copy of your HD and can be run from a floppy disk, so if you trashed your Windows installation you could just Ghost it back from the second partition. Of course, this wouldn't work if your HD itself was broken – but then neither would any other solution, short of replacing the HD and starting again. HD failures, these days, are not very common though. You could use Ghost in conjunction with a PCMCIA/PC Card hard disk to make an identical copy of your original HD, but this isn't a very cheap solution. You could look into plug-in CD or even DVD recorders – Backpack make some very good models now, and you could use one of these to back up all the contents of your HD. All that said, though, I think you'd be better off with a second HD partition for data which you back up regularly using one of the above methods, rather than trying to carry around a permanent clone of your HD.

Chapter 18

Computer Security And Safety

In This Chapter

- ➤ What are viruses, trojans and worms?
- ➤ Anti-virus software
- ➤ Online security threats
- ➤ Things you can do yourself
- ➤ What's a firewall?
- ➤ What to do if you think you're 'under attack'
- ➤ Microsoft updates
- ➤ Other product updates
- ➤ Testing the security of your computer
- ➤ What information to give out
- ➤ Keeping the kids out of your files
- ➤ Safe surfing for kids
- ➤ How to verify that someone is who they say they are/prove that you are who you say you are
- ➤ Spam

It's a sad fact of life that, as soon as you connect your computer to the internet, someone is going to try to get into it for their own nefarious purposes. This chapter looks at securing your computer *before* you put yourself at risk, even before you connect to the internet. In a worst-case scenario if you connect certain types of computer systems to the internet without any additional protection over and above that which comes included with Windows, it can become infected with a virus, trojan or worm.

What Are Viruses, Trojans And Worms?

Viruses And Worms

Viruses are named after the tiny organisms that cause illnesses in humans and other animals because these small programs, when run, do something to change the way your computer works without your permission. Like viruses, worms can replicate themselves from computer to computer. In the same way that a human virus can give you a cold or kill you, computer viruses may be as harmless as just displaying a message on your screen or as harmful as destroying some of your computer's hardware. They also have the ability to replicate and reproduce themselves, replacing files on your computer with a copy of the infected file or spreading out across networks and via the internet, perhaps via e-mail.

Trojan Horses

Named after the wooden horse the Greeks fooled the Trojans with, a trojan horse program insinuates itself onto your computer by pretending to be something harmless like a screensaver or a picture of a celebrity attached to an e-mail. Once installed, it executes malicious code that can do any number of things – destroy data, forward your files on to someone else, send on copies of itself or give its creator access to and control over your PC.

Hoaxes

Although not strictly regarded as viruses, hoax virus messages can have many of the same characteristics. Almost always spread by e-mail, they are replicated by users who don't bother checking up on them first and forward them on to 'everyone they know', i.e. every address in their e-mail address book. As many people don't understand that what they're spreading is a hoax in the first place it means that you can end up receiving a hoax message which has, in the body of the text, hundreds or even thousands of e-mail addresses, and there is a school of thought that some of these messages are spread by spammers (senders of unwanted commercial e-mails) as a way of 'harvesting' others' e-mail addresses. They hope that, eventually, the hoax message will eventually find its way back to them complete with lots of lovely new e-mail addresses for them to spam. Whatever you do, don't forward any warning about viruses to anyone without first checking very, very carefully indeed that it is genuine. Most virus warnings aren't spread this way, if you think about it, and if you follow the instructions later in this chapter the odds are that you won't have a virus on your system that you don't already know about. You can check the genuineness of a virus warning on the Symantec website at www.symantec.com/avcentre/hoax.html or at hoaxbusters.ciac.org, which is run by the US Department of Energy and CIAC (Computer Incident Advisory Capability). There's also www.vmyths.com run by Rob Rosenberger and which is independent of all anti-virus companies. Details of the more common ones are also listed in the 'Virus and Security Warnings' forum on my website at www.drkeyboard.net.

Anti-virus Software

Hopefully it does what it says on the tin: it prevents your computer from being infected by viruses – and worms and trojans. Anti-virus programs work in a number of different ways.

1   They include lists of known viruses – virus 'signatures' – which they scan for through all the files on your computer and in all files which arrive on your PC, whether via e-mail, over a network, on disks, in installation programs and any other way. If they recognise a file as actually being a virus they will swing into action, preventing the virus from running by deleting it or putting it into 'quarantine' – a safe area of your computer where the virus file is kept from doing any harm.

2   They watch for files and programs doing the sort of thing viruses are known to do such as trying to save information to certain parts of your computer's hard disk, deleting or renaming certain types of files or accessing your e-mail program and/or your e-mail address book.

Because new viruses are appearing all the time, it's important to keep updating your anti-virus software. Even AV software you installed last month will be out of date, and you should follow instructions inside the program to update it at something like weekly intervals. If you receive a lot of e-mails, consider updating your AV software daily. One recent virus had the ability to automatically disable the commonest anti-virus programs if they hadn't been updated to make them aware of it. Check in your particular program for details on how to do this and schedule the updates to take place at appropriate intervals. Also, don't run your update program just once – Symantec, for example, recommends that you keep running its LiveUpdate program to update all your Norton Anti-Virus, Firewall and other programs until you get the message that 'No updates are available'. Some updates aren't downloaded to your computer until you've installed an earlier one, so doing this ensures that your machine is really up to date.

Which To Buy

1   Norton Anti-Virus. Now owned by Symantec, www.symantec.com. There are a number of different versions of NAV available, depending on what sort of computer system you use. The latest version for home and SOHO users is Norton Anti-Virus 2003. I've used NAV extensively myself and it works very well. Symantec offers an online anti-virus scan at security2.norton.com/us/home.asp, where you can also download a trial version of NAV (click the 'Symantec Security Check for Home Users' link).

2   McAfee VirusScan, www.mcafee.com, which offers both online scans and software you can use to scan your computer when you're not connected.

3   AVG from Grisoft, www.grisoft.com, is free for personal use although there's no support offered for this version. Again, I've used this product myself for some time and it works at least as well as the paid-for Norton Anti-Virus.

4   Sophos, www.sophos.com, sells its products only to large companies and corporations. You may come across it if your ISP has installed its e-mail scanning software.

5   Trend Micro's PC-cillin 2002, www.antivirus.com is also available as a 30-day 'Evaluation' download.

6   Dr Solomon's, www.drsolomons.com was once the doyen of anti-virus software programs. Now it's part of the McAfee group, although still sold as a separate product.

Online Security Threats

There are potential security problems for you both in the sites you visit while you're surfing the web and in what others are trying to do to your computer while you're connected to the internet.

Safe Surfing

This means being aware of the websites you're looking at and what they're telling you. Look at the address of a site in the **Address** toolbar in your web browser when you've clicked on a link or typed in an address and clicked **Go** or hit **Enter**. For example, when you type in www.chateaukeyboard.com/diary you will be redirected straight away to www.chateaukeyboard.com/2002, my diary for the current year – type in the first address and you'll always be taken to the latest version. This is a genuine redirection, but sometimes a site address may have been 'hijacked' and taken over by someone with nefarious purposes in mind. Also, you'll find that many well-known site addresses, if slightly mis-spelled or mis-typed, will take you to an altogether more unsavoury location than you'd intended. Check what you type carefully, particularly the final portion – the **.com** version of a site may be very different to the **.net** version. This may be more of an annoyance than an actual danger unless the final destination site either tries to take money from you – by pretending to be a commercial website, for example, where you want to buy something. You may also receive e-mails containing strange-looking addresses like 1698542185/yourispname.com/confirm.htm which claim to be, for example, your ISP asking for confirmation of your credit card number. These are almost always fakes and cons – telephone your ISP if you're in any doubt at all. Other potential 'fake' addresses may take the form www.xxxx.someothername.com where **xxxx** is the 'real' place you wanted to visit. URLs read from right to left in the main – first, the **com** tells you that it's a 'commercial' website, then the name immediately to its left tells you who owns the site. Anything between this name and 'www' is a subsection of this site. If the address were, for example, www.microsoft.badperson.com it would not take you to the Microsoft website but to the **badperson** website. Even if the site you arrived at looked like the Microsoft website, it wouldn't be. However, you may see addresses like support.microsoft.com – which *is* a genuine Microsoft website – it's the technical support site. Remember, read the address from right to left to determine who owns it. Finally, be very, very suspicious of URLs with the @ symbol in them. Normally these belong only in e-mail addresses and not those of websites. For example, try typing into your web browser's address the following: www.microsoft.com@drkeyboard.com. You won't go to Microsoft's website but to the Dr Keyboard website – remember, read addresses from right to left.

Keeping Hackers Out

The second area of danger is people trying to access your computer while you're connected to the internet. The risk of someone trying to do this is much greater if you have an 'always-on' connection such as ADSL or a cable modem, but the threat is still a real one even if you connect using a modem and your telephone line. 'Hackers' want to gain access to your computer for a number of reasons. They may find something interesting on it, but this isn't usually the main reason – they could use your credit card number and other personal information – but mostly they want access to the computing resources it offers. Many trojan horses and viruses are designed to give the author control over your computer so they can store information on it – many people have discovered that their PC is an unwitting 'server' of illegal software, music files and worse – or use it in conjunction with dozens or hundreds of other similarly compromised computers to launch an attack on another computer system. These are the so-called DoS, Denial of Service, attacks where, basically, hundreds of computers are used to flood a well-known website like Yahoo! or CNN in the hope that this will cause the site to crash. There are even rumours of various government and terrorist organisations using such tactics. Whatever the reason, you need to take some basic precautions against this happening and, as well as running anti-virus software (see earlier in this chapter) you should also invest in firewall software and/or hardware.

Things You Can Do Yourself

Many of the security threats posed while you're surfing the web come through 'scripts' and 'components' which, simply put, are like small bits of programs. These may be things like Java applets – a game, for example – Flash animations or ActiveX components. ActiveX is a Microsoft technology a little like Java which allows quite complicated programs to run in a web browser, or even run on their own. These scripts, programs and applets can be activated by you just visiting a website and some of them are malicious – they'll try to install trojan horses, viruses and so on on your PC. You can guard against them by turning off scripting in your Internet Explorer and disallowing ActiveX components from running. In IE click **Tools > Internet Options > Security**, make sure the 'Internet' globe is selected at the top then click the **Custom level** button at the bottom. Now check either **Disable** or **Prompt** for the ActiveX controls. If you're very paranoid, select **Disable** for all of them. If you're not quite so suspicious check **Prompt** for the signed components and **Disable** for unsigned ones, or choose **Prompt** for all. Scroll down to the '**Scripting**' section where you'll see the same options again. OK your way out. You can add sites you know to be trustworthy to the 'Trusted sites' list on the **Security** tab of this **Internet Options** dialog box and give them permission to run ActiveX components and scripts if you wish. You will find that very many sites use scripting and a large number use ActiveX components of one kind or another – Flash, for example, counts as one, and you may get fed up having to confirm every time you visit such a site that you want these things to run, so adjust the settings to a comfortable level for yourself. I set signed ActiveX controls to **Prompt** and disable unsigned ones. 'Signed' means that the author of the component can be verified, and it is, generally speaking, safe to run such components.

What's A Firewall?

Named after the metal barrier between the passenger and engine compartments of a car (which was designed, originally, to protect passengers if the engine caught fire), a computer firewall is designed to control both incoming and outgoing traffic – information – on your computer. It should only allow specific programs to access the internet and check all incoming traffic – e-mails, websites and so on – to make sure you asked to receive it and that it's allowed onto your computer. Every program you use which connects to the internet – your e-mail program, your web browser, your anti-virus program when it checks automatically to see if it needs to update itself, programs like the Real Networks music and video player – will need to be given 'permission' to do so by your firewall software. This means that, unless you've specifically given a program permission to access the internet, it can't do so, and this in turn means that you should be warned about trojan horse software trying to 'phone home' and tell its creator that it's invaded your machine. Strictly speaking, there are two types of firewalls – those that check outgoing traffic and 'intrusion detection software', which detects unauthorised attempts to access your computer.

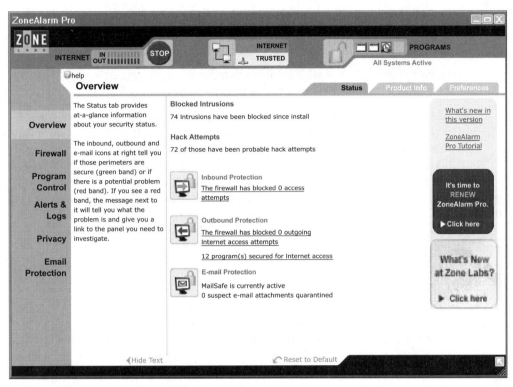

Figure 18.1 ZoneAlarm 'Overview' screen

1   ZoneAlarm, www.zonealarm.com, from Zone Labs is one of the best-known personal firewall programs, and is available as a free-for-personal-use version as well as the paid-for 'Pro' version. I've used this one myself for a considerable period of time – see Figure 18.1 – and it works well.

Figure 18.1 shows the 'Overview' screen from ZoneAlarm version 3.x. This gives an overall view of the current security status of your system, showing that no intrusion attempts have been detected ('Inbound protection'), no unauthorised connections from your computer to the internet have been attempted but that 12 different programs are allowed to access the internet ('Outbound protection') and that ZoneAlarm is monitoring your incoming e-mail ('E-mail protection'). This means that ZoneAlarm is protecting you against attacks on three levels: first, from hackers who attempt to connect to and use your computer for nefarious purposes while it's connected to the internet; second, it protects you against the eventuality that someone has, somehow and despite all your precautions, managed to infiltrate your PC and place on it a trojan program which is allowing them to control it in some way; and third it's watching your incoming e-mails in case any of them might be compromised by including the sort of trojan program which

239

would allow a hacker to take control of it. Other screens show details of attacks or attempted attacks, which programs you're given permission to access the internet (ZoneAlarm asks permission for each one trying to do so) and so on.

2   Norton Personal Firewall 2002 from Symantec, www.symantec.com. This is a fairly new release from the makers of the famous Norton Anti-Virus.

3   BlackICE PC Protection (formerly BlackICE Defender) from Network Ice, www.networkice.com used to be an intrusion detection program only, but now manufacturer Network Ice has added features to detect applications trying to access the internet or other machines on your local network. When installed (on a guaranteed virus-free machine) it takes a 'snapshot' of all the programs on your PC and can then check to see if they've been modified or if another application pretending to be an 'innocent' program is trying to access the internet.

4   McAfee. Like Norton, McAfee, www.mcafee.com, makes a firewall program, Personal Firewall Plus.

5   TINY Software, www.tinysoftware.com, makes the Tiny Personal Firewall. Like ZoneAlarm, it's free for personal use.

6   Microsoft Windows XP comes with a rudimentary built-in firewall. Open **Network Connections** in **Control Panel**, right-click your ISP connection icon and left-click **Properties > Advanced** to find it. Note, ICF, Internet Connection Firewall only protects you against incoming attacks. Unlike some other firewalls, notably ZoneAlarm, it doesn't prevent outgoing connections at all, so if your computer were infected with a trojan or worm ICF wouldn't prevent it sending out any information it wanted to. Also, it doesn't show any information at all about incoming attacks, apart from a pretty cryptic log file, and doesn't offer any help in tracking down those would-be attackers should you feel vengeful. Also, if you connect from home to an office network using VPN (Virtual Private Network) ICF may interfere with this.

7   Hardware firewalls. These are serious pieces of kit and used to be very expensive. With the home and SOHO computing revolution and the advent of cheap, always-on, broadband connections they're becoming more and more popular, especially with those who have small networks all sharing a single internet connection. These usually connect between your PC and the socket connecting you to your ISP via ADSL, cable modem or whatever. Most popular brands include Cisco – at the high, expensive end – www.cisco.com, Sonicwall, www.sonicwall.com, and Linksys, www.linksys.com.

What To Do If You Think You're 'Under Attack'

You will be surprised at the number of potential 'attacks' on your computer detected by your firewall software. Many will be false positives, in fact, echoes coming back from sites you've visited. Also, if you're using a dial-up connection to the internet it's possible that your computer will receive echoes back from websites the previous user of your current IP address visited, accounting for the fact that you're receiving apparent attacks from websites and addresses you've never heard of. But there will be some that make you suspicious and, while you're safe if your firewall and anti-virus software are working and up to date, you may want to just check to see who that person is, especially if you're receiving repeated 'attacks'. There are, of course, websites where you can find out who owns a domain name or even a particular IP address. Try www.netsol.com/cgi-bin/whois/whois and www.internic.org.uk for domain names, and SamSpade, www.samspade.org for domain names, IP addresses, 'obfusticated' URLS (like those mentioned earlier in this chapter in the format http://16985412542) and more interesting things you never knew you wanted to know.

Microsoft Updates

As well as keeping your anti-virus software updated, you should also check for updates to your Microsoft and other software. As the biggest target around, Microsoft tends to attract more attention from the 'hacker' community than other software manufacturers – more, probably, than all the rest added together. Hopefully this means that it's also more closely watched by the good guys, and you should pay attention to updates and security 'patches' (fixes for security 'holes' in software) released for your particular mix of programs.

1   Visit windowsupdate.microsoft.com and click the 'Product updates' link. This will scan your computer (without sending any information to Microsoft) and work out if you need to install any updates. Like your anti-virus software updates, you should re-run the 'Product updates' link until no more updates are available, since some updates won't be shown as available or necessary until after you've installed an earlier one. The Windows Update site divides the available updates into several categories. First, and most important, are 'Critical updates' which affect the security of your machine. Other updates are optional, but you should consider 'Critical updates' compulsory and always install them. You may also be offered the option to install the 'Critical updates notification' program – this connects to the Windows Update site when you're online and automatically checks whether there are any important security updates available for your PC. It's well worth installing it. Note that it may add an item to the 'Scheduled updates' program (which usually appears in the System Tray) which apparently says that 'Critical updates' is trying to connect to the internet every 15 minutes. This isn't actually the case: it

only connects once a day. When you're online after installing the notification program it will check when you go online at intervals to see if there are any critical updates available for your computer and then pop up a notification 'bubble' in the Systray – follow the instructions to install what's being recommended and this will help you stay free from harm.

2   If you have Windows NT4, Windows 2000 or Windows XP you can use the MBSA (Microsoft Base Security Analyser) utility. See www.microsoft.com/security for details and to download it. MBSA goes beyond just telling you what security updates can be installed on your computer (although it does do that), informing you about what's available even before it gets on to the Windows Update website in the form of 'Hotfixes'. It also looks at all aspects of security on your PC including advising you about 'insecure' passwords, who's allowed to log on to it and more. Also, if you have a network of computers MBSA will scan any or all of the computers from one machine. It's well worth running if you have one of the supported versions of Windows. Note that MBSA doesn't run on Windows 95, 98 or Me.

Other Product Updates

Many other program makers are assiduous about updating their software and 'patching' (repairing) security holes in their programs. Others, unfortunately, aren't, relying on the fact that, as the biggest target around, Microsoft will draw all the fire. Pay close attention to any update bulletins issued by makers of any software you use. Visit their website regularly to check for updates – put a note in your diary to remind yourself – and, if they have one, sign up for any e-mail advisory lists they run about such matters.

Testing The Security Of Your Computer

How, you may wonder, can you check to see if all these security measures you've taken are working? How can you be sure that you need any of them in the first place? There are a number of websites where you can test just how secure your computer is, both against intruders and from internal attacks, e.g. from virus-laden e-mails.

1   Gibson Research, grc.com, is run by veteran computer expert Steve Gibson. While he's not shy about promoting his talents and has, on more than one occasion, been castigated for his over-enthusiastic denunciations, Steve runs a very useful website where you can not only test the security of your machine, but you can also find lots of good advice on how to make it more secure. Run his 'Shields Up!' and 'Probe My Ports' tests to start with – if you've not taken any security precautions yet you may well be frightened into doing something immediately.

2   Hacker Whacker, www.hackerwhacker.com. This isn't as thorough or as easy to use

as Steve Gibson's site, and once you've had your 'free trial' – actually just a (very) cut-down version of their full for-sale product – you have to pay to use the full service. But it's a useful test to run – when it comes to computer security you're wise to adopt a belt-braces-and-another-belt-just-in-case approach.

3   Security Space, www.securityspace.com, is, like Hacker Whacker, mainly a paid-for subscribers website. There are some free security tools including one which allows you to probe any website for its basic settings and details, and a 'whois' lookup service to check who owns a domain name or IP address.

4   PC Flank, www.pcflank.com/about.htm offers a battery of tests for your browser and PC, including tests to detect if your PC is already infected with certain trojan programs and how much personal information your web browser may reveal about you.

There are also a couple of sites which will test the security of your personal e-mail.

1   Jason's Toolbox, www.jasons-toolbox.com/test-defenses.asp, will send you a 'test' series of e-mails loaded with harmless 'viruses' designed to probe the security of your e-mail program, whatever it is. The viruses are actually harmless files but they will show up vulnerabilities in your program and give guidance on how to close the loopholes.

2   The GFI e-mail security test at www.gfi.com/emailsecuritytest also sends you 'test' e-mails containing harmless 'viruses' to probe your PC's vulnerabilities. They will show whether or not your e-mail program is set to allow potentially harmful programs and scripts to run and point you to ways to prevent this happening.

What Information To Give Out

You will be amazed at the information people want about you when you start browsing around the world wide web: not just your e-mail address but your name, address and telephone number. People want to know your age, your sex, your favourite author/pop singer/film star and your inside leg measurement. In short, people want to know *everything* about you. They do this 'profiling', as it's called, either to better tailor their own services to their audience or, more likely, to give advertisers more information about their clients and readers. Sometimes the information you give out will be in return for a service they provide to you – tell them a little about yourself and a newspaper website will remain free, for example. Sometimes you'll find the information being collected intrusive but you may have no choice about handing it over if you want to get something. You are the only one who can make up your mind about this. And sometimes you'll have no idea about what information you're handing over – or who's collecting it.

E-mail Addresses

Most people who provide you with information or an online service will want your e-mail address. Sometimes, like on the Dr Keyboard message board, it's a security measure to prevent access to undesirables. In my case, I collect 'real' e-mail addresses and verify that they're real by sending the user's password to that address – you can't post on the board without having a real e-mail address. I guarantee not to use your address for any nefarious purpose, as do most people, but not everyone is as honest as me. It can be a good idea to set up a second, 'throwaway' e-mail address on a free service such as Hotmail, www.hotmail.com, or Yahoo!, www.yahoo.com, or, if your ISP gives you more than one e-mail address, to use one of your 'spare' ones when you sign up for things online. Then, you need only check the alternative address when you're expecting a password or other instructions to be e-mailed to you, keeping your 'personal' e-mail address private and secret. If you own your own domain name you will probably have unlimited 'forwarding' addresses – so, if your domain name is drkeyboard.com you can have help@drkeyboard.com and info@drkeyboard.com but, normally, when anyone types anything before the @ sign it will always be forwarded to one, default address. So you could use this to identify specific people to whom you have to give an e-mail address. I know that if I receive unwanted spam addressed to company@drkeyboard.com where company is the name of an online service to which I've had to give an e-mail address, this means that they have sold my e-mail address on against my wishes.

Credit Card Numbers

If you want to buy something online, at some point you're going to have to hand over your credit card number, and there are three main considerations.

1   Does the site use SSL (Secure Socket Layer) technology? This means that when you send your credit card number off to the seller, it will be encrypted and, in the unlikely event of someone intercepting it, they couldn't read the number. You can usually tell whether or not a site has SSL security by the small 'locked' padlock on the status bar at the bottom of your Internet Explorer screen. Also, the page's address is likely to begin with https:// rather than just http://. In fact, there's no known instance of a credit card number being stolen while it's in transit across the internet. All recorded credit card frauds have happened when someone has stolen numbers and used them fraudulently online or when the security of an online site has been compromised and the numbers have been stolen directly from the site itself.

2   How reliable and well-known is the site? If it's a brand-name you know and trust (and you're sure that the address is really their website – see earlier in this chapter about reading right-to-left to see who a site really belongs to) then you've probably little to worry about. You can always try searching on, for example,

Google for others who've had problems with the website concerned – these days, people aren't shy about voicing their complaints.

3   You'll find online shopping tips at the Visa credit card website, www.visa.com.

Some credit card companies such as Discover in the USA, www.discovercard.com, are offering one-time only credit card numbers for use online – the number can be used once just like a regular credit card and then it becomes invalid.

Other Information

Only you can decide what information you're prepared to give out in return for the services you're offered. You may, for example, want to be wary about publishing your home address and telephone number, too. I now use a PO Box postal address and a telephone number forwarding service after unpleasant experiences in the past.

Keeping The Kids Out Of Your Files

It's inevitable that, if you have only one computer in the house, everyone in the family is (a) going to want to use it at the same time and (b) want to keep all their own stuff private while digging through all of yours. If you have Windows XP it is easy to set up different users who have access to their own files and only their own files. If you have XP look in the Help files under 'Local users and group concepts' for detailed explanations on how it works. Basically, all you do is use the **User Accounts** section of **Control Panel** to set up new users, giving them rights to access either just their own parts of the computer (normal users) or all of it (administrators). As the administrator yourself this means that you can limit the amount of hard disk space the children use and whether or not they can install programs without your specific permission.

If you have Windows 95, 98 or Me then, as you may have discovered, you can set up your computer with different user profiles so that when each different person logs on and uses their own username/password they see their own desktop (look on the **User Profiles** tab in the **Passwords** section of **Control Panel**), set of documents, files and so on. However, enquiring minds and busy little fingers will also have discovered that they can (a) avoid the logon dialog box altogether by hitting **Esc** or clicking **Cancel** when they see it, and (b) browse through everyone else's files anyway. If you want to keep your files private using one of these versions of Windows you need a third-party encryption program – have a look at www.mercury.org.uk for some freeware programs which do just this.

Safe Surfing For Kids

The world wide web can be a dangerous place for children, but you don't want them to lose out on the benefits of new technology, so how can you safeguard them? It's unfortunately easy to stumble accidentally across inappropriate websites – pornographers sometimes use addresses similar to those of popular sites and you only need to mistype one or two letters to find sites you'd rather your under-10s didn't see.

The good news is that there are a number of simple things which you, as parents, can do to safeguard your children and make sure they surf safe.

1 Content Advisor in Internet Explorer only allows your children to view sites rated according to the guidelines from organisations like the ICRA, the Internet Content Rating Association. You can set the levels of language, nudity, sex and violence which can be viewed by different users of your computer and you can have different levels for older children and for yourself. If you're using Internet Explorer 5 or 6, you can do this by clicking on **Tools > Internet Options > Content > Enable** and setting the four sliders to appropriate levels. There's a 'supervisor' password so your settings can't be changed. You can add sites yourself which haven't been rated. Instructions for other browsers are on the ICRA website at www.icra.org.

2 There are also a number of programs you can use which will monitor and guide your children's web browsing. One of the best known is Net Nanny, www.netnanny.com, which costs under £20 to download directly from the internet. It also monitors chat rooms and e-mail. This means that any junk e-mail sent to your children will be screened for inappropriate content before they can open it. Similar programs include CyberPatrol, www.cyberpatrol.com by Mattel and Cybersitter, www.cybersitter.com. Not all of these services are as reliable and useful as you might like, however, and some definitely have their own moral and/or political agendas. There is, in the end, no substitute for parental guidance and spending time online with your children.

3 There are also many places on the world wide web itself which can point you towards places that are safe for children – places like the SafeSurf's Educational Resource Files, www.safesurf.com, BESS, bess.net, which offers links and a search engine of content safe for children to view, Safekids, www.safekids.com, which gives information for parents and children on safe surfing, as does the GetNetWise site, www.getnetwise.org and Yahooligans!, www.yahooligans.com, the child-friendly search engine set up by top search engine Yahoo!

Advice To Give Your Children

It's best to always sit with very young children both to guide them and help ensure they don't accidentally end up somewhere both they and you would rather they didn't. When you and they are happy for them to be left alone, give them a few simple rules – the same sort of things you'd tell them when they're out and about anywhere:

1 Don't tell anyone your real name and/or address or e-mail address without asking permission from the person who looks after you.

2   Always ask the person who looks after you – a parent or guardian – not someone online if there's something you don't understand.

3   If you feel unhappy or uncomfortable about something you've seen or read online, talk to a teacher or the person who looks after you about it. Don't keep it to yourself.

4   Always ask permission from the person who pays the bills before going online.

5   Don't stay online any longer than you've agreed to.

How To Verify That Someone Is Who They Say They Are/Prove That You Are Who You Say You Are

There's an old saying in the online world that, 'On the internet, nobody knows you're a dog' – usually with a pointer to a cartoon of a dog surfing the web (Google has a nice list if you're interested). Which is quite amusing until it's you who has to prove you are who you say you are to someone else online, and this is where digital signatures come in.

A digital signature can be a way to prove that the sender of an e-mail is really who they say they are. Essentially a unique code is added to your e-mails which recipients can check to verify your identity. There are a number of different ways to get yourself a digital ID.

1   In Outlook Express, if you click **Tools > Options > Security** you'll see a button there marked **Get Digital ID**. Click it and you'll be taken to a page on the Microsoft website where you can find more links to providers of digital IDs. Verisign, for example, provides one for $14.95 a year after a 60-day free trial.

2   PGP, Pretty Good Privacy, provides both digital IDs – signatures for e-mails – and encryption of files and e-mails. It works with Outlook, Outlook Express and Eudora automatically, signing and/or encrypting e-mails for you. Signing an e-mail with your PGP key doesn't actually prove you are who you say you are – it proves that the e-mail has been sent from the stated address. You can also encrypt a file you send as an attachment. It works by using public and private keys. Every user has one of each, and the principle is that anything encrypted with one key can only be unlocked with the other. So if you were sending an encrypted e-mail to your friend Sarah, you'd use PGP to encrypt it with her public key and then she would unencrypt it with her private key. You publish your public key for anyone to see – you'll find mine at www.drkeyboard.com/pgp – and never, ever reveal your private one. As long as you can verify the source of a public key, you can be sure that only the owner of the corresponding private key will be able to open and

read any message encrypted with that public key. You'll find lots more information about PGP at www.pgpi.com.

Spam

More properly known as UCE, Unsolicited Commercial E-mail, spam e-mails are, usually, trying to sell you something you don't want and may even be offended to be offered – drugs, pornography, CDs containing millions of e-mail addresses, swampland in Florida, the list goes on and on. Unfortunately for spam recipients, spammers find it tremendously easy and rewarding to send out millions of e-mails selling their products. It costs virtually nothing to send such messages so, even if only a few dozen of the millions solicited respond positively, it's an economically worthwhile venture for them. So the first and absolutely golden rule of spam is: *never, ever reply*. Don't reply positively but also you shouldn't reply demanding to be removed from the mailing list – even if the message contains authoritative-looking rubbish about how it's legal under this, that or the other law, how you can be removed by simply replying with the word 'unsubscribe' in the subject line, how you can be removed simply by 'clicking here and visiting our website'. All these things ever do is confirm that there's a real, live – albeit angry – human being at the end of that e-mail address, and therefore that address will be moved to the top of the list for future spam e-mails and be sold on to other spammers at a premium price. So, replying will only guarantee that you get lots more spam. There are some things you can do to reduce the amount of spam you do receive, though.

1   Be very, very careful about where and to whom you give out your e-mail address. If you use instant messenger programs like AIM from AOL, Microsoft Messenger or ICQ, many others using those systems can discover your e-mail address, so think about using a different address when you sign up with these programs.

2   Set up a 'throwaway' e-mail address with one of the many free e-mail providers which you give out when signing up for online services. Only check that e-mail box when you're expecting something like a password for an online forum to be sent to you, and junk all the spam.

3   In Outlook you can turn on the 'Junk Filters' – these are under the rules wizard; click the **Organize** button on the toolbar to find them. All messages containing potentially adult or junk content will be filtered out if they match one of the existing rules and new messages can be added to the Junk Senders list. Gaznet, www.gaznet.au.com/spam/download.htm publishes new and updated versions of this file, **junk senders.txt** every month. You can send in your additional spammers and benefit from those added by others around the world, too.

4   In Outlook Express you can block individual message senders – left-click the relevant message to select it then click **Messages > Block Sender** (then **Tools > Message Rules > Blocked Senders** to review or change the list). Unfortunately,

spammers rarely send two e-mails from the same address so this can be an exercise in futility. You can block whole domains or even countries using this method, but it does mean that even legitimate messages from these places won't get through.

5 Look at Spamcop, spamcop.net. First, it offers a way to report spam e-mails to those who may be able to do something about it. It will notify all those who have provided services to the spammer – an e-mail address, e-mail servers, web space, whatever – that their service is being abused and ask them to cut off the spammers. This does have an effect – I regularly get messages back from ISPs saying they've cut spammers off after I've complained about them. Unfortunately, these days it's all too easy to find another e-mail address and web space, so in many respects this is an exercise in closing stable doors post-horse bolting. So, Spamcop also offers 'filtered' e-mail accounts which remove a large percentage of the spam you're sent. You can set them up to work in conjunction with your existing e-mail accounts so you don't even need to change e-mail addresses and, in my experience, this definitely works – it cuts out something like 99 per cent of the spam I'm sent on a daily basis.

6 Cloudmark, www.cloudmark.com has a cooperative approach to stopping spam. It puts a button on your Outlook menu bar (other e-mail programs may be included later – at the time of writing support for Outlook Express is promised 'soon') which allows you to 'vote' on whether or not a particular message is spam. If enough people agree that a message is spam, it's added to the program's filters and it'll automatically be excluded in future.

Questions And Answers

Easy Questions And Answers

Some people recommend the BlackICE and ZoneAlarm firewall programs. I already have Norton Internet Security Family Edition. Will these still work and are they still necessary? I have had several Internet Alerts from the Norton Software saying it has blocked trojan SubSeven. I have also run Gibson Research to probe my PC, with clean results.

I recommend BlackICE and ZoneAlarm simply because they're the programs I use and have found to be worth putting my faith in. I don't hear bad things about Norton Internet Security and, as a very happy user of Norton Anti-Virus, I think it's almost certainly a very decent program. Keep it up to date with whatever Norton recommends and you'll be fine, I'm sure. It wouldn't hurt to run BlackICE and ZoneAlarm – I run both simultaneously – because each has its own strengths, but it isn't necessary by any means.

I understand there's now a new trojan/worm/virus/whatever which will execute (install itself onto your computer) if you just look at a web page with it. Is this true?

I've said for some time that the possibility exists that someone will write a virus which can infect users who simply read a web page or receive an HTML e-mail. Now someone's done just that with the JS.Offensive worm which uses ActiveX to run inside a browser window or e-mail preview pane. One variant has a **Start** button which needs to be clicked, the other just needs to have its page viewed. The symptoms include: Start menu items have text file icons; there are no icons on the desktop; you can't start any programs; if you try to shut Windows down you get an error message about security settings. The good news is that most anti-virus software like Norton AV already protects against this threat; if you don't have any AV software, you run the risk of being infected by this one – because, as I say, all you effectively need to do is either view a web page or 'preview' an e-mail containing it.

I have recently started getting error messages on my Windows 98 computer saying that programs such as Netscape and others cannot load because it has run out of memory. I'm not sure why. Programs that do load are slower than they used to be. I am very worried! I downloaded a file off an e-mail (silly – I know) called **psycho** *and it is since then that the problem has occurred. However, I deleted the file and used two virus software programs to try to see if there was a virus but there wasn't. Still I am stuck and I had no problems before as far as memory was concerned.*

Apart from being labelled, 'Warning! This e-mail attachment is actually a virus, do not install it' I'm not sure how it could have been clearer that any attachment called **psycho** is definitely one to avoid. Really. It's a virus, although exactly which one isn't obvious since several include the word 'psycho' in their name. Visit the Symantec website at www.symantec.com/securitycheck, where you can run an online check of your machine which should root out the virus and clean up your computer. You can also download a trial version of Norton Anti-Virus, which I personally use and recommend. Alternatively there's the free anti-virus program AVG from www.grisoft.com which I also use and recommend. And please, *do not* open e-mail attachments you aren't explicitly expecting – if you're ever in doubt, ask the sender if they meant to send it.

My 5-month-old PC has suddenly produced an error message on start-up. It says: 'Registry error. Cannot import C:\windows\kak.reg. Error opening the file. There may be a disk or file system error'. When I click on OK, the message goes away and the PC appears to behave normally. The message appeared on start-up for about 5

days, then it didn't for 10 days or so, and now it has reappeared. What does it mean, and what should I do about it?

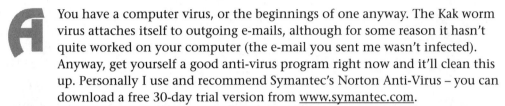

You have a computer virus, or the beginnings of one anyway. The Kak worm virus attaches itself to outgoing e-mails, although for some reason it hasn't quite worked on your computer (the e-mail you sent me wasn't infected). Anyway, get yourself a good anti-virus program right now and it'll clean this up. Personally I use and recommend Symantec's Norton Anti-Virus – you can download a free 30-day trial version from www.symantec.com.

When I open an email attachment on Outlook Express, it prompts me to either open it directly or to save it on to the hard disk. If I open it directly, could an attached virus be undetected by my virus software? If so, how can I open it safely?

It depends on the capabilities of your anti-virus software and how recently it's been updated. Some programs will check your e-mail as it arrives and warn you of any message containing a virus before you open it. Some check files and programs as you open or run them, and again warn you of potential viruses before any harm is done. Other programs rely on you manually scanning each file before opening it. You will need to check the documentation and help files which came with your anti-virus software to see what facilities it offers.

When I switch my computer on and Windows Desktop appears I get a message saying there's a 'Driver Memory Error'. Then I get a message that says something like 'Cannot find server'. This window is the typical window you get when you're on the internet and your browser cannot locate a web address but says it's at res://C:WINDOWS\SYSTEM\SHDOCLC.DLL/ dnserror.htm#res://ie4tour.dll/ welcome.htm. When closing this window I often get this warning: 'Cannot import C:Windows\kak\reg:Error opening the file. There may be a disk or file error'. To use my computer any further I must close this uninvited window (or warning) every time. I find this extremely annoying and would love to resolve the problem.

Two things. First, and most importantly, you have a virus – the Kak worm. If you don't already have an anti-virus program, visit www.symantec.com/ securitycheck where you can run an online virus checker and download a trial version of Norton Anti-Virus. If you do have anti-virus software installed, it isn't working. Update your virus definitions now – check the program's help files for details on how to do this. If this doesn't clear up your virus, visit the Symantec site above – it *will* clear the virus. In the meantime, please don't send out any more e-mails until you've removed the virus, and you would be well advised to notify those you've e-mailed recently that you've probably sent them a virus. The 'Can't find ...' stuff is because your browser thinks the

IE4 'guided tour' page is its home page. Change your home page and this message will go away.

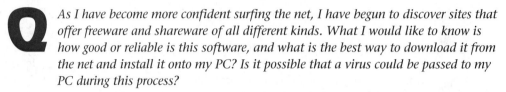

As I have become more confident surfing the net, I have begun to discover sites that offer freeware and shareware of all different kinds. What I would like to know is how good or reliable is this software, and what is the best way to download it from the net and install it onto my PC? Is it possible that a virus could be passed to my PC during this process?

Yes, it is possible your PC could be infected with a virus in this way. Any software is only as reliable as its vendor, and even the most reliable vendors have, in the past, sent out software discs with viruses on them. Magazines, too, have been known to accidentally include viruses on their cover discs so you're not safe wherever you obtain your software from. The only truly safe thing to do is run a virus checker constantly – most nowadays like Norton Anti-Virus will automatically check every file you download and every program you run, not just for known viruses but for virus-like behaviour. This means that, even if you come across a previously unknown virus, the things it tries to do on your PC may alert your anti-virus software.

*Is this warning about the **sulfnbk.exe** virus for real? I had the file on my hard disk and have deleted it, but I have heard of pranks to get people to delete system files.*

Well it's worked on you – it's a hoax but you still deleted this fairly important Windows system file before checking it out, so they've fooled you. **sulfnbk.exe** is a normal part of a Windows installation – it's the program which deals with long file names. You can check it out at hoaxbusters.ciac.org, a site maintained by the US Department of Energy on hoax messages just like this, and at securityresponse.symantec.com/avcenter/venc/data/sulfnbk.exe.warning.html – this is the website of Symantec, makers of Norton Anti-Virus, the anti-virus software I use and recommend myself. If you are worried that you may be infected with any sort of virus go to www.symantec.com/securitycheck where you can perform an online virus scan of your computer, and also download a trial version of Norton Anti-Virus.

*Where this virus came from I don't know. It is listed by Norton as **WAS.mtx** and affects certain internet links. I connect to my ISP no problem, but attempting to visit favourite sites brings up the error message. When Norton scans my files, it finds about 90 infected. I delete its suggestions, clean the rest (leaving 5 still infected; unable to clean) yet when I return 2 hours later and try scanning/cleaning again, all 90 files are still infected, even the so-called deleted ones.*

I think you're referring to the **W95.mtx** virus since one of the things this virus manages to do is prevent you from visiting various anti-virus sites. Clever, for a virus, since it stops you downloading new updates for your AV software. The removal instructions are at service1.symantec.com/sarc/sarc.nsf/html/W95.MTX.html.

My local department store sells Norton Anti-Virus bundled with Firewall, against hackers. Are lowly private individuals, operating their computer from home, at risk from hackers? I must confess that the idea had never occurred to me.

Home users are potentially more at risk of 'attack' from hackers than big companies since the latter are more likely to be running behind firewalls – systems which protect from such attacks. If you're connecting via a dial-up modem the risk only exists while you're connected, of course, but the downside to this is that your ISP (Internet Service Provider) will only have a limited 'pool' of IP (Internet Protocol) addresses to assign to users – the numeric address all computers connected to the internet need to have. Your computer will be assigned one temporarily while you're connected and, because it's from a limited range, hackers may be 'scanning' the entire range of numbers continually for someone to start using one on an unprotected computer. They could then install software on your machine doing various nefarious things. So, this is all a long-winded way to say yes, you should be running some sort of firewall software. I've never used the Norton software myself, I rely on BlackICE from www.networkice.com and others I trust use ZoneAlarm from www.zonealarm.com.

Last night I came home and found my computer screen with an error message. I figured it was a java script or something and clicked OK without reading it. The screen went blank and came back with half of a screen of the Windows 98 load picture (bottom half) and froze. I then turned off the power and waited 15 seconds then turned it back on. The screen was black with picture fuzz and the computer was not booting. I tried to power off again and this time the Windows 98 half screen appeared again and froze. I tried again and it had the boot screen but stopped with the pipeline burst cache at the end and froze. I can turn it off and get any one of these screens at any time but the computer never loads the operating system. What should I look for to see if it's the video card, hard drive, memory or software?

First, as a warning to others – read error messages and other dialog boxes which pop up on your screen. It's quite hard for virus writers to do something nasty to your computer without your permission, but it is possible for them to pop up a message on your screen which looks innocuous – something about your anti-virus software needing updating, for example – and get you to click a button which then launches a horrible attack on your computer. If this has happened, you hopefully have the rescue/boot disks created by your operating system and anti-virus software which will help you work out what's happened. You also need to check the hardware, as you've guessed, to see if anything has worked loose inside such as the video card or some of your memory, for example. And try booting from a floppy disk to see if you can access your hard disk at all. This is a problem which can have many potential causes; if you get stuck, try posting a question on www.drkeyboard.net and we can work through the options with you.

Q *I received today an e-mail with an attachment which had the worm virus. I downloaded Norton Anti-Virus last week and found it with this. I did not extract the attachment and have deleted both the mail and attachment. Was this correct and do I need to do anything else?*

A No, that's all you need to do. Generally speaking you can only infect your computer with a virus by opening and running an attachment, but see comments in the 'Virus and Security Warnings' forum on www.drkeyboard.net about other vulnerabilities. I recommend updating your anti-virus software at least every week – with NAV you just run the 'LiveUpdate' function – and visiting the Windows Update site at windowsupdate.microsoft.com. There's also a good Microsoft security site at www.microsoft.com/security.

Q *When I try to watch a movie clip in IE, I get the message: 'The Java machine would not allow me to open a listening socket. Try changing your security settings. Warning: Applet Window!' Is this a virus?*

A Check your settings under **Tools > Internet Options > Security** then internet or whatever zone the site is in, then **Security > Custom Level > Java**.

Q *Whenever I press a key on the keyboard I hear a small bleep from my tower. I use Windows XP.*

A Look at what Accessibility Options are set in **Control Panel** – it's possible to set the behaviour you describe here. Also, run a check for viruses on your machine – AVG from Grisoft, www.grisoft.com, works well on Windows XP.

Q *After rebooting (or logging off), the POP3 server details have been replaced by 'localhost', and the actual details have been appended to the user name, i.e. myname.isp.com/pop3.isp.com.*

A This will almost certainly be being done by your anti-virus software to allow it to check your incoming e-mails as they arrive. Norton Anti-Virus, for example, changes the e-mail server's address to 127.0.0.1 which is the numeric equivalent of 'localhost'. Leave the settings as they are and your AV software will be able to do its job.

I installed Norton Anti-Virus but it hasn't found any viruses yet. Why not?

Probably because there aren't any on your computer.

I have received and eliminated the W95.Hybris virus contained in an email from an unknown source using Norton Anti-Virus. I obtained the full details, path etc. of the sender from the properties box of the message. Are these details of any use to any organisation?

If your AV program already knows about the virus then the only people interested in it should be those who sent it to you in the first place – tell them what they sent you and how they can get rid of it. You'll find more details on the Symantec site at <u>service1.symantec.com/sarc/sarc.nsf/html/ W95.Hybris.Plugin.html</u>.

I've read of some viruses/worms which only affect computers running Microsoft's Internet Information Server web server software. How can I tell if I have it?

Generally it only runs on the NT, 2000 and XP versions of Windows, but a quick way to tell is to open Internet Explorer and in the Address field type **http://localhost** and hit **Enter**. If you see a web page or get a dialog box asking for a username/password, then you have IIS.

As a pensioner I can't afford an expensive virus checker. How can I find a reliable one on the web?

Try AVG from Grisoft, <u>www.grisoft.com</u> – I use and recommend it myself.

How can I prevent my ISP connecting to premium rate lines when I am surfing the net? This seems to happen with no warning. Is it possible to bar such connections?

It sounds very much as though you have some sort of computer virus. Visit www.symantec.com and download the 30-day trial version of Norton Anti-Virus, which should sort you out. You can also set the connection options in your e-mail program and web browser so they don't automatically connect every time you start them up.

I have heard of a nasty virus circulating in/emanating from Russia called Chernobyl. I use Norton (per your recommendation) Anti-Virus software, but I cannot find if they have protection against it. Do you know if there is also anti-virus software (freeware) in a Russian version which can protect against this one?

Norton protects against the Chernobyl virus – just keep updating your definitions and you should be fine.

Spam Questions and Answers

I received an e-mail recently offering me a disc containing 1 million e-mail addresses for £5. I presume I received this message because I am included on the CD. For several reasons I am unhappy with this. Like most people, I only make my e-mail address available to companies or individuals I believe I can trust. I will only allow them to pass on my address to equally trustworthy sources. I do not expect – or want – it to be made available to anyone who may be willing to pay for it, irrespective of their background. It would be only too easy for someone to obtain this disc and use it to send out computer viruses or material of an offensive nature to all listed. What are your thoughts on this? I have sent a message back to the sender requesting that I am removed from his listing. Is there anything that can be done to prevent this sort of thing?

Unfortunately you've already done the one thing you should never do with spam (unsolicited commercial e-mail, sometimes known as UCE) – you've replied to it. This confirms to the spammer that there's a living, breathing person behind the e-mail account to which they sent their unwanted rubbish, and your address will now be worth more than an unconfirmed account. As for how they got your address in the first place, it could have come from a number of places – newsgroup postings on Usenet, some websites or bulletin boards where you've posted, or they could simply have guessed it. Spamcop, spamcop.net, is a pretty reliable way to report spam, and I also like the GazNET anti-spam filters which unfortunately for many only work with Outlook, not Outlook Express – you'll find them at www.gaznet.au.com/spam/download.htm. Spamcop now has a very good solution, a 'filtered' e-mail account which removes, in my testing, something like 99 per cent of the spam I used to receive. It's a bit of a steep learning curve working out how to use it, but the results are very worthwhile and now, instead of receiving hundreds of spams in my inbox every week I now only see one or two. Best of all, the account only costs $30 a year. Highly recommended.

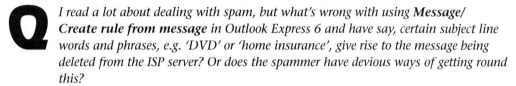 *I read a lot about dealing with spam, but what's wrong with using **Message/ Create rule from message** in Outlook Express 6 and have say, certain subject line words and phrases, e.g. 'DVD' or 'home insurance', give rise to the message being deleted from the ISP server? Or does the spammer have devious ways of getting round this?*

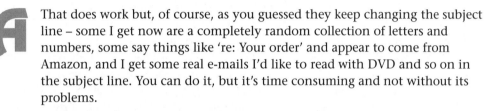 That does work but, of course, as you guessed they keep changing the subject line – some I get now are a completely random collection of letters and numbers, some say things like 're: Your order' and appear to come from Amazon, and I get some real e-mails I'd like to read with DVD and so on in the subject line. You can do it, but it's time consuming and not without its problems.

Harder Questions And Answers

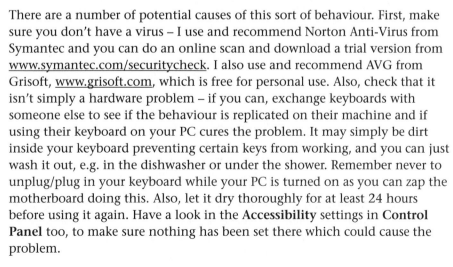 *just a recent problem i have been having with my windows 98 computer involves my shift keys. as you can see the only way to uppercase my letters is by hitting the caps lock every time i need it. i cannot access any symbols, exclamation marks, question marks or anything. however the left shift key is now shortcutting when running programs, and the right shift key is not affecting anything. this is a real bother and i think i may have hit some keys while typing or something. the problem is not with the keys, as the computer is responding to them, but i have no idea what i did and how to fix it. maybe by reinstalling my keyboard, but i have no idea how to do that, and i don't think it would make any difference anyway.*

There are a number of potential causes of this sort of behaviour. First, make sure you don't have a virus – I use and recommend Norton Anti-Virus from Symantec and you can do an online scan and download a trial version from www.symantec.com/securitycheck. I also use and recommend AVG from Grisoft, www.grisoft.com, which is free for personal use. Also, check that it isn't simply a hardware problem – if you can, exchange keyboards with someone else to see if the behaviour is replicated on their machine and if using their keyboard on your PC cures the problem. It may simply be dirt inside your keyboard preventing certain keys from working, and you can just wash it out, e.g. in the dishwasher or under the shower. Remember never to unplug/plug in your keyboard while your PC is turned on as you can zap the motherboard doing this. Also, let it dry thoroughly for at least 24 hours before using it again. Have a look in the **Accessibility** settings in **Control Panel** too, to make sure nothing has been set there which could cause the problem.

257

I was surfing a regular site I visit on the internet when a prompt appeared on my screen from a hacker saying that my connection was insecure and that he had easily gained access to my system. I could not remove the prompt window in any other way than by restarting my system. How can I prevent a hacker gaining access to my system in the future?

Assuming this wasn't just a pop-up advert trying to sell you something (test this by closing your web browser then going back to the same website) your first move should be to visit the excellent Steve Gibson's site at grc.com. Take his 'Shields Up!' and 'Probe my Ports' tests and then read the advice he offers for the problems he may or may not detect. Personally I use a variety of security systems, including (but not limited to, for all you hackers out there) the BlackICE firewall software from Network Ice (www.networkice.com) and this works fine for me. Others swear by ZoneAlarm (and Steve Gibson recommends it highly) – details at www.zonealarm.com. You'll also find a number of other products available – Steve Gibson has a fairly comprehensive list of them on his site.

I heard that Microsoft is releasing a patch for vbs type viruses. I have looked everywhere (at least I think everywhere) for the patch on their site but can't find it. Can anyone direct me?

Start at www.microsoft.com/security and you'll see all they have on this. Of course, the answer to this and all similar viruses is much, much easier than updating your software (although you should still do this) – simply *never* open any attachment which you're not 100 per cent sure is safe. If you're not expecting an attachment, don't open it. If it's from someone you don't know, don't open it. If it's from someone you do know, check with them first that they meant to send it in the first place. I have changed my e-mail signature to add the line, 'This e-mail was sent without attachments – if any arrive, please delete them and notify me.' If I do send an attachment I have to remember to remove this line but that's a small burden for the added security it gives. Fourth, everything I've read about this 'security patch' from Microsoft for Outlook (not OE) indicates that it's next to useless. It makes Outlook virtually unusable for many groups of users and doesn't offer enough options during the install to make it usefully customisable. Worse, it's a search-and-destroy install – once installed there's no uninstall option, apart from completely removing Outlook and starting over. Read what Woody's Office Watch has to say about it at woodyswatch.com/office/archives.asp – click on the 25 May 2000 date and scroll down to item 5 for the full details.

My Norton Anti-Virus picked up the fact that the Kak virus was present in an email which came from an online group to which I belong. But the Norton program could not repair it or take it off my computer – and I had kept my anti-virus downloads

up-to-date. First of all the worm gets in through a security hole in Outlook Express only. Secondly, there is a patch available from Microsoft, and thirdly Symantec has complete instructions on how to eradicate the thing. I have sent copies of what I wrote to my group, as well as the instructions from Norton. As you can imagine, several members of my group were badly affected by the thing – I was lucky and warned right away, but I still had to do some investigating.

 You're right, Norton Anti-Virus isn't able to wipe the Kak worm from e-mails, but it should be able to pick it up on the way in and warn you about it before it does any harm. Follow the instructions on-screen to quarantine the infected attachment and then delete it from within NAV itself. You won't be able to read the e-mail so tell the person who sent it to you about the problem and get them to re-send it. If you've installed the update from Microsoft (either via www.microsoft.com/TechNet/IE/tools/scrpteye.asp or start at the general updates page at windowsupdate.microsoft.com) then – assuming NAV hasn't already intervened – you'll get a pop-up box telling you that there's an unsafe control on the page, i.e. the Kak worm. You're quite right to urge your friends to take precautions too – some mailing lists filter out this sort of problem but quite a few don't.

 Yesterday I received an e-mail from an unknown named 'HaHaHa' which I immediately deleted. However, having OE as my e-mail manager I assume it was probably downloaded on my PC before I deleted it, as the content of the message appeared in the message box below. Shortly after that my PC crashed. Tonight I went to close down my PC, having disconnected from the net and closed all programs running, and a message box appeared saying that I was trying to close a 'hidden window' and did I want to end the task? I'm assuming the two incidents are connected – is it likely that my machine's picked up a virus, or even a hacker? And is there any (free) e-mail management software that will let you read who your e-mail is from, giving you the option to delete it without reading as you can with the online services such as Yahoo!?

 It's theoretically possible to become infected by a virus by just previewing an e-mail – one called Bubbleboy tried to do this. See www.symantec.com/avcenter/venc/data/vbs.bubbleboy.html for more information. Bubbleboy exploited a security weakness in Outlook Express which Microsoft fixed some time ago – check the links on the Symantec page for details. The name 'HaHaHa' is associated with the W95.Hybris.gen worm. See www.symantec.com/avcenter/venc/data/w95.hybris.gen.html for more information. You can take a fairly basic precaution against this sort of thing by setting up a 'rule' in Outlook or Outlook Express to move anything with an attachment to a folder of its own on arrival, and then set this folder to not show you a preview of the message automatically. This allows you to save the message off elsewhere and scan it with an anti-virus program and to check with the sender that they

259

meant to send you an attachment without any chance of it being opened. You can download a trial version of Norton Anti-Virus from the Symantec site above, or try the free AVG from Grisoft, www.grisoft.com.

I have a Pentium II with 256 MB of RAM and an 8 GB hard disk running Windows 98. Response to keyboarding or mouse clicking has slowed way down, to the point where I have to wait maybe ten seconds for a word to appear after it has been typed or for a mouse click to take effect. It happens in all applications but is especially noticeable when typing e-mail messages in Outlook Express.

First, check you don't have a virus. If you already have some anti-virus software, update it and run a thorough scan over your hard disk. If you don't have any, visit www.symantec.com/securitycheck where you can perform an online scan and download a trial version of Norton Anti-Virus, the program I personally use and recommend. I also use and recommend AVG from Grisoft, www.grisoft.com, which is free for personal use. Next, have a look at how many programs are running and what they're doing. Click **Start > Run** and in the dialog box which pops up type **msconfig** and click **OK**. Look on the **Startup** tab for a list of what's run when your machine is turned on. Notorious system hogs include Microsoft's own Find Fast utility – uncheck the box next to it if you see it to prevent it running when you restart. Note, you may want to change settings inside miscreant programs to stop them running if this shows them to be the culprit, or even uninstall them completely. You'd also be doing yourself a favour by clearing out temporary files – do a **Start > Find** for ***.tmp** files and delete them all. They usually hide in **C:\Windows\temp** or similar. If you come across one or two which refuse to be deleted, don't worry – it just means they're currently in use, so they can be left. This may clear up a fair bit of space on your hard disk, which could be causing some of the problem. If none of this helps much, though, come over to the Dr Keyboard message board at www.drkeyboard.net and we'll run through a few more options.

My virus checker informed me that 92 files have been infected. It could only clean 87, which had all returned an hour later after another attempted clean. The virus is named w95.mtx and is affecting my internet sites. Is any advice or download available? I don't know where this came from as I don't open e-mail attachments.

You can read lots more about this virus on many sites. Symantec, which makes the Norton Anti-Virus program I use and recommend, has a page devoted to it at securityresponse.symantec.com/avcenter/venc/data/ w95.mtx.html, a removal tool at www.sarc.com/avcenter/venc/data/w95. mtx.fix.tool.html and an interactive tutorial on how to get rid of it and a number of other common viruses and trojans at www.symantec.com/ techsupp/virusremoval/virusremoval_info_tutorial.html.

I am getting an Internet Explorer Script Error, RichTextBox1 on all URLs now. I have run Norton Anti-Virus twice and it does not pick up any virus. Does this sound like a virus to you? Any suggestions on how to remove this blasted curse?

I don't think this is a virus and I can't find any reference to it being a known problem with IE. RichTextBox1 is a standard name for what it says – a box with text in it on a web page of some kind. Somehow your browser has got stuck into a loop somewhere, possibly with a script or other web page component, and is always trying to open some box of text. Open **Control Panel** and then **Add/Remove Programs**, click **Remove** under Internet Explorer and then choose the 'Repair' option, which may fix the problem.

I received an e-mail from my friend's computer, an attachment with no message. The attachment was FIKUMUJI.JPG.vbs (11.1). I ran it from its location and nothing happened so I exited Outlook Express and began to browse around and in my photo album I found that all my photos have been converted into VBS script format that won't open or generate an image on my computer. Also I can still save a file in format the way it's supposed to save it, but soon it converts over to a VBS script file. How can I get my computer to format back to the right script and not this VBX script format?

You've infected your computer with a virus which may well have destroyed irreparably the files you're trying to open. The only good news is that you haven't managed to infect yourself to the point where you're now sending it on in your e-mails – the mail you sent me was clean. Go to www.symantec. com/securitycheck where you can perform an online virus scan of your computer, and also download a trial version of Norton Anti-Virus. The simple rule about any attachment is *don't open it* unless you're expecting it and you're sure that the person sending it meant to do so. Don't open anything on the basis that it's from someone you know – that's no guarantee of security. I still, incredibly, get dozens of virus-infected e-mails a week from people who know me in various ways despite spending a fair amount of my time banging on about the dangers of viruses, worms and so on. Install anti-virus software – I use and recommend Norton Anti-Virus – and intrusion detection and firewall software like BlackICE (from www.networkice.com) and ZoneAlarm (www.zonealarm.com) and keep them up to date. You owe it to everyone around you, not just yourself.

I have been sent a virus on my computer via e-mail. Once alerted via the sender I checked the attachment sent with my virus checker which didn't find anything. However, I then went on to the Symantec site and by stumbling about managed to do a virus check and found a W32.Magistr.24876@mm virus. When I chose the repair option it just scanned again and said there were no viruses. I did then update my Norton software but it still says I have no viruses. There were however four files

*in the backup folder of the Norton application which I have deleted. My computer is still behaving strangely – it is difficult to log off the internet and when I do **Ctrl-Alt-Del** there seem to be two or three versions of Internet Explorer running. The below-mentioned is an error message I received. 'EXPLORER caused an invalid page fault in module <unknown> at 0000:01a78a90.'*

If you run a regular Norton AV scan of your hard disk after updating the virus definitions, you can be pretty sure you don't have a virus. Quite how you found one via the Symantec site is a bit of a mystery to me. Try doing a 'Repair install' of Internet Explorer. Click **Start > Settings > Control Panel** and then double-click **Add > Remove Programs**. On the **Install > Uninstall** tab, click Microsoft Internet Explorer 5 then **Add > Remove** and 'Repair the current installation of Internet Explorer' and **OK**. Follow the wizard through.

Part 7
Resources

Although PCs often resemble those useless, inflamed organs you'd like a professional to take out and burn, the appendices to this book are rather more useful than that.

First, there's a complete listing of all the problems solved and questions answered in the book that should give you quick access to solutions to your own difficulties. Appendix 2 points you to websites you might find useful in your quest to beat your PC into a lump of something more useful than just an expensive paperweight. And Appendix 3 is where all the geek language is explained, all abbreviations expanded and all gibberish fully described.

Quick Answer Guide

Chapter 1: What's Gone Wrong?

1 'Illegal operations' – what's so illegal?

2 What's the very first thing I should do when something goes wrong?

3 Dr Keyboard's list of Really, Really Obvious Things To Check First.

4 There's power but my PC won't start up.

5 What are all these beeps on startup?

6 I see the 'Starting Windows' splash screen but nothing else.

7 I get to the Windows desktop but then get lots of error messages.

8 Why has my program/bit of hardware suddenly stopped working? It was fine yesterday.

9 My hardware's plugged in fine but why won't it work?

10 You may need new 'drivers' for your hardware if it works fine elsewhere.

11 Why do I need new drivers? What are drivers anyway?

12 What should I do when nothing cures the problem?

13 Dr Keyboard's List of How To Make Sure It Doesn't Go Bang (or, if it does go bang, how to make it all better again).

Chapter 2: Identifying The Source Of The Problem

18 My old laptop gives the error 'I/O Error ... abort, retry, fail'.

19 Why do Scandisk and Disk Defragmenter always stop 10 per cent (or 3 per cent or anything less than 100 per cent) of the way through checking my hard disk?

20 Why do I get the error message 'Bad or missing Keyboard Definition File'?

21 What does the error message, 'Stuck key. Press ESC to continue' mean?

22 Why does my computer randomly restart all on its own?

23 I've installed an earlier version of a program over a newer one and now neither works.

24 I keep getting the error message 'This site contains frames and your browser doesn't support them'. How do I turn frames on?

25 I get an error about 'RUNDLL32' when I start Outlook Express or Windows Explorer.

26 My computer made a lot of noise and then displayed a message about a 'missing operating system'.

27 I always get a 'Driver memory error' on start-up. What does this mean?

28 I've downloaded a program and get an error message saying, 'Extracting File Problem. It is most likely caused by low memory or corrupted cabinet file.'

29 What does an 'Abnormal termination' error mean?

30 I can't access a CD-R disc.

31 My web browser says it's got 'internal errors'.

32 My computer keeps going to a blue error screen. It is not when any particular action or program is running. Pressing any key or **Ctrl-Alt-Del** does not do anything, so I have to reboot the machine.

Chapter 3: Setup And Start-up

1 What should I check when I get a new computer?

2 What goes where? Which things should I concentrate on first?

3 Where can I look for more help if it just won't work?

4 What should I do first when it's all set up and working properly?

5 What software should I install?

Chapter 4: Inside Your PC

1 What does the inside of a PC look like?

2 What do all the different things inside the box do?

3 What precautions do I need to take before opening up my PC?

4 I'm getting an error with my scanner's SCSI card.

5 My computer won't start consistently and sounds as though it's not accessing the hard disk.

6 My PC won't work since I moved house from the USA to Europe.

7 The fan on my PC's power supply cuts out after a few seconds.

8 When my computer turns on it does nothing – it doesn't boot, nothing shows up on the monitor, the monitor acts as if the computer is not on.

9 I have a broken keyboard plug.

10 My computer locks up at the splash screen.

11 Can I add USB sockets to a PC or should I go on using a SCSI card for my scanner?

12 How do I disable the 'on-board' graphics on my PC so I can use an add-in video card?

13 What do the beeps I hear on start-up mean?

14 Can I upgrade the RAM on my computer?

15 How can I protect my PC (and other electronic equipment) against lightning strikes and power surges?

16 I've changed my PC case and now it won't work.

17 My PC resets itself for no reason.

18 Can I add a third hard disk to my PC?

Chapter 5: Monitors And Displays

1 What should I know about my computer screen's size, resolution and capabilities?

2 How can I tell if my computer screen is at the optimal settings, and what can I do if it isn't?

3 How can I find out what kind of video card my computer has if it isn't recognised automatically by Windows?

4 Where can I find drivers for my video card even if the card manufacturer no longer exists?

5 What's that line across my screen?

6 Why can't I see anything?

7 Why does everything look so huge and grainy?

8 Can I watch movies on my PC and use a TV as a computer monitor?

9 Can I disable 'on-board' graphics to add a new video card?

10 Why does my computer screen insist on sticking to 640×480 resolution?

11 Why is my monitor getting darker and flickering?

12 What's DirectX and how can I improve the quality of computer game pictures?

13 Where can I find out what's the latest, greatest, hottest graphics card?

14 My screen goes purple, and jiggling the connectors doesn't help.

15 Why when I minimise a window does the screen freeze and graphics from the previous window remain on-screen?

16 Why does my computer screen freeze while I'm surfing the net?

17 When my PC is turned on the message appears, 'There is a problem with your display settings. The adapter type is incorrect or the current settings do not work with your hardware'.

18 I installed the video card drivers from the Windows 98 CD but things haven't improved.

19 I installed Windows Me and now I get a very poor quality picture on my screen.

20 Can you tell me what the specification of an Intel 815E Internal Graphics card is?

21 My video capture card is too big to fit into the slots in my new PC.

22 Can I download and record video from the TV on to my PC?

23 When I play video games the screen looks really dark.

24 How can I have two computer monitors on my laptop?

25 I've installed the correct software for my computer monitor but the image is still stuck at 640×480 resolution with just 16 colours.

26 My monitor takes up to five minutes to come on when I start up my PC.

27 I've been notified that my Windows 95 video card drivers are obsolete.

Chapter 6: Sounds, CDs And DVDs

1   Why doesn't any sound come out of my PC's speakers?

2   What cables should I check?

3   My PC produces 'beep' noises from inside and will play sounds in games but not music CDs.

4   I've checked all the hardware – what about the drivers?

5   I've checked the hardware, software and drivers – what next?

6   How can I improve the quality of sound coming from my PC?

7   Is the built-in audio on my PC good enough? What else is available?

8   Is it worth adding better speakers?

9   Can I plug my PC into my hi-fi?

10   How else can I improve the sound quality?

11   Where can I find out more about the sound capabilities of my PC?

12   What about surround-sound from DVD films?

13   Can I transfer music from CDs, LPs and cassettes to my PC?

14   What can I legally do with MP3 files?

15   My keyboard makes sounds every time I type on it.

16   My computer can't detect my sound card.

17   How can I put streaming video files on my website?

18   CDs are very quiet unless I turn the volume way up, but then Windows' sounds distort.

19   Only one of my speakers works.

20   How can I get sounds from old DOS games in Windows Me?

21   Audio from internet radio stations keeps breaking up.

22   I can't get Sound Recorder to work in Windows 98.

23   I've lost all sound after installing QuickTime.

24   I only hear sounds from DVD films – I see no picture.

25   My sound card drivers are 'disabled 0'.

26   What should I use to clean my CD/DVD drive?

27 What are the main problems with CD/DVD drives?

28 My PC suddenly refuses to recognise a disc, what should I do?

29 It looks like the problem's my CD/DVD drive. What next?

30 The hardware's fine, now what?

31 What types of CD and DVD drives are available?

32 I uninstalled my CD burning software and now can't access my CD drive at all.

33 Can I fit a second CD drive so I can have permanent access to my reference CD?

34 Can I copy the contents of a CD to my hard disk so I don't have to keep it in the drive all the time?

35 What can I do with out-of-date CD-ROM discs?

36 My PC won't play music CDs.

37 Why do I get a 'Load from CD failed' message when I start my PC?

38 Can I boot my PC from a CD?

39 Can I add a CD drive and sound card to my old laptop?

40 My CD drive has suddenly stopped reading any discs.

41 Can I read my old CD-ROMs and play music CDs in a DVD drive?

42 How can I read DVD discs in a CD-ROM drive?

43 How can I reformat the CDs from computer magazine covers?

Chapter 7: Printers And Printing

1 What's the choice between different types of printers?

2 How can I choose between different types of printer?

3 What are the differences between laser printers and inkjets?

4 What brands do you recommend?

5 What should I look for when buying a printer?

6 Things to check when your printer won't print: the cables, the ink, clean the printer, the drivers.

7 How to work out what facilities and features you really need when buying a printer.

8 How to make the most of the printer you already have.

9 What to do if you've checked the basics and it still won't print.

10 Why do I get 'Insufficient memory' messages when I print?

11 Can I run one printer on my parallel port and a second via USB?

12 I get a 'Communication error – printer out of paper' when it's got lots of paper.

13 The salesman who sold me my printer said the ink would last for 'several months' but it's run out after two.

14 What are the limits on daisy-chaining devices off the printer port of my PC?

15 Why does my screen wobble when it's next to my printer?

16 How can I connect a laser and inkjet printer at the same time to one printer port?

17 How can I print web pages without the background pictures?

18 How can I print headers and footers on the first page only of a document?

19 Where can I download fonts from the internet?

20 Can I print out my contacts book from Outlook?

21 How do I use the 'print screen' key?

22 My printer doesn't work properly since I upgraded to Windows 98.

23 How can I print out all of a web page?

24 When I print a Word document with my e-mail address as a blue hyperlink, it doesn't show on the paper.

25 The Maintenance Wizard on my printer doesn't work since I upgraded to Windows 98.

26 I get the error message 'There was an error writing to LPT1'.

27 How can I print a web page with its background colour?

28 How do I strip out all the >>>> symbols in e-mails before printing them?

29 My printers work on the parallel port but not the USB socket.

30 How can I send a document to someone to print if they don't have the program it comes from?

31 How do I print my Outlook Express address book?

32 I can't print at all from Outlook Express.

33 Word takes ages to start printing.

34 How do I print comments in Excel 2000?

35 Underlined text looks strange when I print it.

36 I have to reinstall my printer each time Windows crashes.

37 How can I print from DOS?

38 How do I print my Outlook contacts on to Filofax-sized paper?

39 My printer produces a single page with strange characters on it when I turn it on.

40 How can I connect two computers to the same printer?

41 How do I print just the data for a form in Word, not the form itself?

42 Can I install a second printer port on my computer?

43 How can I print out Favorites website addresses in IE5?

44 How can I get Outlook Express to print in portrait mode?

45 How do I obtain a print out of my list of Internet Explorer Favorites?

46 If I write a letter and after printing it I cancel it, does some file remain on my hard disk?

47 Any e-mails I print from Outlook Express have a black border.

48 How do I print long single scrolled web pages?

49 My computer doesn't recognise my scanner. I was told it's a SCSI (whatever that is) and the cable it came with fits my printer socket.

50 Can I print more than one e-mail on the same page?

51 Is it correct that there are different size cartridges for the HP895Cxi inkjet printer?

52 My son's school have been given a Star LC200 dot-matrix. Where can they get a printer driver?

53 How can I make the 'Printer' icon appear on my taskbar?

54 How can I print my own e-mails?

Chapter 8: Operating Systems

1 What's an operating system for?

2 What versions of Windows might I come across?

3 What's Windows NT? How is it different to Windows 9x?

4 Are there any operating systems other than Windows?

5 How can I keep Windows up to date?

6 Is it worth upgrading every time a new version of Windows comes out?

7 How do I upgrade? Do I lose everything on my PC when I do so?

8 I reinstalled Windows XP and now have two versions on my PC.

9 Where do I load programs on a multi-operating system PC?

10 When I reinstall Windows XP, how can I avoid having to reactivate it?

11 Where can I find troubleshooters for problems with Windows?

12 Can Windows start up without a keyboard attached to the PC?

13 What kind of Windows does my Apple Mac use?

14 Is there a cure for the 'memory leak' problem in Windows?

15 How can I upgrade to Windows Me and change my partitioned hard disk back into a single C :drive?

16 If I buy a computer abroad could I install an English language version of Windows?

Chapter 9: Application Software

1 What software comes on new computers?

2 Are deals offering a thousand pounds worth of free software really worthwhile?

3 Are there any alternatives to Microsoft Office that can read and write files in the Office format?

4 What are shareware and freeware?

5 Where can I find all this free software that's supposed to be available on the internet?

6 What shareware/freeware do you use and recommend yourself?

7 I want some educational software which will fit in with my children's school curriculum, where can I find some details?

8 I want games. Where should I start?

9 I loaded Microsoft PowerPoint separately from Office and now it won't use the Office dictionary.

10 Where do I load the programs on a multi-operating system computer?

11 How can I get my computer to produce the Euro € symbol?

12 Is there a self-help user group for Microsoft Office?

13 How can I get rid of the Microsoft Office Assistant for ever?

14 How can I read Office 97 format documents in Office 95?

15 If I want to reload the upgrade version of Office 2000 do I need to reinstall Office 95 and 97 first?

16 How do I copy the AutoText Office files from one PC to another?

17 What are all these files ending in **.rbf**?

18 I have a copy of Word 2000. Will it work with Office 97?

19 I can't load WMF files in Office 97.

20 How can I open Ami Pro and other word processor format files in Word?

21 How can I change the contents of one Excel spreadsheet and have those updates applied automatically to other spreadsheets?

22 How can I update the 'OEM' version of my anti-virus software?

23 How can I type maths formulae in Word 2000?

24 When I create a new document in Word I get a whole new instance of the program on my toolbar – what am I doing wrong?

25 How can I open Wordstar 4 files in Word?

Chapter 10: Connecting To The Internet

1 How does a connection to the internet work?

2 What do I need to get connected to the internet?

3 How can I find an Internet Service Provider?

4 What criteria should I judge ISPs by?

5 How do I get connected to my first ISP?

6 What are the different kinds of connection available?

7 Can I have more than one ISP?

8 Why should I have more than one ISP?

9 What's the difference between the internet and the world wide web?

10 How can I connect automatically when I want to go online?

11 How can I stop my computer going online every time I open my web browser or e-mail program?

12 What are the alternative methods of connecting to the internet?

Chapter 11: E-mail

7 How to add e-mail addresses to your Outlook or Outlook Express address book.

8 How can I send an e-mail to more than one person at the same time?

9 Can I send a copy of an e-mail to someone without the main recipient knowing?

10 The alternatives to Microsoft e-mail software.

11 Can I collect my e-mails when I'm away from home? Even abroad?

12 Can I collect my e-mails when I'm using a different ISP?

13 Why can I collect my e-mails but not send them when using another ISP?

14 How can I set up an 'Out of office' reply?

15 Hotmail, Outlook Express and MSN.

16 My e-mail progam says 'Receiving 1 of 3 messages' but nothing arrives.

17 Why do I get e-mails for someone who's not me at a domain name I own?

18 How can I look up an e-mail address?

19 How do I back up my Outlook Express e-mails?

20 My e-mail program doesn't hang up the line when it's finished collecting mail.

21 I can't connect to my e-mail server.

22 I keep getting the message: 'MSIMN Application error'.

Chapter 12: Now You're Online

1 How can I speed up my internet connection?

2 How do I download stuff from the internet? Where is all this free stuff?

3 Who's in charge of how people behave on the internet?

4 Are there any rules for behaving on the internet?

5 What are 'chatting' and 'instant messages'?

6 If I use AOL's AIM, can I talk to my friend using Microsoft Messenger?

7 What's a 'message board'?

8 What are 'newsgroups'?

9 How can I change the page I see when I start up my web browser?

10 Can I save web pages and read them when I've disconnected from the internet?

11 Will turning off pictures in Internet Explorer speed things up?

12 Some internet sites don't fit on my screen.

13 Can I remove some sites from the drop-down History list in Internet Explorer?

14 Why does my internet connection drop after 5 or 10 minutes?

15 Outlook Express gives an error when I move from one newsgroup to another.

Chapter 13: Connecting To A Network

1 Why would I want a network anyway?

2 What do I need to network two computers?

3 What hardware is involved?

4 Can I set up a network without opening up my PC?

5 What are 'wireless' networks?

6 What's 'Ethernet'?

7 What are 'network protocols'?

8 How do I start setting up a network?

9 What's the easiest way to set up a network?

10 What do I need to do to my PC?

11 Are there any security considerations?

12 Where can I find more detailed information on setting up a network?

13 How can I automate logging on to my networked PC?

14 What implications are there for my network if I change drive letters?

15 What are IP addresses and how do they work?

16 Is it possible to use one set of Outlook Express folders across a network?

17 The Microsoft 'Critical Updates Notification' seems to be telling my networked computer to go online every five minutes.

18 How can I share a single-user 'broadband' internet connection between two PCs?

19 What's a 'crossover' cable? Don't you need a hub to connect two computers?

20 My Windows Me and Windows 2000 computers won't network together.

Chapter 14: Additional Storage

1   What types and sizes of additional storage are available for my PC?

2   Can I use a CD writer or DVD writer as additional storage for my programs and data?

3   What about the 'giant floppy' devices like Iomega's Zip drive?

4   What are 'external hard disks'?

5   What are 'hard disk caddies'?

6   Can I use tape and other backup devices for additional storage?

7   What about backing up over the internet?

8   My Zip drive just clicks and won't read any disks.

9   What's the best way to transfer data between my work and home PCs?

10   Where can I find support for my Iomega Zip drive?

Chapter 15: Speeding Up Your Computer

1   Is there anything I can do to speed up my computer apart from spending money?

2   Eight simple things you can do to your computer to speed it up again.

3   If I have to spend money on something, how can I work out the most effective way to spend it?

4   Is it worth upgrading my hardware, software or both?

5   Is it always worth upgrading software?

6   How can I find free updates?

7   What should I be doing regularly to my PC to keep it running at optimum speed?

8   I have to wait about 10 seconds for my PC to respond to any mouse click or keyboard press, what's the matter?

9   I have a 'winmodem'. Will it slow my PC down?

10   My disk defragmenting always stops at 10 per cent – why?

11   Typing in Word 97 slows and then grinds to a halt.

12   How can I stop programs like RealPlayer and AOL running in the Systray?

13   Why does my computer claim it's 'Out of resources' even though I've loads of RAM?

279

14 My Windows 98SE machine seems to slow down throughout the day. What can I do about this?

15 Can my CPU temperature being too high slow my PC down?

16 Will Find Fast really slow my computer down?

17 If I move my data files to another hard disk, will the programs still be able to open them?

18 Why does Word take longer and longer to open existing files?

19 Will I notice any difference if I add more RAM to my computer?

20 I deleted my internet temporary files in Windows Explorer. Now Internet Explorer won't work properly.

21 What programs can I turn off to speed up my computer?

22 What can I do about these warnings I get from CrashGuard?

23 What's most cost-effective, more RAM or a new processor?

24 Which order should I upgrade the components of my PC?

25 Is my computer too old to upgrade?

26 Should I reformat my hard disk to speed things up?

27 Moving things round on my PC seems very slow.

28 How can I speed my Celeron PC up a bit?

29 Where can I sell my old PC to buy a faster one?

30 Will having a picture as my Desktop wallpaper slow it down?

31 Does having 700 fonts slow my PC down?

32 I have so many icons on my Desktop I can't find them.

Chapter 16: Managing Disks And Files

1 Why should I bother organising how I store the files on my PC?

2 What's a hierarchical filing system?

3 Where can I find my files in Windows and from programs?

4 How can I change the application which opens certain kinds of files?

5 Why would I want to have more than one hard disk?

6 I can't afford two hard disks, what can I do to protect my data?

7   What do FAT16, FAT32 and NTFS mean?

8   Can I put files and folders on to another hard disk?

9   How can I find missing files if I can't remember their names?

10   What do ScanDisk and Disk Defragmenter do?

11   I'm trying to keep my hard disk in good condition by using ScanDisk and Disk Defragmenter but they both stop at 10 per cent.

12   What's Disk Cleanup?

13   How can I recover files deleted from a SmartMedia Card?

14   What are these files ending in **.chk**?

Chapter 17: Backups And Archiving

1   Why should I bother backing up at all?

2   Is it possible to restore backups from one version of Windows in a later version?

3   What are the essential things to back up?

4   How do I back it up? Do I need to buy new stuff?

5   Are there any considerations about backing up when I buy a new computer?

6   Apart from my documents, are there other things I should back up?

7   How can I back up my e-mails?

8   Can I back up my personalised program settings?

9   How do I back up my web browser bookmarks or Favorites?

10   Is it possible to back up my ISP internet connection settings?

11   Why should I bother saving files I download?

12   What information should I keep about my computer?

13   How can I find out what's inside my computer?

14   What are the alternative ways to back up? What hardware and software do I need?

15   Can't I just copy this all on to floppy disks? (No, you can't.)

16   What's a 'Grandfather, father, son' backup strategy?

17   Why do I need a 'backup strategy'?

18   Can I use a second hard disk to back up my original one?

19   How do I put a shortcut to 'Backup' on my Desktop?

Chapter 18: Computer Security And Safety

16 Why do all these people want to know personal information about me online?

17 Is it safe to use my credit card online?

18 How can I protect my personal files from my children?

19 How can I keep my children safe while they're online?

20 What advice can I give my children about using the internet?

21 How can I verify someone is who they say they are online? How can I prove I am really who I say I am?

22 What is spam?

23 How can I stop all this junk e-mail being sent to me?

24 Is there anything I can do with my e-mail program to filter out this spam?

25 how come i can't type any capital letters?

26 A prompt appeared on my screen from a hacker saying he'd gained access to my system. How can I prevent this?

27 Where can I find patches for my Microsoft programs?

28 Norton Anti-Virus found the Kak virus on my computer but couldn't delete it.

29 Can I be infected with a virus just by previewing an e-mail in Outlook Express?

30 Is Norton Internet Security any good? Why don't you recommend it?

31 Can I be infected with a virus by looking at a web page?

32 It can take up to 10 seconds for a word to appear after I've typed it, especially in Outlook Express.

33 My virus checker says I had 92 infected files but it could only clean 87 and now I have W95.MTX.

34 I opened an e-mail attachment called 'Psycho' and now I keep getting 'out of memory' errors.

35 My PC gives an error message on startup about 'kak.reg'.

36 If I open an e-mail attachment directly and it's a virus, will my anti-virus program detect it?

37 I get a 'Driver memory error' when I start my computer.

38 How good and reliable is this 'freeware' and 'shareware' I find on the internet?

39 Is this warning about 'sulfnbk.exe' for real?

40 I'm getting a warning about 'RichTextBox1'.

283

41 Norton Anti-Virus gives me a warning about 'WAS.mtx' and finds 90 infected files, even after scanning them.

42 Are lowly private individuals at home really at risk from hackers?

43 I saw an error message on my screen and clicked OK without reading it, now my PC won't start up at all.

44 I opened an attachment on a friend's e-mail called FIKUMUJI.JPG.vbs and now all my photos have been converted to VBS script format.

45 Norton Anti-Virus on my computer finds no viruses but an online check found a W32.Magistr.2487@mm virus.

46 I was sent a virus as an attachment which I've deleted. Do I need to do anything else?

47 When I try to watch a movie clip I get a 'Warning: Applet Window!' message. Is this a virus?

48 Every time I press a key my PC beeps.

49 My e-mail server name in my e-mail program has been changed to 'localhost'.

50 Why hasn't Norton Anti-Virus found any viruses on my PC?

51 I've eliminated a virus from my machine and know where it came from. Would anyone be interested in this information?

52 How can I tell if my PC is vulnerable to the worms that infect Microsoft's internet server?

53 Can you recommend a free anti-virus program?

54 How can I prevent my ISP connecting to premium-rate phone lines?

55 Does Norton Anti-Virus protect against the Chernobyl virus?

56 I received a spam e-mail offering me a CD containing a million e-mail addresses, including mine presumably – I've written demanding my name be removed. What else can I do?

57 Why can't I just use the 'Create Rule' option in Outlook Express to prevent spam?

Resource Guide

Finding Stuff

Google, www.google.com (and also www.google.co.uk and www.google.fr) has become the best search engine on the web by far. It has a specialised section where you can search for images, too, at images.google.com/images (or via the 'Images' link on the front page). Google also has a 'Groups' service with a 20-year archive of posts to the usenet newsgroups and a 'Directory' section, showing listings similar to those on Yahoo! (www.yahoo.com and www.yahoo.co.uk).

AltaVista, www.altavista.com, including the Babel Fish translation site, babelfish.altavista.com.

Software Updates

Microsoft Windows, windowsupdate.microsoft.com.

Symantec (Norton Anti-Virus), www.symantec.com/techsupp.

Grisoft (AVG anti-virus), www.grisoft.com.

Microsoft support, support.microsoft.com.

Advice On Hardware

Hardware Guys, www.hardwareguys.com, is run by the authors of *PC Hardware in a Nutshell*, Robert Bruce Thompson and Barbara Fritchman Thompson.

Overclockers, www.overclockers.com, will help you find the outer limits of performance of your PC.

Tom's Hardware, www.tomshardware.com, for regular comparative reviews of new hardware.

Driver Guide, www.driverguide.com. Has more than 60,000 drivers for current hardware and also for items which are no longer made – even some for products from long-disappeared manufacturers. There's also a 'driver request' board where you can ask others for missing drivers.

Video drivers, www.video-drivers.com, has many drivers for graphics cards, both current and past models.

Eric's BIOS POST codes page, www.webenet.net/~ntuser.

Useful Stuff

Shareware.com, www.shareware.com, a great place to find free and 'try before you buy' software.

Tucows, www.tucows.com, another source of shareware and freeware.

Mercury Freeware, www.mercury.org.uk, for some very useful tried-and-tested freeware.

Dr Keyboard message board for readers of this book, www.drkeyboard.net/trouble, where you can ask as many questions as you like relating to this book and any difficulties you have in understanding any of it.

Glossary

16/32/64-bit   The number of bits of information a computer can process at once. DOS and Windows 3.xx were 16-bit programs, Windows 9x a mixture of 16- and 32-bit and Windows NT, 2000 and XP fully 32-bit.

Applet   A small program or part of a program such as those you find in *Control Panel*.

Application   Another name for a program or software. Microsoft Word is an application or program.

Bandwidth   The carrying capacity of e.g. your connection to the *Internet*, usually measured in bits per second, bps. The more bandwidth you have available, the more information you can copy at once and the quicker you'll receive e-mails and browse through web pages.

BIOS   Basic Input Output System. When you turn on the power to your PC the BIOS chip detects this and takes control of the start-up process, working out what types of devices like hard disks and memory are contained within your system. You can change settings in the BIOS by pressing a combination of keys when your machine starts up, e.g. **Ctrl-F12** or **Shift-F1** – check your documentation for the correct combination or watch for a message on-screen when your machine starts up.

Bit   The smallest amount of information that a computer can use. A bit can be either a 1 or a 0, on or off, yes or no.

Bluetooth   A short-range wireless networking technology designed to replace the wires that connect the various components of your PC, so there will be Bluetooth keyboards, mice and printers.

Boot up   To start up your computer. The phrase comes from the idea of 'pulling yourself up by your bootstraps' – a PC can't start up without any software telling it what to do, but the software which tells it what to do can't run until the computer has started up. PCs use a small *BIOS* chip to start the process which, when it has finished its duties, hands the running of your PC over to your *operating system.*

Bps   Bits per second, a measurement of the speed of connection between e.g. your modem and the internet.

BSOD   Blue Screen Of Death, named after the background colour of Windows error message screens. Usually pushing the *reset button* on your computer is the only way to get out of such a screen.

Bugs   Errors, mistakes and faults in software which can cause it to run badly, slowly or not at all. Named after a very early valve-based computer was stopped from running when a moth caused a short-circuit. The moth was removed from the machine and stuck into the fault-reporting log-book and labelled a 'bug' in the computer.

Burn   The process of creating a *CD* or *DVD* yourself using some sort of writer drive, so called because these drives use a laser to 'burn' pits into the substrate of the blank disc, storing your data or music.

Byte   Eight bits of information. Computer memory is built from blocks of 8, starting with 8 *bits* making one byte. You may notice that computer memory always comes in multiples of 8 – 32 MB, 256 KB and so on.

CD   Compact disc. In PCs they're usually CD-ROMs (CD-Read Only Memory), CD-R (CD-Recordable, which can be recorded on once only) or CD-RW (CD-ReWritable) which can be recorded over many times.

Click   Click the left button of your mouse (see also *double-click*).

Click One > Two > Three   Left-click your mouse on the item labelled **One** and then you'll see one or more options, one of which is called **Two**. Click this and you'll see more options, including **Three**, which you should click, i.e. this is the sequence of options you should left-click with your mouse, first one, then two, then three. A typical sequence might be **Tools > Options > Spelling** – click **Tools** on the menu bar, then click the **Options** item on that menu, then click the **Spelling** tab on the dialog box which opens.

Command line   Where you type in commands manually at a DOS or command prompt rather than using the Windows *GUI* to perform various functions.

Control Panel   Accessed by clicking **Start > Control Panel** or **Start > Settings > Control Panel**. Contains small *applets* to change various settings on your PC, e.g. the quality of the display on your screen.

Database   A program which organises data in a searchable format allowing 'queries' or questions to be asked of it, such as 'show me all the people in the database aged 25–35 who own a car more than five years old'.

Default   The option which a program automatically chooses if you don't specify an alternative. For example, Microsoft Word's 'default' file location is the **My Documents** folder on your *Desktop*.

Desktop   The area of your screen you see when you have no programs running or when they're all minimised. It's usually what you see when you first start up your PC, and it has icons on it for the **Recycle Bin**, **My Computer** and others. Also sometimes used to differentiate between those computers used by individuals and *server* computers, as in 'a desktop computer'.

Device Manager   A listing of all the *hardware* components installed in your computer with information about the internal resources they use and their *drivers*.

DirectX   A way for computer games to interact with Windows designed by Microsoft. See www.microsoft.com/windows/directx for more details.

Double-click   To click quickly twice in succession with your left mouse button. This usually opens a file or folder. It can be difficult at first to work out what needs one click and what needs to be clicked twice to make it do something interesting. Generally, files and folders need a double-click to make them open, hyperlinks on the internet only need one click.

Download   To copy a program or file from the internet onto your PC, e.g. to download a new driver for your computer's sound card.

Drivers   Small programs that tell your computer's *software* how to interact with its *hardware*.

DVD   Digital Versatile Disc.

E-mail   Electronic messages sent from your computer to another over the internet.

External device   Something you attach to your PC which sits outside the main system box, e.g. a printer or scanner (see also *internal device*).

Female   Used in conjunction with Male to describe a type of plug which fits into a socket on your PC. Male plugs or sockets have pins sticking out of them, as in an electrical power plug. Female plugs or sockets have receptacle holes as in the electrical outlet socket on the wall.

File format   A file's specific type, e.g. Microsoft Word documents are in DOC format, RTF means Rich Text Format, MP3 is a type of music file format. You can associate a specific type of file format with a particular program so that, for example, Microsoft Word always opens DOC format files.

Firewire   Also known as 1394 after its IEEE (Institute of Electrical and Electronics Engineers) designation number, this is a method of connecting peripheral devices such as hard disks or video cameras to your PC which can communicate very quickly with it (400 Mbps). Apple owns the Firewire standard, www.apple.com/firewire, and charges licence fees to anyone who wants to use it, which can make it expensive for some purposes, unlike *USB*.

Floppy disk   Removable disk in a hard, plastic case. 'Standard' 3.5 inch floppy disks can hold 1.44 MB of information, and there are a number of 'super floppies' which can hold much more information, including Iomega's Zip disks (100 or 250 MB) and LS120 discs which can hold 120 MB. They're called 'floppy' because originally 8" and 5.25" discs came in thin, flexible plastic sheaths. The discs inside 3.5" floppy disk cases are also still flexible. They're useful for transferring small files between unconnected computers but are *very* prone to data loss and should *not* be used to keep the only copy of any file. You *will* lose the data on a floppy disk sooner or later, no exceptions. If you've been using the same floppy disk for the past five years and not lost a byte of data yet, you're going to learn this lesson the hard way real soon now, I'm afraid.

Format   To prepare a disk, e.g. a floppy disk, to make it ready to have files, programs and other information saved on to it. Formatting a disk will remove any information already on it. See also *file format*.

GB   A gigabyte.

Gb   A gigabit.

Gigabyte   A million megabytes.

Google   The web search engine at www.google.com, which is, by far, the best available.

GUI   Graphical User Interface, e.g. Windows which uses *WIMPs* to allow you to interact visually with the operating system.

Hard disk   Usually internal (inside the main system box of your PC) but can be external, hard disks are where your PC stores your programs and data. Their capacity nowadays is measured in gigabytes, e.g. 20 GB, 80 GB. Aka HD, HDD, Hard Disk Drive, Hard Drive.

Hardware   The physical components which make up your computer. See also *software*.

Hot-swap   To plug in or remove devices from your PC without having to turn it off. *USB* devices are hot-swappable, as are those connected by Firewire. PS/2 keyboards (those with small, round plugs) are *not* hot-swappable, meaning you have to power off your PC before plugging in or unplugging a keyboard. If you're in any doubt, always turn off your PC first.

IDE Integrated Drive Electronics, the most popular type of hard disk found in PCs.

Internal device Something attached to your PC which sits inside the main system box, e.g. a hard disk, CD-ROM drive or video card.

Internet Worldwide network of computers, the 'plumbing' which allows you to access the *world wide web* and use *e-mail*.

IP address Every computer accessing the *internet* is assigned a numerical address, in the format xxx.xxx.xxx.xxx where xxx is a number between 0 and 255 (1–254 in the final group of numbers). When you connect to your *ISP* your computer will automatically be assigned an IP address. Every website you connect to has an IP address, too – when you type in an address like **www.drkeyboard.net** it looks up the numerical equivalent of this address and uses that to find the appropriate website.

ISP Internet Service Provider, the company via which you connect to the internet.

Kb Kilobit, a thousand (more accurately 1024) bits.

KB Kilobyte, a thousand bytes or, more accurately, 1024 bytes.

Male See *Female*.

Mb Megabit, a million (more accurately 1,048,576) bits.

MB Megabyte, either a million bytes or, more accurately, 1,048,576 (1,024 × 1,024) bytes.

MIDI Musical Instrument Digital Interface, a format for editing and playing music on your computer. This is the 'industry standard' format for computerised music.

Motherboard The basic system component inside your PC to which everything else connects.

Network To connect two or more computers together, either with wires or by *wireless* connections so that they can share resources such as printers and your internet connection.

Offline When your computer is disconnected from the internet.

Online When your computer is connected to the internet.

Operating system The bottom layer of software in your computer, e.g. Windows, that performs basic functions like dealing with hardware, saving data, displaying information on your monitor screen and running software programs.

OS Operating system.

Partition A section of a hard disk. A single physical hard disk can be divided up into one, two or more separate 'partitions'. Two partitions called C: and D: could occupy one hard disk, for example, and be used for different operating systems or to allow Windows and your application software to be installed on C: and all your data on D:.

Patch   Small addition to a program which corrects a *bug* or fixes a security problem.

PC   Personal computer, usually taken to mean an IBM-compatible computer running Microsoft Windows.

Peripheral device   Something you attach as an 'optional extra' to your computer, usually an *external device* such as a scanner or printer.

Program   See *application* and *software*.

Properties   Folders, programs, files and most things on your computer have 'Properties', attributes specific to them. You can see the 'properties' for many things like files by right-clicking them and then left-clicking Properties on the menu that pops up.

Radio button   Found on forms on websites and on dialog boxes in programs, these are usually round and a small black 'dot' appears in the centre when you click them to choose between multiple options. You can usually only choose one radio button, as you would if you were pressing station selection buttons on your car radio (hence the name).

RAM   Random Access Memory, where your computer runs programs stored on your hard disk. Typically computers have 32, 64, 128 or 256 MB of RAM, or multiples thereof.

Reboot   To restart your computer, either by clicking **Start > Shutdown > Restart** or, if that doesn't work, pushing the *reset button* on the front panel of your PC or, if that doesn't work, by turning off the power completely by removing the power cable and/or unplugging it.

Reset button   Usually on the front of your computer, pushing it turns your computer off and back on again. If you push it with programs open you will lose any unsaved information.

Right-click   Click the right button of your mouse.

SCSI   Small Computer System Interface, a method for connecting hard disks, scanners and other devices to a PC. These devices can be internal (inside the main computer box) or external. SCSI hard disks and optical drives (CDs and DVDs) are generally regarded as being faster than *IDE* drives, particularly for applications such as video and music since the SCSI interface does much of the work itself, rather than relying on your PC's CPU. SCSI devices are also usually more expensive than alternatives.

Search   Do a search on your computer by clicking **Start > Search > For Files or Folders** (**Start > Find > For Files or Folders** on earlier Windows versions). If you were looking for all your Outlook Personal Storage (PST) files, for example, you'd type in the 'Search for files or folders named' box, ***.pst**. ***** is a 'wildcard' meaning 'anything at all', and you could find **outlook.pst**, **backup.pst** or **archive.pst**. If you know that a filename includes the word 'lawyer' but you're not sure if it's lawyers.doc, lawyer.doc or lawyer1.doc you could search for **lawyer*.doc** which will find both **lawyers.doc** and **lawyer letter October 2000.doc**. You can narrow it down by using a question mark (**?**) instead of an asterisk (*****). ? means 'look for only one character in this location', so a search for **lawyer?.doc** will find **lawyers.doc** but not **lawyer letter October 2000.doc**.

Server   A computer used for 'serving up' e.g. files or websites. A server is accessed by *desktop* or *workstation* computers sharing a resource such as a *database* or collection of documents, a website or hardware such as a printer.

Software   The programs and *operating system* which run on your computer's *hardware*.

System Tray   The area of your *Taskbar* next to the time display. You'll see icons here for programs which are running in the background such as your anti-virus software and your internet connection.

Taskbar   The area at the bottom or to the side of your screen where you see the **Start** button and time display. By default it's docked (stuck) at the bottom of your screen, but you can click-and-drag it to any edge of the screen. You can also hide it when it's not in use – right-click it and left-click **Properties** and then **Auto hide**. You bring it back by moving your mouse to the edge of the screen where it's hidden.

Tool tip   When you hover your mouse over a link on a web page or an icon in a program, you may see a box appear describing where the link goes or what the icon does.

Upload   To copy a file from your PC on to a site on the internet, e.g. to put a picture on to your personal website.

USB   Universal Serial Bus, a way of connecting external peripherals including mice, keyboards, scanners and printers to your PC. Owned and promoted on a royalty-free basis by Intel, the original USB 1 standard connects devices at 12 Mbps while the newer USB 2.0 standard works at speeds up to 480 Mbps while remaining compatible with USB 1, making it a less expensive and even faster competitor to the Firewire standard. Most new PCs ship with USB 1 ports and increasingly with USB 2.0.

Video/graphics card   The names 'graphics card' and 'video card' are interchangeable and refer to the add-in or built-in card which connects to your computer monitor and is responsible for putting the picture on it which you see.

Website   A page or collection of pages on the world wide web. There are personal sites (e.g. my diary at www.chateaukeyboard.com/diary) and business sites (e.g. www.eu.microsoft.com) and everything in between. There are websites for more or less anything you can think of now.

WIMPs   Windows, Icons, Mouse (or Menu), Pointers (or Pull-down Menus) as used in the Windows and Macintosh operating systems.

Windows 9x   The 'x' stands for 5, 8 or Me as in Windows 95, 98 or Me (OK, you have to delete the 9 yourself for Me). This 'family' of Windows has essentially the same underpinnings and is only distantly related to the Windows NT line, which started for most people with Windows NT 3.51 and graduated through NT 4.0 and Windows 2000 to Windows XP.

Wireless   Usually means to connect two or more PCs in a network using a wireless system instead of wires and cables. The commonest standard is called 802.11 (a, b and g) and runs at speeds of between 11 and 54 Mbps. 802.11b, which runs at 11 Mbps, is the commonest.

Wizard   Small program which guides you through a procedure such as installing software or exporting information from one program to another.

Workstation   A computer you work at, as opposed to a Server. It used to refer to specialised machines designed for specific purposes, for example video editing, but now is generally applied to most desktop computers.

WWW or world wide web   Made up of millions of individual *websites* devoted to millions of different topics, you use a web browser (e.g. Microsoft Internet Explorer, Netscape) to access the sites and view 'pages' on them containing words, pictures, animations and sounds.

YMMV   Your Mileage May Vary. Particularly used in statements like, 'I find that Windows XP runs just fine with 64 MB of memory, but YMMV'.

Index